# Mixed Blessings

# Mixed Blessings

Indigenous Encounters with Christianity in Canada

*Edited by Tolly Bradford
and Chelsea Horton*

UBCPress · Vancouver · Toronto

25 24 23 22 21 20 19 18 17 16    5 4 3 2 1

Printed in Canada on FSC-certified ancient-forest-free paper
(100% post-consumer recycled) that is processed chlorine- and acid-free.

---

**Library and Archives Canada Cataloguing in Publication**

Mixed blessings : indigenous encounters with Christianity in Canada / edited by Tolly Bradford and Chelsea Horton.

Includes bibliographical references and index.
Issued in print and electronic formats.
ISBN 978-0-7748-2939-7 (hardback). – ISBN 978-0-7748-2940-3 (pbk.). –
ISBN 978-0-7748-2941-0 (pdf). – ISBN 978-0-7748-2942-7 (epub). –
ISBN 978-0-7748-3083-6 (mobi)

1. Native peoples – Missions – Canada – History. 2. Missions – Canada – History.
3. Canada – Church history. I. Bradford, Justin Tolly, editor. II. Horton, Chelsea, editor

E78.C2M59 2016          266.0089'97071          C2016-900148-2
                                                C2016-900149-0

---

Canadä

UBC Press gratefully acknowledges the financial support for our publishing program of the Government of Canada (through the 'Canada Book Fund), the Canada Council for the Arts, and the British Columbia Arts Council.

This book has been published with the help of a grant from the Canadian Federation for the Humanities and Social Sciences, through the Awards to Scholarly Publications Program, using funds provided by the Social Sciences and Humanities Research Council of Canada.

UBC Press
The University of British Columbia
2029 West Mall
Vancouver, BC V6T 1Z2
www.ubcpress.ca

# Contents

# Acknowledgments

THIS COLLECTION IS the outgrowth of a workshop, "Religious Encounter and Exchange in Aboriginal Canada," held at the University of Saskatchewan in May 2011. For facilitating this initial workshop, we gratefully acknowledge the financial assistance of the Social Sciences and Humanities Research Council of Canada and the Department of History and the Faculty of Arts and Science at the University of Saskatchewan. We likewise extend our warm gratitude to University of Saskatchewan Elder Walter Linklater (Anishinaabe) and historians Jim Miller and Susan Neylan for their valuable contributions to that gathering. Thank you, further, to all the participants, who made the workshop truly meaningful. We appreciate your work and (to the contributors here) your patience as we pulled all the pieces together. It has been an honour working with all of you, and we look forward to continued conversation. Thank you also to Taiaiake Alfred, Emma Anderson, Darcy Cullen at UBC Press, and the anonymous reviewers of the manuscript for their helpful input on the project. Finally, the editors express their appreciation to their families and to each other. We are two historians of somewhat different training and approach and have both learned much through the shared process of producing this collection together.

# Mixed Blessings

# Introduction:
# The Mixed Blessings of Encounter

*Tolly Bradford and Chelsea Horton*

ON SUNDAY, 21 OCTOBER 2012, over three hundred years after her death and nearly a century and a half after campaigns for her canonization began, Mohawk woman Kateri (or Catherine, as she is known to some) Tekakwitha was formally invested as a Catholic saint. During his homily at the Vatican that Sunday, Pope Benedict XVI declared, "Saint Kateri, Protectress of Canada and the first Native American saint, we entrust to you the renewal of the faith in the first nations and in all of North America! May God bless the first nations!"[1] This was a charged statement in light of current investigations into the history of residential schools in Canada, a history in which the Catholic Church is intimately implicated and for which it has yet to issue a formal apology on the scale offered by the Anglican, Presbyterian, and United Churches in Canada.[2]

Indeed, it is tempting in this context to read the timing of Kateri's canonization and the pope's statement as a shrewd political effort to curry sympathy with Indigenous peoples or, perhaps more charitably, as an "act of atonement" for past sins.[3] It would also be easy to read Kateri's biography, which Jesuit missionaries composed as hagiography upon her death in 1680 and settlers of various stripes subsequently deployed to promote the image of the "ecological Indian" and more, as a straightforward narrative of colonial victimization.[4] After all, this was a woman who lost immediate family members, including her parents, to smallpox, and was herself disfigured by the disease. Displaced from her natal settlement in what is now New York State, Kateri died in the Mohawk missionary village of Kahnawake, near Montreal, at the age of twenty-four. And yet, as her well-documented acts of Christian piety attest, Kateri was an ardent Catholic. And she made Indigenous meanings of Christianity.[5]

Because of her deep Catholic faith, Kateri was largely isolated from her people and remains an ambivalent figure among the Mohawk, a growing number of whom are focused on the resurgence of Haudenosaunee spiritual teachings and nationalism.[6] At the same time, Kateri is a source and symbol of strength to many Indigenous people, Mohawk and not. Indigenous Catholics, many of them women, were key advocates for her canonization. And it was the healing of a young Lummi boy in Washington State from a potentially fatal skin infection that finally propelled Kateri to formal saintly status.[7] This boy, Jake Finkbonner, together with his parents and Indigenous Catholics from across North America, was among the thousands who travelled to Rome to witness Kateri's canonization ceremony in person. So were several Kahnawa'kehro:non (Mohawk people of Kahnawake), including Alex McComber, whose late mother was a long-time devotee of Kateri's. For McComber, the significance of the ceremony extended beyond "the politics of religion" to the people of Kahnawake and "people of spirit." As he was cited in a newspaper article published the day of the canonization, "it makes me feel good knowing that so many indigenous peoples look to Kateri on that spiritual level: that faith, that strength, that positive spiritual energy."[8]

The title of this book, *Mixed Blessings,* is informed by the stories of people like Kateri Tekakwitha and the complex implications of her canonization.[9] The book's cover image, a detail of a statue at the National Saint Kateri Tekakwitha Shrine, located at the Caughnawaga village site in Fonda, New York, where Kateri lived for several years in her youth, similarly invokes this layered and contested history.[10] Though contributors do not discuss Kateri specifically, this collection is an interdisciplinary effort to explore the meanings and legacies that her living history so effectively limns. It asks how and why some Indigenous people historically aligned themselves with Christianity while others did not. It plumbs processes and politics of religious combination. And it reflects on the role of Christianity in Indigenous communities and Canada today. This is a timely endeavour. Current public discussions concerning the history of residential schools and attendant intergenerational trauma are a stark reminder of Christianity's core role in this country's ongoing colonial history.[11] From the time of early contact (indeed, before modern Canada itself), Christian missionaries of diverse denominations were deeply imbricated in efforts to alter the lifeways of Indigenous peoples in North America. Moreover, missionary outreach is ongoing in Indigenous Canada, as is the structural and symbolic violence of settler colonialism. At the same time, many Indigenous people continue to interpret and live Christianity in ways meaningful to them, just as others, and sometimes the same people, persist in the practice of specifically Indigenous forms of spirituality. Christianity, this collection illuminates, has proved a flexible, while always deeply freighted, site of colonial encounter and exchange.

This book is the outcome of a workshop organized by the editors, both of whom are historians of white settler heritage, during which participants spent three days in close discussion of each other's work. Bringing together emerging and established scholars in history, Indigenous studies, religious studies, and theology, this workshop stimulated rich, sometimes difficult, dialogue about the details of Indigenous interactions with Christianity, diverse disciplinary approaches to the topic, and the pressing imperative of decolonization. Although contributors do not share any one single approach to the process, this project is nevertheless animated by a shared commitment to connect past and present. As editors, we are wary of making a facile claim to decolonization, an emergent process that "centers Indigenous methods, peoples, and lands" and, as contributor Denise Nadeau argues in her chapter here, that bears on Indigenous and settler peoples alike and is "profoundly different for both."[12] In engaging and promoting dialogue across disciplinary boundaries and between Indigenous and settler scholars, peoples, and methodologies, however, we understand and offer this project in a decolonizing spirit and aim to spark ongoing innovative investigation of Indigenous-Christian encounter in Canada.

## The Study of Encounter

During recent decades, scholars of colonized territories outside of North America have dissected the intricate and powerful roles played by Christianity in the colonization and transformation of Indigenous societies. Challenging established narratives of the missionary-as-hero and the missionary-as-villain, these critical reappraisals of religious encounter have hinged on such concepts as cultural imperialism, hybridity, and, especially, Indigenous agency and action.[13] More recently, scholarship about the United States, which on the surface shares so much with the Canadian story, has included similar innovative analysis of Indigenous-Christian encounter. A key work consolidating this shift is the volume *Native Americans, Christianity, and the Reshaping of the American Religious Landscape.*[14] This book, like *Mixed Blessings*, had its seeds in a workshop. Editors Joel W. Martin and Mark A. Nicholas sought out leading scholars from several disciplines whose work they felt reflected a reappraisal of Indigenous-Christian interaction that had been underway in the United States for several years. As Martin explains in the introduction to the volume, although most scholars of American history readily recognize that Christianity and "Native American conversion is inextricably interwoven with a brutal history of colonialism and conquest," there has been a discernible shift towards examining the complex, and often contradictory, role of missionaries and Christianity in the construction of the Native American religious landscape.[15]

Some scholars of Canada have shared in such rethinking. In an innovative study of the life of one Innu youth taken from his home and then returned from

France by early-seventeenth-century Recollect missionaries, for example, religious studies scholar Emma Anderson helps shift interpretive focus from white missionary actors and categories to Indigenous peoples and perspectives.[16] As historian Allan Greer illustrates in a compelling "dual biography" of Kateri/ Catherine Tekakwitha and Jesuit missionary Claude Chauchetière, this shift in turn promotes deepened understanding of Indigenous and European actors alike.[17] Other scholars of Canada similarly reject restrictive interpretations of religious encounter that reduce Indigenous interactions with Christianity, and conversion especially, to inevitable acts of assimilation or sheer survival strategy. Focusing on regions to the north and west, for example, studies by Kerry Abel (examining the Dene) and Susan Neylan (studying the Tsimshian) show how encounters were shaped by colonial power, Indigenous agency, and spiritual and political dynamics internal to specific Indigenous communities.[18] Still other scholars have effectively examined encounter through the lens of individual Indigenous missionaries and converts.[19] Most of this literature focuses on the early contact period and nineteenth-century contact zones.[20] There are some, however, including Muscogee (Creek) religious studies scholar James Treat, anthropologists Frédéric B. Laugrand, Jarich G. Oosten, and Clinton Westman, and the collaborative team of anthropologist Leslie A. Robertson and the Kwagu'ł Gixsam Clan, who have offered vital insights on more recent events, experiences, and memories of Indigenous interactions with Christianity.[21]

While such works provided important inspiration for this collection, they are few and far between in scholarship about Canada. On the whole, the place of Christianity remains somewhat peripheral to major narrative threads in Canadian Indigenous history and studies. Church historian John Webster Grant's 1984 book, *Moon of Wintertime: Missionaries and the Indians of Canada in Encounter since 1534,* is still the sole overview text on the subject.[22] Canadian historical literature, meanwhile, has tended to either overlook Christianity or reduce its role to one of two dichotomous poles: a wholesale instrument of colonialism or a force with little bearing on the "real" (read: economic and political) vectors of colonial exchange.[23] This volume, then, like the Canadian context more broadly, differs from the consolidation work undertaken by Martin and Nicholas. Where they set out to bring together specific leading scholars to reflect on an interpretive shift well underway in the United States, this book emerged from a gathering that aimed to gauge interdisciplinary interest and approaches to the topic in Canada. In this sense, readers should approach this collection as a reconnaissance project that seeks both to sketch out basic terrain and encourage ongoing research and dialogue.

Another critical issue sets this book, and Canadian scholarship, apart from studies of religious encounter in other colonial contexts. Over the past several decades, and especially through the work of the Truth and Reconciliation Commission of Canada (TRCC), awareness of the history of Indian residential schools in this country has grown. Canadians, and those studying Canada, have been forced to confront some of the most traumatic moments of Indigenous-Christian encounter in modern history. They must grapple with the TRCC's finding that church-run residential schools were a crucial institution in a wider government policy of cultural genocide that aimed to eliminate Aboriginal peoples as a distinct element in Canadian society.[24] In sharing these stories and analysis, the TRCC has helped produce a powerful narrative about religious encounter in Canada, a narrative in which commanding white missionaries suppress and abuse powerless Indigenous children, families, and communities.[25] Confronting the histories of violence and abuse associated with residential schools is critical to understanding the workings and living legacies of colonialism in Canada. Yet contributors here seek to complicate singular stories of powerful churches and powerless Indigenous subjects. Indeed, most scholars would now challenge the white colonizer/Indigenous victim binary that tends to be reproduced in the Canadian media's current coverage of residential schools.[26] In place of such dichotomous depictions, scholars of Indigenous-Christian interaction, including many in this volume, have increasingly stressed Indigenous agency and explored how Christianity had, and continues to have, real meaning for many Indigenous people. Such arguments, however, can ring hollow, even meaningless, when considered in relation to the experiences and testimonies of former residential schools students. It became apparent during the workshop that led to this collection and during the subsequent editing process that every scholar of Indigenous-Christian encounter in Canada, whether exploring interactions in the seventeenth century or the twenty-first, must reconcile his or her commitment to recognizing Indigenous agency, and the reality of Indigenous Christianities, with the traumatic histories of violence associated with Christian missionaries, churches, and the residential schools. This volume does not offer any single prescriptive method for resolving this tension. In taking up this challenge, however, this collection is concerned with exploring connections across time and with contemplating the roles and responsibilities of scholars of religious encounter.

## Sites and Patterns of Encounter

This collection coheres around the concept of encounter. Dictionary definitions of this term carry a certain negative valence (the idea of collision, clash, and hostility) that resonates, in part, with Christianity's colonial histories and legacies.[27] Scholars have also engaged encounter as a power-laden process of exchange.[28] Not all contributors to this volume explicitly engage this formulation, and some actively eschew it. Likewise, contributors employ a range of terminologies to identify Indigenous groups. Indeed, the dynamism of this collection derives from its wide-ranging composition and refusal to reduce analysis to any single interpretive approach.

This text is organized according to several shared sites of encounter. Part 1, "Communities in Encounter," explores how Christianity shaped, often in unpredictable ways, the politics, identities, and organization of Indigenous communities in the past. Here, contributors emphasize how Indigenous communities and leaders interacted with representatives of Euro-Canadian Christianity, how these interactions were informed by particular contexts of colonialism, and how they informed dynamics within Indigenous communities themselves. Part 2, "Individuals in Encounter," considers how specific individuals in the past – in this case, a white missionary wife, a prominent Métis leader, and a nêhiyaw (Cree) Anglican minister and leader – engaged Christianity in creative, even contradictory, ways. This approach allows for the examination of interactions with, and uses of, Christianity from a close, intimate perspective. Here, we learn about not only the political contexts that shape encounter but also the personal motivations and experiences that do so. Part 3 shifts the focus to a trio of present-day sites of exchange. "Contemporary Encounters" grapples directly with the challenge of acknowledging the complex living legacies of Christianity and colonialism among Indigenous peoples in Canada and actively contemplates strategies for reconciliation and decolonization.

**Encounters of Power**

While highlighting the distinctive nature of community, individual, and contemporary sites of encounter, *Mixed Blessings* simultaneously illuminates several shared patterns of encounter that extend across all three sites. First, contributors are united in the recognition that Indigenous interactions with Christianity were intimately shaped by colonial politics and struggles for power, both spiritual and political, in specific contexts of exchange. Over the past three decades, scholars have come increasingly to explore the political motivations inspiring Indigenous interactions with Christianity.[29] While this marks a welcome move away from casting Indigenous converts to Christianity in the role of passive "dupes," it has also tended to reduce Indigenous response to the pragmatic, parsing the spiritual and the political in a way not in keeping with Indigenous worldviews.[30] Chapters in this book reveal that the political and the spiritual were and remain interwoven, and responses by Indigenous peoples to Christianity were shaped by searches for political and spiritual power alike.[31]

This search for power did not and does not occur in a vacuum. In the opening chapter of this volume, for instance, historian Timothy Pearson examines

Indigenous-Catholic interactions in the seventeenth-century northeast through the lens of ritual. Drawing carefully on Jesuit records and other colonial documents, Pearson finds a world animated on all sides by "powerful spiritual forces, potentially both divine and dangerous." For French missionaries and Huron and Algonquin people alike, he argues, "ritual contributed to the creation of real and metaphorical spaces where people experienced the sacred and negotiated religious and social differences."[32] In this context, religious expression was a process of individual and community definition and thus clearly a political process. Ethnohistorian Amanda Fehr's chapter about the Stó:lō in southwestern British Columbia in the 1930s advances a similar argument. With the reserve system and the Indian Act as a backdrop, Fehr argues that Stó:lō leaders looked to the I:yem memorial, a Catholic monument, as a way to empower themselves and their community. She underscores, at the same time, that Stó:lō community and identity were in no way static, monolithic entities. In Chapter 7, religious studies scholar Siphiwe Dube reiterates that encounters with Christianity should never be seen as neutral. In questioning the role of Christian churches, and of Christian discourse more broadly, in the Truth and Reconciliation Commission of Canada, Dube brings into relief the same conundrum faced by the Huron and Algonquin in the seventeenth century and the Stó:lō in the 1930s: that it is nearly impossible to separate the "message" of Christianity from the colonial context in which it is delivered. For Dube, recognition of this conundrum, and the relationship between colonialism and Christianity, is critical if Indigenous and settler peoples in Canada are to move towards a more constructive spiritual and political relationship.

While this emphasis on the political forces framing encounters between Christianity and Indigenous communities is prevalent in most chapters, no contributors reduce the story to one informed by political concerns alone. In fact, one of the novel features of this collection is the concern for taking more seriously the role of spiritual experiences and knowledge in academic writing about Indigenous peoples, Christianity, and colonialism more broadly. At the workshop that led to this collection, some contributors characterized spirituality, both Indigenous and Christian, as something of a "technology" that was, along with furs and firearms, exchanged between European and Indigenous peoples. Writing from her perspective as a historian, Elizabeth Elbourne presents a fruitful framework for how to explore this dynamic. Focusing on Haudenosaunee interactions with Christianity, and Anglicanism specifically, from the late eighteenth century to the early nineteenth century, Elbourne argues that Christianity was seen as a force that had spiritual, political, and economic significance. The Haudenosaunee, argues Elbourne, saw Anglicanism as a source of spiritual power (accessible through baptisms and other rituals) and a source of secular power that granted them access to military, political, and economic support from the British. She argues, further, that the Haudenosaunee saw danger in Christianity, believing that Christian texts and particularly the Bible could be damaging to the internal strength and unity of their communities. Elbourne explains that for many Haudenosaunee, the encounter with Christianity was mainly about "managing" the religion. The goal of this management was to gain the benefit of the "powers" while avoiding the pitfalls or the "dangers" of Christianity. This framework moves scholarship away from a focus on the question of Indigenous agency alone (did Indigenous people have the ability to respond to Christianity?) and turns our attention to specific methods (how did Indigenous people use their agency to respond?), doing so in a way that more accurately reflects the connected nature of spirituality and politics in Indigenous contexts.

Indigenous studies scholar Tasha Beeds illustrates this interconnectedness in her study of early-twentieth-century nêhiyaw Anglican minister Edward Ahenakew. Situating Ahenakew in the context of acute colonial violence and nêhiyawi-mâmitonêyihcikan (Cree consciousness/thinking) alike, Beeds demonstrates how Ahenakew contributed to the "preservation of nêhiyawiwin" (Creeness) through his engagement with Anglicanism, the English language, and settler education and scholarship. In situating her own self and scholarship within nêhiyawi-mâmitonêyihcikan and language, Beeds, who is of nêhiyaw (Cree) Métis and Caribbean ancestry, contributes to this process of preservation and resurgence. For Heiltsuk theologian and United Church of Canada minister Carmen Lansdowne, whose chapter is a revealing personal reflection on her experience conducting research in missionary archives, the ultimate goal is to articulate Indigenous Christian theologies. How Indigenous people have managed and experienced the spiritual and political powers of Christianity, and how we as scholars can and should describe this process, are constant themes throughout this book.

## Transnational Encounters
Given the global spread of both Christianity and European colonialism during the past several hundred years, all of the chapters in this collection also implicitly or explicitly situate their subjects in a transnational context. That is to say, all of the chapters recognize that encounters between Indigenous peoples and Christianity were shaped by, and shaped, forces and events that extended beyond the local region or national boundaries of Canada. This recognition, broadly informed by a range of scholarship falling under the banner of postcolonial theory, is reflected to varying degrees throughout the chapters in this volume.[33]

Historian Cecilia Morgan's chapter on Eliza Field Jones (the English wife of Ojibwa missionary Kahkewaquonaby/Peter Jones), for instance, sheds light on how people that were part of this encounter were living transnational lives themselves. In Morgan's chapter we see that both husband and wife, but especially Eliza, approached the task of mission work in Upper Canada from a transnational (and, more specifically, transatlantic) perspective. Although focused on cultivating Indigenous Christians in Canada, both husband and wife were closely supported and informed by family members and cultural expectations in imperial Britain. For this missionary couple, the encounter between Indigenous and Christian worlds was at once intimate and international, local and global.

Two more historians, Jean-François Bélisle and Nicole St-Onge, likewise employ a transnational and comparative history approach to offer a fresh interpretation of Métis leader Louis Riel leading up to the 1885 North-West Resistance or Rebellion. By re-reading Riel's writings with an eye to the influence of broader hemispheric processes on his thought, the chapter attempts to move beyond the dichotomous depiction of Riel as either political leader or religious visionary. Instead, Bélisle and St-Onge argue that Riel was constructing a "church-state" that reflected not only the neo-ultramontane ideas then current in French Canada, but also those of García Moreno, Ecuadorian statesman and creator of the most comprehensive church-state society in the nineteenth century. By linking Riel with this Ecuadorian context, while also exploring what they describe as the parallel historical example of the Mayan free state known as Cruzob, Bélisle and St-Onge argue that Riel was not unique, nor was his resistance simply the expression of an isolated political or messianic movement. Rather, they suggest that Riel saw himself not just as a Métis nationalist, a champion of western Canadian rights, or an anti-colonial revolutionary, but as a leader in a hemispheric movement to construct a theocratic ultramontane state in the Canadian Northwest. Like Kateri's canonization in Rome or the shrine dedicated to her in Fonda, New York, this repositioning of Riel in a hemispheric context underscores that Indigenous encounters with Christianity were closely interconnected with ideas, events, people, and power outside of Canada as well as inside.

## Methodological Encounters

All contributors to this collection recognize that Christianity, and its imbrication in European and Canadian colonialism, has had deep, often devastating, effects on Indigenous people and communities in contemporary Canada. The legacies of the residential school system has made it clear that many of the struggles that Indigenous peoples are facing in Canada today are directly linked to a long history of colonialism at the hands of Christian missionaries and the Canadian state. However, as became evident during the workshop leading up to this publication, and as we hope is revealed in this book, the actual history of the missionary enterprise is far more complex than first imagined. Encounters between missionaries and Indigenous peoples were multifaceted and replete with contradiction and surprising innovation. As noted above, a challenge for the reader of this collection – and a constant point of discussion at our original workshop – is how to explain (and perhaps reconcile) the subtlety and diversity of Indigenous responses to Christianity while simultaneously recognizing the painful living legacies of Christian missions and colonialism in Canada. Contributors themselves navigate this tension through the application of several distinct, sometimes conflicting, methodologies.

For many of the historians here, focus falls on that space that literary critic Mary-Louise Pratt has influentially dubbed the "contact zone," a site of colonial encounter shot through with uneven relations of power but also animated by agency and contingency on all sides.[34] These historians, further, focus their efforts predominantly on archival research and evidence. Contributors readily recognize the difficulty of accessing Indigenous voices and experiences, especially spiritual ones, in a documentary record overwhelmingly produced by white male missionaries and colonial officials (and populated also by Indigenous "elites" such as the famed Brant family in the case of Elizabeth Elbourne's chapter). Engaging such sources, Elbourne avers, requires humility. Still, while they acknowledge the limitations of their sources, many here are committed to reading archival records both for what they reveal and for what they obscure. As noted, Bélisle and St-Onge offer fresh perspective on the spiritual state that Riel envisioned by revisiting his abundant writings and positioning them in the context of consonant Catholic developments in Latin America. Morgan similarly situates Eliza Field Jones in a transatlantic context and finds in writings like Jones's diaries and an 1838 memoir of her niece, Elizabeth Jones, a perspective that at once reproduces and undermines dualism current in other contemporary missionary texts. Working with a much more limited source base, Pearson elects to clearly foreground the contingency of the Jesuit records on which he is dependent by distinguishing between "ritual as it appears in text" and "ritual as it may have originally been performed." Though her focus is the much more recent past, and she draws on oral as well as archival sources, ethnohistorian Fehr is likewise explicit, and effective, in pointing out the inevitably partial nature of her interpretation.

Other contributors are more explicit in their challenge of established Western research and teaching methods. Denise Nadeau, for example, offers insight into the context of university pedagogy, detailing her efforts to help decolonize the field of religious studies by incorporating Indigenous ways of knowing and learning into an undergraduate course on Indigenous traditions, women, and colonialism. Nadeau explains that while she engaged contact zone scholarship in early iterations of her course, she found that this literature functioned to turn focus back onto the colonizer rather than foregrounding generative Indigenous agency and action. Her more recent teaching, by contrast, has explicitly centred the historical experiences and contemporary resurgence work and writings of Indigenous women. While the class that this chapter reflects on does not contain "Christian" in the title, this piece is entirely germane to the topic of Indigenous-Christian encounter. It suggests how Christianity, both in the author's own personal background as a theologian of mixed heritage and in the implicit assumptions and worldviews of other scholars and undergraduate students, continues to inform Indigenous-settler relations in Canada today. It deals directly with the challenge of how to engage students with the living legacies of historical Christian encounters discussed elsewhere in the volume and, through thoughtful and honest reflection on the author's own teaching practice, offers insights on the process of decolonization that scholars and teachers in many fields stand to learn from.

Carmen Lansdowne's chapter likewise offers personal reflections that both straddle and challenge disciplinary boundaries. Here, the author herself is both site and subject of analysis. Through the method of autoethnography, Lansdowne offers raw reflection on her experience of seeking out, and her pain and disappointment at not finding, Indigenous theologies in the written missionary record of the Methodist church on the Northwest Coast. Lansdowne's chapter is in large measure a meditation on her discomfort and dissatisfaction with academic history – a discipline, she argues, that draws insufficient connection between past, present, and colonial power, and in the face of which she fears her autoethnographic reflections will be dismissed as too personal. Like both Lansdowne and Nadeau, Tasha Beeds opens her chapter by declaring her own social and spiritual location, an act through which she positions herself in place and within ties of relationship and responsibility. Beeds writes as "a woman of nêhiyaw Métis and mixed Caribbean ancestry" and situates her work intimately in the inseparable contexts of nêhiyaw Métis land and language.[35] She simultaneously draws on the theory of Indigenous scholars of other ancestry as well, stressing, as she did at the workshop that led to this volume, that Indigenous people are producers of knowledge, not simply subjects of study.

While Beeds, Lansdowne, and Nadeau engage Indigenous theories as well as methodologies, and the imprint of postcolonial concepts such as hybridity and liminality are evident throughout the volume, most chapters in this collection are more applied than theoretical. By contrast, Siphiwe Dube's analysis of the Truth and Reconciliation Commission of Canada (TRCC) draws on a range of philosophical and other theories to consider the role of Christian discourse (which he defines, in this case, as both Christian institutions and language) in addressing both aporia and atrocity in the TRCC. For Dube, theory creates potentially liberatory spaces to posit questions and possibilities that do not easily issue from either the historical record or the TRCC as currently articulated. He argues that Christian discourse as used in the TRCC has a double meaning: it is characterized and mobilized as both a colonial tool used in the residential schools to support assimilation and a language that offers hope, forgiveness, and reconciliation. In laying bare such ambiguity, an attribute he extends metaphorically by using an intentionally ambiguous writing style, Dube examines the relationship between Christianity and colonial power addressed in previous chapters. He openly questions whether and how the TRCC can contribute to the process of reconciliation given its use of a Christian discourse that is deeply implicated in colonialism. In so doing, Dube offers an important critical reading of the TRCC and further brings the story (or, better, stories) of Indigenous-Christian encounter into the twenty-first century.

## Mixed Blessings

This collection neither aims for nor claims comprehensiveness, and there are gaps in regional, thematic, and temporal coverage. For example, the volume does not consider Indigenous-Christian exchange in the North or the Maritimes, nor does it deal with relatively recent and widespread Indigenous interactions with Pentecostal, Evangelical, and charismatic forms of Christianity or with non-Christian faiths such as the Baha'i religion.[36] Rather than providing comprehensive coverage, this collection seeks to convey the energy and dynamism of a specific set of interdisciplinary conversations and case studies, and to spark, in the process, ongoing research and dialogue.

The distinct sites and common patterns of encounter illuminated throughout the pages that follow offer a fresh way forward. Together, the community, individual, and contemporary sites of encounter considered in this collection confirm the exceedingly complex and charged nature of Indigenous-Christian interactions in Canada (interactions, these chapters simultaneously reveal, that were connected with events and processes outside Canada as well). From the moment European Christian missionaries arrived in the territories now known as Canada, encounters were informed by colonial power and Indigenous efforts to engage with new religious frameworks in a way that would allow them to retain, or even enhance, their own spiritual and political strength. These complex relations persist. The legacies of residential schools, in particular, reminds us that along with living histories of Indigenous agency, resistance, and resurgence are those of colonial violence and affiliated cultural loss and community instability. The challenge for scholars, and the one taken up by this book, is to acknowledge and contemplate connections between these complex pasts and presents and, in so doing, promote a more complete understanding of Indigenous encounters with Christianity in Canada.

## Notes

1 "Homily of His Holiness Pope Benedict XVI," Saint Peter's Square, 21 October 2012, http://w2.vatican.va/content/benedict-xvi/en/homilies/2012/documents/hf_ben-xvi_hom_20121021_canonizzazioni.html.

2 For a succinct overview of church apologies, residential school history, and current context, including the Truth and Reconciliation Commission of Canada, see Erin Hanson, "The Residential School System," *Indigenous Foundations, Arts, UBC,* http://indigenousfoundations.arts.ubc.ca/home/government-policy/the-residential-school-system.html.

3 Reporter Eric Reguly employed the language of atonement explicitly: "In An Act of Atonement, Vatican makes Kateri Tekakwitha First Native Canadian Saint," *Globe and Mail,* 21 October 2012, http://www.theglobeandmail.com/news/national/in-an-act-of-atonement-vatican-makes-kateri-tekakwitha-the-first-native-canadian-saint/article4626652/. Kateri's canonization drew extensive media coverage from outlets ranging from *CBC News, BBC News,* and the *New York Times* to *The Eastern Door* [Kahnawake], the *Montreal Gazette,* and *Indian Country Today.*

4 For a thorough biography and analysis of Jesuit hagiography and settler myth making in relation to Kateri, see Allan Greer, *Mohawk Saint: Catherine Tekakwitha and the Jesuits* (New York: Oxford University Press, 2005). See also Nancy Shoemaker, "Kateri Tekakwitha's Tortuous Path to Sainthood," in *In the Days of Our Grandmothers: A Reader in Aboriginal Women's History in Canada,* ed. Mary-Ellen Kelm and Lorna Townsend (Toronto: University of Toronto Press, 2006), 93–116. For a Mohawk perspective, see Darren Bonaparte, *A Lily among Thorns: The Mohawk Repatriation of Káteri Tekahkwí:tha* (Akwesasne, QC: Wampum Chronicles, 2009).

5 Religious studies scholar Michael McNally uses the language of "making meaning" (in contrast to strictly "making do"): *Ojibwe Singers: Hymns, Grief, and a Native Culture in Motion* (New York: Oxford University Press, 2000), 6.

6 See the observations of Mohawk scholar Orenda Boucher cited in Cordelia Hebblethwaite, "Kateri Tekakwitha: First Catholic Native American saint," *BBC News Magazine,* 21 October 2012, http://www.bbc.co.uk/news/magazine-19996957. See also Christina Colizza, "A Mixed Blessing: Kahnawake Reacts to Kateri Tekakwitha's Canonization," *McGill Daily,* 14 November 2012, http://www.mcgilldaily.com/2012/11/a-mixed-blessing/. For context on and call for resurgence of Indigenous (and, more specifically, Mohawk) nationalism, see the work of Mohawk scholar Taiaiake Alfred: *Heeding the Voices of Our Ancestors: Kahnawake Mohawk Politics and the Rise of Native Nationalism* (Don Mills, ON: Oxford University Press, 1995); *Peace, Power, and Righteousness: An Indigenous Manifesto* (Don Mills, ON: Oxford University Press, 1999); *Wasáse: Indigenous Pathways of Action and Freedom* (Peterborough, ON: Broadview Press, 2005). See also the work of Mohawk scholar Audra Simpson, *Mohawk Interruptus: Political Life across the Borders of Nation States* (Durham, NC: Duke University Press, 2014).

7   Hebblethwaite, "Kateri Tekakwitha"; Greer, *Mohawk Saint*, 200–5.

8   Steve Bonspiel, "A Boost for All Mohawk People of Spirit,'" *Toronto Star,* 21 October 2012, http://www.thestar.com/news/insight/2012/10/21/a_boost_for_all_mohawk_people_of_ spirit.html. Bonspiel is editor of the Kahnawake newspaper *The Eastern Door.*

9   This title is further and, more specifically, inspired by the title of journalist Christina Colizza's "A Mixed Blessing: Kahnawake Reacts to Kateri Tekakwitha's Canonization." A similar metaphor is applied in the title of another edited collection on religious encounter: Jamie S. Scott and Gareth Griffiths, eds., *Mixed Messages: Materiality, Textuality, Missions* (New York: Palgrave Macmillan, 2005).

10  The shrine's website readily reveals a patchwork of Indigenous and Catholic iconography (and merchandise): http://www.katerishrine.com/. The shrine is also a meaningful location for Indigenous Catholics of various backgrounds. See, for example, http://www.catholic register.org/faith/item/14884-kateri-feast-day-draws-native-american-catholics-eager -for-own-saint; http://www.timesunion.com/local/article/Kateri-canonized-to-cheerful -crowds-3969837.php; Emma Anderson, *The Death and Afterlife of the North American Martyrs* (Cambridge, MA: Harvard University Press, 2013), 297–302.

11  For various perspectives on residential schools and reconciliation, see the Aboriginal Healing Foundation series: Marlene Brant Castellano, Linda Archibald, and Mike DeGagné, eds., *From Truth to Reconciliation: Transforming the Legacy of Residential Schools* (Ottawa: Aboriginal Healing Foundation, 2008); Gregory Younging, Jonathan Dewar, and Mike DeGagné, eds., *Response, Responsibility, and Renewal: Canada's Truth and Reconciliation Journey* (Ottawa: Aboriginal Healing Foundation, 2009); Ashok Mather, Jonathan Dewar, and Mike DeGagné, eds., *Cultivating Canada: Reconciliation through the Lens of Diversity* (Ottawa: Aboriginal Healing Foundation, 2011). These publications are available online, http://www.ahf.ca/publications/research-series.

12  Aman Sium, Chandni Desai, and Eric Ritskes, "Towards the 'Tangible Unknown': De-colonization and the Indigenous Future," *Decolonization: Indigeneity, Education and Society* 1, 1 (2012), http://decolonization.org/index.php/des/article/view/18638/15564. Denise Nadeau, "Decolonizing Religious Encounter? Teaching 'Indigenous Traditions, Women, and Colonialism,'" this volume. As Sium, Desai, and Ritskes further observe in their introduction to the inaugural issue of this eponymous journal, decolonization "is a messy, dynamic, and a contradictory process," definitions of which remain open, even unknown. "Towards the 'Tangible Unknown,'" ii. For further reflection on settler roles and responsibilities for decolonization, see Paulette Regan, *Unsettling the Settler Within: Indian Residential Schools, Truth Telling, and Reconciliation in Canada* (Vancouver: UBC Press, 2010).

13  Consider, for example, the rich literature on Christianity in Africa, which includes the following studies: Richard Gray, *Black Christians and White Missionaries* (New Haven: Yale University Press, 1990); Jean Comaroff and John L. Comaroff, *Of Revelation and Revolution: Christianity, Colonialism and Consciousness in South Africa,* vol. 1 (Chicago: University of Chicago Press, 1991); Janet Hodgson, "A Battle for Sacred Power: Christian Beginnings among the Xhosa," in *Christianity in South Africa: A Political, Social, and Cultural History,* ed. Richard Elphick and T.R.H. Davenport (Berkeley: University of California Press, 1997), 68–88; J.D.Y. Peel, *Religious Encounter and the Making of the Yoruba* (Bloomington: Indiana University Press, 2000); Adrian Hastings, *Christianity and the African Imagination: Essays in Honour of Adrian Hastings,* ed. David Maxwell and Ingrid Lawrie (Leiden: Brill, 2002); and Elizabeth Elbourne, *Blood Ground: Colonialism, Missions, and the Contest for Christianity in the Cape Colony and Britain, 1799–1853* (Montreal/ Kingston: McGill-Queen's University Press, 2002). Several recent edited collections are

testament to this rethinking in areas beyond Africa as well: see Peggy Brock, ed., *Indigenous Peoples and Religious Change* (Leiden: Brill, 2005); David Lindenfeld and Miles Richardson, eds., *Beyond Conversion and Syncretism: Indigenous Encounters with Missionary Christianity, 1800–2000* (New York: Berghahn Books, 2012).

14 Joel W. Martin and Mark A. Nicholas, eds., *Native Americans, Christianity, and the Reshaping of the American Religious Landscape* (Chapel Hill: University of North Carolina Press, 2010).

15 Martin, "Introduction," in ibid., 2.

16 Emma Anderson, *The Betrayal of Faith: The Tragic Journey of a Colonial Native Convert* (Cambridge: Harvard University Press, 2007).

17 Greer, *Mohawk Saint*, x.

18 Kerry Abel, *Drum Songs: Glimpses of Dene History*, 2nd ed. (Montreal/Kingston: McGill-Queen's University Press, 2005); Susan Neylan, *The Heavens Are Changing: Nineteenth-Century Protestant Missions and Tsimshian Christianity* (Montreal/Kingston: McGill-Queen's University Press, 2003). Several recent doctoral theses likewise focus on specific Indigenous groups: Catherine Murton Stoehr, "Salvation from Empire: The Roots of Anishinabe Christianity in Upper Canada, 1650–1840" (PhD diss., Queen's University, 2008); Nicholas May, "Feasting on the AAM of Heaven: The Christianization of the Nisga'a, 1860–1920" (PhD diss., University of Toronto, 2013).

19 See the works by Anderson, Greer, and Neylan mentioned above, as well as the following: Donald B. Smith, *Sacred Feathers: The Reverend Peter Jones (Kahkewaquonaby) and the Mississauga Indians* (Toronto: University of Toronto Press, 1987); Winona Wheeler, "The Journals and Voices of a Church of England Native Catechist: Askenootow (Charles Pratt), 1851–1884," in *Reading beyond Words: Contexts for Native History*, ed. Jennifer S.H. Brown and Elizabeth Vibert, 2nd ed. (Peterborough, ON: Broadview, 2003), 237–62; Susan Neylan, "'Eating the Angels' Food": Arthur Wellington Clah – An Aboriginal Perspective on Being Christian, 1857–1909," in *Canadian Missionaries, Indigenous Peoples: Representing Religion at Home and Abroad*, ed. Alvyn Austin and James S. Scott (Toronto: University of Toronto Press, 2005), 88–108; Lesley Erickson, "Repositioning the Missionary: Sara Riel, the Grey Nuns, and Aboriginal Women in Catholic Missions of the Northwest," in *Recollecting: Lives of Aboriginal Women of the Canadian Northwest and Borderlands*, ed. Sarah Carter and Patricia McCormack (Edmonton: Athabasca University Press, 2011), 115–34; Peggy Brock, *Many Voyages of Arthur Wellington Clah: A Tsimshian Man on the Pacific Northwest Coast* (Vancouver: UBC Press, 2011); Tolly Bradford, *Prophetic Identities: Indigenous Missionaries on British Colonial Frontiers, 1850–75* (Vancouver: UBC Press, 2012).

20 In addition to the literature cited above, see, for example, Tracy Neal Leavelle, *The Catholic Calumet: Colonial Conversions in French and Indian North America* (Philadelphia: University of Pennsylvania Press, 2012).

21 James Treat, ed., *Native and Christian: Indigenous Voices on Religious Identity in the United States and Canada* (New York: Routledge, 1996); James Treat, *Around the Sacred Fire: Native Religious Activism in the Red Power Era: A Narrative Map of the Indian-Ecumenical Conference* (New York: Palgrave Macmillan, 2003); Frédéric B. Laugrand and Jarich G. Oosten, *Inuit Shamanism and Christianity: Transitions and Transformations in the Twentieth Century* (Montreal/Kingston: McGill-Queen's University Press, 2010); Clinton Westman, "Pentecostalism among Aboriginal People: A Political Movement?" in *The Liberating Spirit: Pentecostals and Social Action in North America*, ed. M. Wilkinson and S. Studebaker (Eugene, OR: Wipf and Stock, 2010), 85–110; Leslie A. Robertson and Kwagu'ł Gixsam Clan, *Standing Up with Ga'axsta'las: Jane Constance Cook and the Politics of Memory, Church, and Custom* (Vancouver: UBC Press, 2012). See also Steve Heinrichs,

ed., *Buffalo Shout, Salmon Cry: Conversations on Creation, Land Justice, and Life Together* (Waterloo, ON: Herald Press, 2013).

22  John Webster Grant, *Moon of Wintertime: Missionaries and the Indians of Canada in Encounter since 1534* (Toronto: University of Toronto Press, 1984).

23  Regional surveys of the Canadian West are illustrative of these approaches. See, for instance, Gerald Friesen, *The Canadian Prairies: A History* (Toronto: University of Toronto Press, 1984), and Sarah Carter, *Aboriginal People and Colonizers of Western Canada to 1900* (Toronto: University of Toronto Press, 1999). Another more recent example of a reductionist depiction of religion and the missionary in western Canada is found in James Daschuk's discussion of food and health among Plains Aboriginal people, in which he positions missionaries as agents of both the Hudson's Bay Company and the Canadian state. Such a depiction downplays the complex role of missionaries during the fur trade era and at treaty, when Indigenous leaders often used missionaries as crucial allies as they sought to oppose or subvert the goals of the Hudson's Bay Company and the state. James William Daschuk, *Clearing the Plains: Disease, Politics of Starvation, and the Loss of Aboriginal Life* (Regina: University of Regina Press, 2013), 70–71, 95.

24  Truth and Reconciliation Commission of Canada, *Honouring the Truth, Reconciling for the Future: Summary of the Final Report of the Truth and Reconciliation Commission of Canada,* 2015, 1, http://www.trc.ca/websites/trcinstitution/File/2015/Honouring_the_Truth_Reconciling_for_the_Future_July_23_2015.pdf.

25  Scholars of South Africa have made similar observations about the Truth and Reconciliation Commission in that country. Deborah Posel, for example, argues that although the South African TRC created space for the voices of victims of Apartheid-era violence, the commission's final report also produced a simplistic narrative and historical memory of Apartheid. Deborah Posel, "The TRC Report: What Kind of History? What Kind of Truth? A Preliminary Report" (presented at the Wits History Workshop "The TRC: Commissioning the Past," 11–14 June, Johannesburg, 1999), 1–30, http://wiredspace.wits.ac.za//handle/10539/8046.

26  For samples of mainstream media coverage, see http://globalnews.ca/tag/residential-schools/; http://news.nationalpost.com/tag/residential-schools; http://www.huffingtonpost.ca/news/residential-schools-canada/; http://www.cbc.ca/news/canada/a-history-of-residential-schools-in-canada-1.702280. For an example outside of news media that reproduces this binary depiction, see Sarah Milroy's visual essay "What Emily Carr Saw: An Unsettling Journey through the Archives," *The Walrus,* May 2015, 37–42.

27  Definitions in the *Oxford English Reference Dictionary,* for example, include, in verb form, "meet as an adversary" and, as a noun, "a meeting in conflict." Judy Pearsall and Bill Trumble, eds., *Oxford English Reference Dictionary,* 2nd ed., revised (Oxford: Oxford University Press, 2002), 463.

28  The term figures, for example, in the title of Webster Grant's *Moon of Wintertime: Missionaries and the Indians of Canada in Encounter since 1534.* "Encounter" is a concept deployed by historians in particular. Ethnohistorian James Axtell has characterized encounters as "'mutual, reciprocal – two-way rather than one-way streets,' 'generally capacious,' and 'temporally and spatially fluid.'" Cited in Daniel M. Cobb, "Continuing Encounters: Historical Perspectives," in Daniel M. Cobb and Loretta Fowler, eds., *Beyond Red Power: American Indian Politics and Activism since 1900* (Santa Fe, NM: School for Advanced Research Press, 2007), 57. As Cobb notes, scholars of Axtell's generation tended to apply "encounter" to early contact periods; however, the concept retains purchase in more recent contexts, where both colonialism and Indigenous engagement with – in the case of this volume – Christianity continue.

29 James Axtell's studies of religious encounter in northeastern North America were among the first to consider closely how Indigenous Christian conversion was as much about politics as religion. See James Axtell, "Some Thoughts on the Ethnohistory of Mission," *Ethnohistory* 29, 1 (1982): 35–41, and *The Invasion Within: The Contest of Cultures in Colonial North America,* Cultural Origins of North America 1 (New York: Oxford University Press, 1986). Webster Grant's *Moon of Wintertime* also hints at the pragmatic and political aspects of Indigenous interactions with Christianity, although it does not explore this issue in great depth.

30 For a thoughtful critique of this tension, and an alternative analytical model focused on practice, see Michael D. McNally, "The Practice of Native American Christianity," *Church History* 69, 4 (December 2000): 834–59. The inseparability of the spiritual and the political in Indigenous contexts was a point that Tasha Beeds, Carmen Lansdowne, and Denise Nadeau stressed throughout the workshop that led to this volume. On this point see also Lee Irwin, "Native American Spirituality: An Introduction," in *Native American Spirituality: A Critical Reader,* ed. Lee Irwin (Lincoln: University of Nebraska Press, 2000), 3. Critiques of sacred/secular binaries are not confined to Indigenous contexts. Some scholars of Christianity in Canada have likewise challenged historians to take spirituality seriously rather than reducing it to social or political frameworks. See, for example, Ruth Compton Brouwer, "Transcending the 'Unacknowledged Quarantine': Putting Religion into English-Canadian Women's History," *Journal of Canadian Studies* 27, 3 (Fall 1992): 47–62; Michael Gauvreau, *The Evangelical Century: College and Creed in English Canada from the Great Revival to the Great Depression* (Montreal/Kingston: McGill-Queen's University Press, 1991); Marguerite Van Die, *An Evangelical Mind: Nathanael Burwash and the Methodist Tradition in Canada, 1839–1918* (Montreal/Kingston: McGill-Queen's University Press, 1989).

31 That secular and sacred power stood at the centre of this kind of encounter is a point made in regards to other colonial contexts as well. See, especially, Hodgson, "A Battle for Sacred Power."

32 Timothy Pearson, "Reading Rituals: Performance and Religious Encounter in Early Colonial Northeast North America," this volume.

33 A recent collection reflecting this transnational approach to Canadian history at large is Karen Dubinsky, Adele Perry, and Henry Yu, eds., *Within and Without the Nation: Canadian History as Transnational History* (Toronto: University of Toronto Press, 2015). For discussion and critique of such a move towards the transnational, see Gerald Friesen, "Critical History in Western Canada," in *The West and Beyond: New Perspectives on an Imagined Region,* ed. Sarah Carter, Alvin Finkel, and Peter Fortna (Edmonton: Athabasca University Press, 2010), 3–12. Canadian historians of religion have long positioned their subjects in a transnational context. See, for example, Alvyn J. Austin, *Saving China: Canadian Missionaries in the Middle Kingdom, 1888–1959* (Toronto: University of Toronto Press, 1986); Austin and Scott, *Canadian Missionaries, Indigenous Peoples*; Ruth Compton Brouwer, *New Women for God: Canadian Presbyterian Women and India Missions, 1876–1914* (Toronto: University of Toronto Press, 1990) and *Modern Women Modernizing Men: The Changing Missions of Three Professional Women in Asia and Africa, 1902–69* (Vancouver: UBC Press, 2002); Rosemary Gagan, *A Sensitive Independence: Canadian Methodist Women Missionaries in Canada and the Orient, 1881–1925* (Montreal/Kingston: McGill-Queen's University Press, 1992). Likewise, historians of Indigenous peoples have examined Indigenous mobility across colonial state borders and transnational, or transregional, Indigenous connections. See, for example, Tolly Bradford, "World Visions: 'Native Missionaries,' Mission Networks and Critiques of Colonialism in Nineteenth-Century

South Africa and Canada," in Peter Limb, Norman Etherington, and Peter Midgley, eds., *Grappling with the Beast: Indigenous Southern African Responses to Colonialism, 1840–1930* (Leiden: Brill, 2010), 311–33; Paige Raibmon, "Meanings of Mobility on the Northwest Coast," in Ted Binnema and Susan Neylan, eds., *New Histories for Old: Changing Perspectives on Canada's Native Pasts* (Vancouver: UBC Press, 2007), 175–95. For emerging theoretical formulations and analyses of Indigenous transnationalism, see also Paul Lai and Lindsay Claire Smith, eds., "Special Issue: Alternative Contact: Indigeneity, Globalism, and American Studies," *American Quarterly* 62, 3 (September 2010); Hsinya Huang, Philip J. Deloria, Laura M. Furlan, and John Gambler, eds., "Special Forum: Charting Transnational Native American Studies: Aesthetics, Politics, Identity," *Journal of Transnational American Studies* 4, 1 (2012).

34   Mary Louise Pratt, *Imperial Eyes: Travel Writing and Transculturation* (London: Routledge, 1992), esp. 6–7.

35   Tasha Beeds, "Rethinking Edward Ahenakew's Intellectual Legacy: Expressions of nêhiyawi-mâmitonêyihcikan (Cree Consciousness or Thinking)," this volume.

36   For existing studies on these topics, see, for example, Abel, *Drum Songs*; Chelsea Horton, "All Is One: Becoming Indigenous and Baha'i in Global North America" (PhD diss., University of British Columbia, 2013); Laugrand and Oosten, *Inuit Shamanism and Christianity*; Westman, "Pentecostalism among Aboriginal People."

# Part 1
# Communities in Encounter

# 1

# Reading Rituals:
# Performance and Religious Encounter in
# Early Colonial Northeastern North America

*Timothy Pearson*

> *For I do not call it religion if there be not some ritual* (latrie) *or*
> *divine service.*
>
> – Marc Lescarbot, 1609[1]

Many early modern peoples, both Indigenous North Americans and Europeans, considered the social group and ritual to be, to a significant degree, isomorphous.[2] The lawyer and adventurer Marc Lescarbot, who travelled to Acadia in 1606–07, suggested in his *Histoire de la Nouvelle-France* that cultural practice fundamentally characterizes and, therefore, differentiates, all nations. All people, he said, enter and leave the world in much the same way, and what divides them into groups is behaviour, customs, and ceremonies that involve everything from naming practices to ways of worshipping the divine.[3] This idea was not significantly different from that of a Montagnais man called Makheabichtichiou from the region of Tadoussac, who told the Jesuit missionary Paul Le Jeune during a conversation in 1637 that "all nations have something peculiar to them. Baptism is good for you others, and not for us."[4] Makheabichtichiou recognized the spiritual power of baptism, but believed it was particular to French needs and ways of living. The Montagnais had their own ritual forms to engage the cosmological forces of the universe. For both Makheabichtichiou and Lescarbot, religious practices – rituals – even more than whatever beliefs or doctrines they may have entailed, were universal and essential constituents of diverse social and cultural identities.

The fundamental role that Indigenous peoples as well as European Catholics granted to serialized performances as objects that did not just reflect but actually constituted social groups calls attention to ritual as something more than just symbolic practice. While hermeneutical readings of ritual tend to emphasize the meaning behind the performance, in practice, belief is generally not separate from ritual but part of the experience of the sacred – the other-than-human –

shared by participants.[5] As I aim to show in this chapter, ritual contributed to the creation of real and metaphorical spaces where people experienced the sacred and negotiated religious and social differences in the early colonial Northeast. This chapter examines the place and function of ritual in encounters between Indigenous peoples and French Catholic missionaries in the first half of the seventeenth century. In doing so, it engages with some key issues of religious encounter that are of collective interest to the contributors to this volume: religion as a locus of cross-cultural communication, the challenge of new and alternative spiritual systems and their practices, the relationship of religion to daily life, the meaning of conversion, and the difficulties involved in reading Euro-Canadian sources for evidence of Indigenous spirituality. In response to concerns raised by some contributors here and at the workshop that preceded the publication of this volume regarding the limitations that colonial texts place on understandings of Indigenous histories, I hope to contribute to the development of ways of reading that emphasize ritual in both its performed and written forms. Like Elizabeth Elbourne, I see ritual as an instrument used by all participants in colonial exchange to manage a religious encounter that itself stands as a "contact zone" infused with power as potentially great as it was dangerous.[6] For both French newcomers and Indigenous peoples alike, metaphysical understandings of the world were a fundamental part of daily life in the early seventeenth century, and I try to place both parties under the same analytical lens. Therefore, I will refer to "spiritual lifeways" rather than religious beliefs in an effort to reduce the conceptual difference between theology and practice – a Euro-American sense of bounded religion and the complete integration of the metaphysical with daily life common among many Indigenous nations.[7] By focusing on ritual practices that did not merely reflect, but actually constituted, the sacred in various ways, I aim to show how French, Huron, and Algonquin social groups negotiated religious encounter through inclusive and exclusive ideals of shared spiritual lifeways from the late 1630s to 1650.

## History, Anthropology, and the Problem of Ritual

First, however, it is necessary to problematize ritual by exploring some of its difficulties as a religious, historical, and anthropological object. In the first half of the seventeenth century, religion, along with trade and diplomacy, formed primary points of contact between Indigenous nations and French newcomers. Several recent studies show how rituals of trade, war, violence, and diplomacy animated intercultural communication and cultural change.[8] Historians have also focused on religious encounter in ways that complicate and challenge traditional notions of Christian conversion, showing how the creative appropriation of aspects of Christianity resulted in dynamic and multiple Indigenous

Christianit*ies*.[9] My strategy here is to concentrate on the first phases of encounter, when Indigenous and French interlocutors each tried to entice the other to become participants in their own culturally specific performances and thereby begin the process of reconstituting the social identities of the other.[10]

The challenge of examining ritual in this way is the disagreement shown in historical sources over just what constituted a ritual and, furthermore, current questions over the suitability of the term for describing a broad range of ceremonies and spiritual practices. As Lescarbot makes clear in the quotation that opens this chapter, Catholics tended to discriminate between rituals that created the divine for participants and were, therefore, properly religious *(latrie)* and what settlers often regarded as the superstitious ceremonies of Indigenous peoples. *Latrie* refers specifically to the worship that all Catholics owed to the divine presence contained in the mystical transubstantiation of the bread and wine into the body and blood of Christ during the Mass.[11] It is, therefore, differentiated from other serialized performances by what it does – in effect, making the divine immanent, (re)creating God within the ritual of the Mass for people who already shared a fundamental belief-set. In comparison with this divine mystery, Lescarbot could see no evidence of what he considered real worship in the rituals of the Mi'Kmaq he observed in Acadia. He judged accordingly that the Mi'Kmaq had no religion and, therefore, could be expected to convert easily to Christianity.[12]

This distinction between ritual that was properly religious and mere ceremony continued in later Jesuit texts from the Huron mission. In a single chapter of the 1639 *Jesuit Relation,* for example, missionaries defined Huron *ceremonie* as superstition and play, as something associated with and inspired by the devil, as "mal-heureuses" (wretched) and as a form of servitude and slavery to diabolical forces.[13] For Jesuits, *ceremonie,* even though it accessed metaphysical forces, was not properly religious because it did not create the Catholic divine but, rather, engaged spiritual forces that missionaries tended to regard as devilish in origin and nature. For the Huron and other Indigenous groups, however, the purpose of ritual was not to create the divine for participants who shared certain a priori beliefs but rather to negotiate and manage the spiritual forces that were already everywhere in the world. These were fundamentally different understandings of and approaches to spiritual power and the purposes and actions of the rituals that engaged them.[14]

Further complicating matters, Indigenous peoples in North America today tend to use "ceremony," not "ritual," to refer to practices and performances that create those shared sacred experiences, while for some Catholics the form (and reform) of ritual practice has continued to court controversy since the changes instituted by the Second Vatican council in the 1960s. Competing definitions and conceptual slippages of this sort make ritual, like religion and belief, a difficult historical subject of study. Some may prefer to avoid the term "ritual" because of these complicated historical and contemporary associations. For my purposes, which are decidedly historical in orientation and rooted in early encounters between Europeans and Indigenous peoples, however, the term remains useful. Both European newcomers and Indigenous peoples instantly recognized the ritual practices of the other as significant and powerful even if they did not see them as necessarily proper or legitimate. It is in this limited sense that anthropologist Roy A. Rappaport regards ritual as universal, as the social act basic to all humanity and distinguishable to all outside observers everywhere. This mutual recognition of what he calls "performative events of more or less invariant sequences and utterances not entirely encoded or scripted by performers" marks ritual as an important contact zone between Europeans and Indigenous peoples in the early days of encounter.[15] Religious rituals tended towards the creation of an awareness of spiritual power among participants, whether celebrants or members of congregations, and observers. They offer, therefore, a broad framework for understanding how that power was generated, shared, and, most importantly, experienced by Europeans and Indigenous peoples alike in early interactions. Finally, ritual allows for an examination of the ways people tried to include or exclude others from the social group or the bounded group of the faithful through carefully crafted collective experiences that did not just symbolize, but actually created, shared experiences and social identities.

Ritual evokes another problem, however, which likewise shapes this chapter. As something intended to be performed, ritual lacks the stability of written archives with which historians are generally familiar and comfortable. Furthermore, historical performances are generally available only through European sources. These factors both open up the possibility of ritual for destabilizing traditional colonial histories and point towards its limitations. When missionaries described Indigenous rituals in their writings, they did so from a particular vantage point and according to their own purposes and assumptions. As a result, numerous meanings have crept into their written interpretations, intentionally or otherwise, that were likely not present in the original performance. The danger here, as historian Philippe Buc has pointed out, is that the process of creating archives introduces distortions so significant that the performance itself is lost and all that can be recovered is what the commentators saw, or rather, believed they saw.[16] In an effort to confront this challenge, I divide ritual into two categories: "ritual as it appears in text" and "ritual as it may have originally been performed." Although in the case of past ritual events both categories can be accessed only through historical records, my aim in making this division and exploring its possibilities is to unsettle missionary texts by deploying multiple ways of reading the rituals described in them. The examples I relate here, of course, represent only a tiny fraction of the ritual performances that survive in colonial sources, but they are nevertheless broadly representative of the kinds of rituals that appear in early encounter narratives and the ways Indigenous peoples and Europeans alike may have deployed them, participated in them, challenged them, and shared them.

## Ritual in Text

Early on in the religious contact zone of the colonial Northeast, missionaries often looked to the ritual performances of Indigenous Christian neophytes and converts to prove what they hoped were the sincere beliefs of new Christians. For example, when a new Christian at the mission village of Sillery, located near Quebec, held a traditional Algonquin Eat-All Feast in 1638 to announce his acceptance of the new religion, Jesuit observers carefully examined his performance for evidence of Christian virtue, trying to read the outward ritual for signs of true inward belief. "I do not know whether he has Charity [love of God]," wrote the missionary Paul Le Jeune after watching the feast, "but I do know that he shows strong indications of it."[17] Despite Le Jeune's critical scrutiny, the Eat-All Feast was in fact an integral part of traditional Algonquin ritual life and carried significant religious overtones. It celebrated the capture of a large animal, thanking it for giving itself so that others could eat, and simultaneously celebrating the successful hunter who served as host. The feast, as Emma Anderson describes it, offered a practical manifestation of Algonquin social values of gifting and solidarity, granting to the host, who abstained, respect as a hunter and political influence.[18] Accordingly, this recent convert, called Ignace by the missionaries, did not partake in the feast but rather took the opportunity to speak to his guests, encouraging them to try out Christianity. Jesuit commentators generally tended to regard Eat-All Feasts as the worst kind of base gluttony, and hoped Ignace's abstention showed evidence of his new faith and rejection of the ways of life of his kin and countrymen. The "ritual-in-text," therefore, presents only a partial view, and perhaps a complete misunderstanding, of what Ignace may have intended or achieved on this occasion, and does so from the perspective of a bounded Christian belief rather than Montagnais social values.

In addition to reinterpreting Indigenous rituals, missionaries also tried to draw Indigenous participants into specifically Christian ritual practices, but again could only guess at the meanings expressed and understandings received. On Holy Thursday of 1640, for example, missionaries, hospital nuns, and leading men of the colony converged on the tiny hospital at Sillery run by the

Augustinian Sisters, where they proceeded to wash the feet of unsuspecting Algonquin and Montagnais patients. The governor washed the feet of the male patients, and the nuns those of the female ones, "as it is the custom of well-regulated hospitals [in France] to wash the feet of the poor."[19] This ritual, the *pedilavium,* was a common act of Christian humility and contrition in preparation for Easter that mirrored Christ's washing of his disciples' feet on the eve of his crucifixion. In contemporary Europe the ritual inverted the usual social hierarchies. "We explained to them why we performed these acts of humility," wrote Paul Le Jeune. "God knows whether these poor barbarians were touched, seeing persons of such merit at their feet."[20] The missionaries feared, with due cause, that the meaning of the *pedilavium,* so rooted in Christian history and French customs and social hierarchies, would be misunderstood or lost completely on Indigenous participants who did not share the same beliefs, social experiences, or spiritual lifeways. Le Jeune's confusion about the ritual's impact stems from the same misconceptions that led him to question Ignace's conversion: the inability to entirely trust outward performance as an indicator of what he considered to be truly important, that is, internal belief.

Rituals in text such as these included Indigenous peoples in Christian performances more as subjects to be scrutinized than as participants in a shared experience. The tendency of the ritual in text to focus on symbolism generally left missionaries hoping and guessing. It also, however, left them free to reinterpret performances in any way they saw fit for reading audiences back home.[21] In 1650, when Mohawk warriors captured and subsequently executed a young Algonquin warrior from Sillery named Onaharé, Jesuit missionaries interpreted his death as a Christian martyrdom even though he was killed as a war captive and therefore within Indigenous rituals of war and adoption. Like other ritual performances, martyrdom is a loosely scripted event rooted deeply in Christian history and belief. Medievalist Alison Elliot describes it as a drama defined not by death but by the dramatic scene that precedes death, when the martyr confronts his or her persecutors in a theatrical display that is rich in meaning. It is this drama, heavily governed by tradition and expectation, which makes the martyr and allows the victim to speak well beyond immediate audiences to a wider community.[22] To the Jesuits, Onaharé's death showed all the signs of just such a drama; its importance, they believed, could be found in hermeneutical readings of its elements.

The execution of a war captive, closely linked to adoption practices, was likewise a formalized event recognized as powerful and significant by all nations of the Northeast. For more than a decade prior to Onaharé's death, the Iroquois had been capturing so many people in war and adopting them at such a rate that by 1650 it is estimated that upwards of two-thirds of the population of the

Five Nations may have been adoptees.[23] Warfare for Indigenous peoples of the Northeast was a significant religious and cultural affair. The captivity and adoption rituals that led to so many, especially Hurons, joining the Iroquois League, and also to the deaths of Onaharé and many others through ritual torture and execution, held a sacred logic for Mohawks, Algonquins, and others that made them meaningful as much more than an expeditious way of dealing with enemies. For those captives who were adopted rather than put to death, the ritual offered the unity and strength of a shared community. For warriors who were executed, the ritual provided the chance to exhibit personal bravery and affirm key cultural values.[24] All nations of the Northeast were deeply familiar with these practices, including Jesuits whose own brethren, Jean de Brébeuf and Gabriel Lalemant, among others, suffered and even died as captives in the 1640s. That some of these missionaries subsequently became Christian saints merely reaffirms the shared acknowledgment of the power of these rituals and the power of text to impose meanings upon them.

No Christian missionary witnessed Onaharé's death. Rather, two Huron men, taken captive with him and later freed, reported what had happened to Jesuits in Quebec.[25] They told them that Onaharé began to pray loudly as soon as he was captured and that he did not cease to do so throughout the journey from the site of his ambush to Mohawk country. Once there, he continued to pray aloud through three days and nights of torture. As the pre-death drama unfolded, a Huron captive found an opportunity to speak to Onaharé on the scaffold.[26] Onaharé asked the man to send a message to his Algonquin kin: "If ever, my dear friend, you return to the country of the Algonquins, assure them that the Iroquois, with all their tortures, have not succeeded in stifling the prayer on my lips, nor the faith in my heart. Tell them that I died in happiness, in the hope of going very soon to heaven."[27]

In the *Jesuit Relations,* Onaharé's fight against the Iroquois becomes a holy war in which death provides sufficient cause to claim the martyr's palm.[28] His vow to suffer and even die, if necessary, and his performance of the Christian ritual of confession before setting off for war, ensured in Jesuit minds that he died free of sin. A Huron warrior who accompanied Onaharé's war band and then defected to the Iroquois in order, it seems, to join friends and family who had already been adopted and were living among them, is painted as a traitor – the Judas figure who made Onaharé's subsequent death all the more heroic against a backdrop of Christian martyrdom narratives.[29] Onaharé's final message to his Algonquin kin the Jesuits regarded as an act of thanksgiving, "for the grace that [God] had given him to suffer as a Christian and not as a common savage."[30] The ritual in text transformed Onaharé from a "savage" who lived without faith into a Christian, and from a warrior into a martyr.

Because of the symbolic meanings it imposes, however, the ritual in text also leaves questions about Onaharé's experience and what he may have hoped to share with others through his ritual death. In the final hours of his life, hours rich in drama and meaning, Onaharé called on Algonquins, not Jesuits, to recognize the power of his death. Perhaps he hoped that it would serve as evidence that Christianity could become part of Algonquin spiritual lifeways without jeopardizing key Algonquin cultural values – he died as a Christian and also as an Algonquin. Perhaps Onaharé intended to use the shared experiences generated by rituals of captivity and adoption/death to express notions of community membership and social solidarity with his Christian and Algonquin kin alike. In their reinterpretation of events, however, the Jesuits bypass these efforts, instead reading outward signs, familiar to them from key Christian hagiographic texts, as evidence of the inward transformation of a prized neophyte from "common savage" to Christian saint, according to the conventions of the martyrological narrative and the conversions as well as calamities they expected to find in North America.

## Ritual in Performance

Distance, separation, and aloofness from Indigenous ritual performances did not prevent Jesuit writers from drawing their own conclusions about the hidden meanings behind outward events. For this reason, the "ritual in performance" and the experience of participants in them are generally much harder to access through colonial texts than the ritual in text. In the *Jesuit Relation* of 1639, Jérôme Lalemant, the superior of the Huron mission, describes a series of rituals performed in the Huron village of Ossossané (called La Conception by the Jesuits) that illustrate this aloofness but also show how these same sources, when read against other texts, reveal some of the ritual in performance and its essential role in religious encounter between Hurons and Jesuits – alleviating in part the temptation to read rituals only as outward symbols. In a particular example that dominates the chapter, Lalemant relates how Jesuit missionaries residing close to the village refused to participate in a dream-fulfillment ritual held for a woman named Angoutenc. Hurons regarded dream fulfillment as essential for the maintenance of individual and collective health.[31] Angoutenc, when she fell ill, dreamed that all the surrounding nations, including the Jesuits, brought her gifts so that she might recover. When the dream was made known to her community a total of twenty-two gifts were gathered, but the Jesuits refused to hand over a blue blanket she asked of them.[32] The healing ritual proceeded regardless, and the Jesuits withdrew to their cabin located "a musket shot" from the main village. At the nearby Huron village of Ihonatiria, we are told, the door of the Jesuit cabin had been repeatedly broken down during similar ritual celebrations and the missionaries at Ossossané were determined to avoid the same problem. By establishing themselves at some distance from the main village, they signaled their intention to remain apart from the community and its rituals.[33]

Hurons, like Algonquins, generally regarded spiritual power as morally neutral and capable of both good and evil. Aloofness from community and ritual life was considered evidence of negative intentions, especially when adopted by those like the missionaries, who potentially held significant spiritual knowledge and power.[34] Missionaries, on the other hand, believed in the Christian duality of good and evil and regarded Indigenous ritual practices as both inspired by and dedicated to diabolical forces. Confronted with rituals of gift-giving prompted by the dream/vision of Angoutenc, the Jesuits fell back upon well-worn explanations. "The authors of this feast, as well as of all the other ceremonies of the country, and especially of the nude dances and like performances, are no others than the demons," Lalemant wrote.[35] When the village council called upon the missionaries to offer their opinion on fulfilling Angoutenc's dream, their response to the community was that it "could not do a worse thing for the country: that they were continuing to offer homage to evil spirits, through which they more and more confirmed their empire over them and their country, and nothing good could come of continuing to serve such a bad master."[36] In the *Jesuit Relations,* Huron ritual practices are characterized as unsophisticated devilry, while the Jesuits meticulously maintain their distance and try to draw potential converts away from traditional practices.

Accessing the ritual in performance requires decentring these interpretations. At least one French commentator took issue with Jesuit assumptions. Louis-Armand Lom d'Arce Baron de Lahontan, was a military officer in Canada from roughly 1683 to 1693, during which time he learned the Algonquin and Huron languages, lived at the French post of Michilimackinac, and befriended the Huron headman Kondiaronk, who, under the name Adario, became his main informant and interlocutor in accounts of his travels that he later published.[37] His ethnographic works skewered many widely held European beliefs about Indigenous peoples:

> I have read a thousand Ridiculous Stories Writ by our Clergymen, who maintain that the Savages have conferences with [the devil], and not only consult him, but pay him a sort of Homage. Now all these advances are ridiculous; for in earnest, the Devil never appear'd to these Americans ... In fine, after using all possible means for a perfect knowledg [sic] of this matter; I concluded that these Ecclesiasticks did not understand the true importance of the great word Matchi Manitou, (which signifies an Evil Spirit, Matchi being the word for evil and

Manitou for Spirit;). For by the devil they understand such things as are offensive to "em, which in our language comes near to the signification of Misfortune, Fate, Unfavourable Destiny, etc. So that in speaking of the Devil they do not mean that Evil Spirit that in Europe is represented under the figure of a Man, with a long Tail and great Horns and Claws."[38]

Lahontan goes on to explain that where Christians placed their faith in laws found in books, reason lay at the heart of Huron spiritual lifeways. It was the Christian talent for believing out of faith, rather than the evidence provided by living, and taking the writings of men for divine truth, rather than experience, that seemed senseless to Hurons and prevented their conversion to Christianity: "Their prejudice [against Christianity] proceeds from this, that they can't be convinc'd that the Infallibility of the Scripture is to be made out by the Light of Reason. The Word Faith is enough to choak them; they make a jest of it, and alledge that the writings of past Ages are false, supposititious and alter'd."[39] In other words, Hurons had much the same problem with Christian scripture that historians now have with missionary descriptions of ritual; they may have been altered to serve or reflect a particular interest that was held on faith and not the evidence provided by living. Hurons preferred to construct spirituality out of tangible things, the world around them, and dreams, through which they believed the metaphysical forces of the world spoke to them. Spirituality was linked to life through experience.

Hurons understood that Christianity precluded the kinds of tangible and shared numinous experiences their rituals generated for all participants, regardless of faith. Ritual was essential, not for the religious duty of worshipping the divine *(latrie)* and recreating it for the faithful, but for accessing and negotiating with spiritual power. Its importance was not as a symbol but as an event that brought people together. Even the Jesuits were consulted and invited to join in. In response to their refusal to hand over the blue blanket and their general objections to carrying out Angoutenc's dream, however, the headman of the Ossassané council urged the community to have courage and to persist with what was "so necessary and important according to the customs of our ancestors."[40] Joining people together in common cause and creating a shared experience of the sacred drew from the ritual the power necessary to unify the social group, overriding the warnings of those determined to maintain their distance.

The missionaries were welcomed, and even encouraged, to participate in this healing ritual, but when they refused and withdrew to the perceived safety of their cabin, the ritual proceeded nonetheless. On the first night, Angoutenc visited all the cabins in Ossossané. Barefoot and supported by a man on each side she walked through the centre of each longhouse and directly through each of the fires that occupied the central gallery – more than two or three hundred in all – without burning herself. As she passed, the gathered participants followed her in a dance that meandered from longhouse to longhouse. This dancing and feasting lasted three days, during which time the normal rules of society did not apply. Anthropologist Victor Turner describes such ritual time and space as liminal. Here, "betwixt and between" established and normal social states, participants entered into what he calls "communitas" with each other – a state of heightened emotional awareness of the fragility of the community.[41] The ritual suspended social norms and offered opportunities to renew solidarities. Each person had the chance to present his or her own special desires or dreams (*ondinonc*) to the community, which was done in the form of a riddle.[42] Participants then took turns trying to solve the riddle and discover what the person wanted. Once the riddle was solved, the entire community tried to satisfy the individual's desire and thus put to rest any potentially destructive or self-serving behaviour.

As a result, the ritual gave vent and offered resolution not only to Angoutenc's needs, but also to those of the entire community. More than one hundred riddles were offered and solved on this occasion.[43] After three days of feasting and celebration, and with the missionaries still barricaded in their cabin, Angoutenc made a final pass through all the longhouses to mark the end of the feast. It was her turn to present a riddle that the entire community tried to solve. All then strove to satisfy this final request, capping the celebration and reinforcing their unity, strength, and shared experience.[44]

Sometime after emerging from their cabin at the end of this three-day celebration, one of the missionaries spoke with Angoutenc, who told him what had transpired. She also told him that Jesuit refusal to participate had not jeopardized the effectiveness of the ritual: "The devil [in Jesuit reckoning] – after our refusal to give her the blanket that he had ordered and that was asked of us – had appeared to her in the night, and had told her that we remained aloof, and that therefore, notwithstanding our refusal she would not fail to recover if the rest went well; that moreover, thenceforward he would no longer have us participate therein."[45] Angoutenc recovered her health following the feast. Surrounding nations contributed the gifts her dream had demanded, no doubt reinforcing the alliances that were so important to Huron political and spiritual life. All participants contributed to the resolution of potentially destructive desires. The Jesuits' refusal to participate had merely managed to communicate their willful self-exclusion from the community.

The ritual in performance, even when precariously accessed through the ritual in text, reveals an inclusiveness that seems in direct conflict with the exclusionary search for individual internal meaning the missionaries sought in symbolic ritual, and reinforces the importance of the shared experience. The celebrants had attempted to draw the Jesuits into their ritual, offering solidarity and extended political alliance to the newcomers. Even after the Jesuits refused to participate, however, Lalemant noted that the Huron did not cease to try to include them in such events, but that it was "always with little success."[46] The determination of the missionaries to refuse these invitations and to recast Huron rituals as the work of diabolical forces likely contributed to a growing perception among the Huron that these strangers were dangerous and powerful outsiders, adding to accusations of witchcraft made against them, which became increasingly frequent as disease and warfare began to take a devastating toll in the late 1630s. The healing ritual in performance, read through some of the Jesuits' more ethnographic reporting and complementary sources such as Lahontan's, provides a glimpse of the close connection between Huron spirituality and social identity at a historical moment when the fragility of the community was starting to become painfully apparent.

## Conclusion

For Christians and Indigenous peoples alike, mid-seventeenth-century Canada offered a world rife with powerful spiritual forces, potentially both divine and dangerous. Ritual could make these other-than-human forces immanent and generate a shared sense of the sacred for both parties to the encounter, or it could reveal the inner faith and allegiances of participants. Christian rituals did so, however, only for the initiated who shared a predetermined set of beliefs. Outsiders were treated as subjects, not participants, as the recipients of favours rather than as members of a shared solidarity. Meanwhile, missionaries remained aloof from Indigenous ritual performances they did not control but nevertheless claimed the right to pass judgment on through the ritual in text. The exclusivity of Christian ritual practice is, therefore, mirrored in missionary writing. The refusal of missionaries to join in the rituals of others, even when invited, and to restrict participation in theirs (as subjects rather than as objects, for example, of the *pedilavium*) to only those who professed certain beliefs, established Christianity for Hurons and Algonquins as an exclusionary and abstract belief system, disconnected from the realities of everyday life, and as a tool for the differentiation and categorization of people, thus creating suspicion rather than building solidarity.

The ritual in performance, however, takes us beyond hermeneutical readings offered by Jesuits even in their more ethnographic texts. In performance, the rituals Hurons and Algonquins deployed in early contact zones attempted to generate a shared experience of the sacred that built on existing social solidarities to extend the limits of the community to all willing participants. For Hurons and Algonquins, the divine was already present everywhere in the world so ritual wasn't needed to create it but, rather, to manage it in such a way as to maintain solidarity and ameliorate potentially divisive social behaviours that might have negative outcomes for the group. All participants in a ritual performance, not just those initiated into a particular abstract belief, might share in the collective experience of sacred power. Onaharé called on his Algonquin relatives to recognize the power of his death according to Algonquin and Christian ethics and narratives. The Huron did not ask Jesuit missionaries to change their fundamental beliefs in order to join them in the ritual celebration of gift-giving that fulfilled Angoutenc's dream. Rather, they asked them to share in the common fate of all members of the community. The Jesuits' refusal to do so, however, could not destroy the efficacy of the ritual for those who did participate.[47]

Today ritual remains a social act basic to human societies, whose possibilities for fostering shared experiences and cross-cultural communication are enormous. When Max Gros-Louis, Chief of the Huron-Wendat Nation of Wendake, Quebec (descendants of Angoutenc's people), appeared in 2007 before the Bouchard-Taylor Commission then exploring the contentious issue of cultural accommodation of new immigrants and minorities in Quebec, he reminded the commissioners that it was the Indigenous nations who first accommodated Europeans in North America, only to lose their rights, lands, and ways of life over time. Yet the lesson of this history, he argued, teaches neither the complete rejection nor accommodation of newcomers as a strategy of encounter but rather the need to refrain from imposing the exclusive laws and values of one group upon another and the need to follow the Wendat model of inclusivity to accept and cultivate cultural differences and foster communication, not fear, among peoples. "This is what our people have always practiced," Gros-Louis concluded, "and it is a virtue."[48]

## Notes

1  Marc Lescarbot, *Histoire de la Nouvelle-France* (Paris: Jean Milot, 1609), 676. All translations are my own unless otherwise noted.
2  See Philippe Buc, *The Dangers of Ritual: Between Early Medieval Texts and Social Scientific Theory* (Princeton, NJ: Princeton University Press, 2001), 169–71, and "The Monster and the Critics: A Ritual Reply," *Early Medieval Europe* 15, 4 (2007): 447. On the correspondence between religion and early modern French political culture, see Alain Tallon, *Conscience nationale et sentiment religieux en France au XVIe siècle* (Paris: Presses Universitaires de France, 2002).
3  Lescarbot, *Histoire,* 662.
4  *The Jesuit Relations and Allied Documents,* ed. Rueban Gold Thwaites (Cleveland: Burrows Bros., 1896–1901), 11:163 (1637). *The Jesuit Relations* refers to a set of annual mission reports written in Canada and published in France between 1633 and 1672. For most years prior

to 1650, each *Jesuit Relation* was composed in two parts, one written by the superior of the Jesuit mission in Huronia and the other by the superior of the Canadian mission located in Quebec. All references to the *Jesuit Relations* come from the Thwaites edition (hereafter *JR*). I have retranslated most passages. The *Jesuit Relations* and many other documents pertaining to the Jesuit mission can also be found in Lucien Campeau, *Monumenta Novae Franciae* (Quebec: Les Presses de l'Université Laval, 1967–) (hereafter *MNF*). In reference to terminology, I have decided to use the names for Indigenous nations that are found most commonly in French colonial texts, rather than contemporary names (for example, "Montagnais" rather than "Innu"). My purpose is to avoid confusion with contemporary names that do not always correspond to the historical groupings referenced in the sources. I do so, however, in the recognition that some of the terms I use are no longer used or are used differently by Indigenous people today, and that in many cases these are colonial terms imposed by outsiders and as such reveal biases, misunderstandings, and operations of power.

5  On the creative force of ritual beyond symbolism, see Roy A. Rappaport, *Ritual and Religion in the Making of Humanity* (Cambridge: Cambridge University Press, 1999), 52–58; Michael Lambek, "Rappaport on Religion: A Social Anthropological Reading," in *Ecology and the Sacred: Engaging the Anthropology of Roy A. Rappaport,* ed. Ellen Messer and Michael Lambek (Ann Arbor: University of Michigan Press, 2001), 262–64; Victor Turner, *Dramas, Fields and Metaphors: Symbolic Action in Human Societies* (Ithaca, NY: Cornell University Press, 1974), 260.

6  Marie Louise Pratt develops the notion of a contact zone in order to move away from the idea of contact as a singular event and instead to see contact moving out over space and time. The idea could be expanded to include the zone of ritual, performed and recorded, in and through which religious contact took place. Marie Louise Pratt, *Imperial Eyes: Travel Writing and Transculturation* (London: Routledge, 1992). See also John Sutton Lutz, *Myth and Memory: Stories of Indigenous-European Contact* (Vancouver: UBC Press, 2007), 4.

7  This term draws on Michael McNally's "lifeways" and his critique of Christian missionaries' obsession with internal belief over external and integrative religious practices among Indigenous North Americans. See *Ojibwe Singers: Hymns, Grief and a Native Culture in Motion* (Oxford: Oxford University Press, 2000), 10–11. It also references Lutz's defence of the word "spiritual" in "First Contact as Spiritual Performance: Encounters on the North American West Coast," in *Myth and Memory,* 31.

8  For example, Peter Cook, "'Vivre Comme Fréres': Native-French Alliances in the St. Lawrence Valley, 1535–1667" (PhD diss., McGill University, 2008); Juliana Barr, "Rituals of First Contact in the 'Land of the Tejas,'" *William and Mary Quarterly,* 3rd ser. 61, 3 (July 2004): 393–434; George Sabo III, "Rituals of Encounter: Interpreting Native American Views of European Explorers," *Cultural Encounters in the Early South: Indians and Europeans in Arkansas,* ed. Jeannie Whayne (Fayetteville: University of Arkansas Press, 1995), 76–87; Patricia Seed, *Ceremonies of Possession in Europe's Conquest of the New World, 1492–1640* (Cambridge: Cambridge University Press, 1995); and Bruce M. White, "Encounters with Spirits: Ojibwa and Dakota Theories about the French and their Merchandise," *Ethnohistory* 41, 3 (1994): 369–405.

9  For example, Tracy Neal Leavelle, *The Catholic Calumet: Colonial Conversions and Indian North America* (Philadelphia: University of Pennsylvania Press, 2012); Emma Anderson, *The Betrayal of Faith: The Tragic Journey of a Colonial Native Convert* (Cambridge, MA: Harvard University Press, 2007); Allan Greer, *Mohawk Saint: Catherine Tekakwitha and the Jesuits* (New York: Oxford University Press, 2005); and Kenneth Morrison, "Baptism

and Alliance: The Symbolic Mediations of Religious Syncretism," *Ethnohistory* 37, 4 (1990): 416–37.
10 An example of the latter strategy is Lutz, "First Contact as Spiritual Performance," 30–45.
11 T. Scannell, "Latria," in *The Catholic Encyclopedia* (New York: Robert Appleton Company, 1910).
12 Lescarbot, *Histoire*, 676–77. This narrative of lack is common in European assessment of Indigenous peoples throughout the Americas and elsewhere. See Robert F. Berkhofer, *The White Man's Indian: Images of the American Indian from Columbus to the Present* (New York: Alfred A. Knopf, 1978), 10; Takao Abé, *The Jesuit Mission to New France: A New Interpretation in the Light of the Earlier Jesuit Experience in Japan* (Leiden: Brill, 2011), 48–59, 67–77.
13 *JR* 17:146, 148, 152, 160 (1639).
14 Belief in a divine god, then, can be seen as a particularly Christian notion that has often been imposed upon or translated into Indigenous spiritual lifeways due to the limitations of language and understanding available to outside, generally European, observers and interpreters. On the problems of belief in anthropology, see Catherine Bell, "'The Chinese Believe in Spirits': Belief and Believing in the Study of Religion," in *Radical Interpretations in Religion*, ed. Nancy Frankenberry (Cambridge: Cambridge University Press, 2002), 100–16. Also McNally, *Ojibwe Singers*, 10–11.
15 Rappaport, *Ritual and Religion*, 24–27. Rappaport makes little distinction between ritual and ceremony, except that ritual tends to be more formal than ceremonies (ibid., 35, 39). On Rappaport's definition and its influences, see Michael Lambek, "Rappaport on Religion," 253–56.
16 Buc, *The Dangers of Ritual*, 8–9. On the relationship of performance, memory, and archives, see Diana Taylor, *The Archive and the Repertoire: Performing Cultural Memory in the Americas* (Durham, NC: Duke University Press, 2003), 19–27. On the challenge of ritual/performance, see Geoffrey Koziol, "The Dangers of Polemic: Is Ritual Still an Interesting Topic of Historical Study?" *Early Medieval Europe* 11, 4 (2002): 367–88.
17 *JR* 14:98 (1638). For Jesuit reinterpretations of the Eat-All Feast as charity, see *JR* 16:48 (1639).
18 Anderson, *The Betrayal of Faith*, 43. On the close relationship between persons, power, and gifting in Algonquin society, see Kenneth Morrison, "The Cosmos as Intersubjective: Native American Other-Than-Human Persons," in *Indigenous Religions: A Companion*, ed. Graham Harvey (London: Cassell, 2000), 13–15, 23–26.
19 *JR* 19:22 (1640).
20 Ibid.
21 On the capacity of ritual to create insiders and outsiders, see James Peacock, "Belief Beheld – Inside and Outside, Insider and Outsider in the Anthropology of Religion," in *Ecology and the Sacred: Engaging the Anthropology of Roy A. Rappaport*, ed. Ellen Messer and Michael Lambek (Ann Arbor: University of Michigan Press, 2001), 207–26.
22 Alison Goddard Elliott, "The Power of Discourse," *Medievalia et Humanistica*, 11 (1982): 40.
23 Daniel Richter, *The Ordeal of the Longhouse: The Peoples of the Iroquois League in the Era of European Colonization* (Chapel Hill: University of North Carolina, 1992), 61–66.
24 Anderson, *Betrayal of Faith*, 49–50.
25 I have considered Jesuit reactions to this news elsewhere. See "'Nous avons esté fait un spectacle aux yeux du monde': Performance, texte et création des martyrs au Canada, 1642–1652," in *De l'Orient à la Huronie: Du récit de pèlerinage au texte missionnaire*, ed. Guy Poirier, Marie-Christine Gomez-Géraud, and François Paré (Quebec: Les Presses de

l'Université Laval, 2011): 103–22. For a more detailed exploration of Onaharé's "martyrdom," see Timothy G. Pearson, *Becoming Holy in Early Canada* (Montreal/Kingston: McGill-Queen's University Press, 2014).

26  On captivity rituals, see Daniel Richter, "War and Culture: The Iroquois Experience," *William and Mary Quarterly* 40, 4 (1983): 542; and Richter, *The Ordeal of the Longhouse*, 66–74.

27  *JR* 35:224–26.

28  *JR* 35:222. R. Hedde, "Martyre," *Dictionnaire de théologie catholique*, vol. 10 (Paris: Letouzey et Ané, 1951), 231.

29  *JR* 35:218. Theologically, all Christian martyrdom is an *imitatio christi*. See Thomas Heffernan, *Sacred Biography: Saints and Their Biographers in the Middle Ages* (New York: Oxford University Press, 1989), 126–33.

30  Ibid., 224.

31  Georges E. Sioui, *Huron/Wendat: The Heritage of the Circle*, trans. Jane Brierly (Vancouver: UBC Press, 1999), 155–56; Elizabeth Tooker, *An Ethnography of the Huron Indians, 1615–1649* (Syracuse: Syracuse University Press, 1991), 86–91. For an ethnography of the Huron, the best is still Bruce Trigger, *The Children of Aataentsic: A History of the Huron People to 1660* (Montreal/Kingston: McGill-Queen's University Press, 1976, 1987).

32  *JR* 17:170–73 (1639).

33  Given ongoing controversy over the toleration of Chinese rites within Catholicism in the seventeenth century, Jesuits were particularly sensitive to questions about the legitimacy of Indigenous ritual practices within nascent Churches. On the Chinese rites controversy, see Joseph Brucker, "Matteo Ricci," *The Catholic Encyclopedia*, vol. 13 (New York: Robert Appleton Company, 1912); George Minamiki, *The Chinese Rites Controversy from Its Beginning to Modern Times* (Chicago: Loyola University Press, 1985). On Jesuit rigour in Canada, see Peter Goddard, "Augustine and the Amerindian in Seventeenth-Century New France," *Church History* 67, 4 (1998): 662–81.

34  Those with power who chose to remain aloof from the community were often regarded as dangerous sorcerers and accused of witchcraft. On the designation of sorcerers and witches and how the Huron dealt with them, see *JR* 19:82–87.

35  *JR* 17:195.

36  Ibid., 168. Demonology helped missionaries explain the power they observed in Indigenous rituals. Any spiritual power not attributable to the Christian God, in monotheistic cosmology, must come from the devil. See Abé, *The Jesuit Mission to New France*, 76–77.

37  Here "Canada" refers specifically to the French colony of the St. Lawrence River Valley from south of Montreal to north of Tadoussac, and other claimed territories in the *pays d'en haut* or upper country of the Great Lakes region.

38  Louis Armand de Lom d'Arce, Baron de Lahontan, *New voyages to North America giving a full account of the customs, commerce, religion, and strange opinions of the savages of that country with political remarks upon the courts of Portugal and Denmark and the present state of the commerce of those countries*, vol. 2 (London: H. Bonwicke, 1703), 30–31. For Lahontan's publishing history, see David M. Hayne, "Lom d'Arce de Lahontan, Louis-Armand de," in *Dictionary of Canadian Biography*, vol. 2 (Toronto/Quebec: University of Toronto/Les Presses de l'Université Laval, 2003–), http://www.biographi.ca/en/bio/lom_d_arce_de_lahontan_louis_armand_de_2E.html; A. H. Greenly, "Lahontan: An Essay and Bibliography," *Papers of the Bibliographical Society of America*, 48 (1954), 334–89. Lahontan is regarded as a precursor of modern anthropology and a reliable counterweight to missionary writings about native peoples. See Georges E. Sioui, *For an Amerindian Autohistory: An Essay on the Foundation of a Social Ethic* (Montreal/Kingston: McGill-Queen's University Press, 1992), 61–81.

39  Ibid., 24.

40  *JR* 17:171.

41  Turner, *Dramas, Fields and Metaphors*, 38–41. Bobby C. Alexander, *Victor Turner Revisited: Ritual as Social Change* (Atlanta: Scholars Press, 1991), 27–44.

42  *Ondinonc* is described in the *Relations* as information and enlightenment acquired through dreams. *JR* 17:155, 179. It was a cure for diseases or illness caused by desires of the soul. Tooker, *An Ethnography of the Huron Indians*, 82–83.

43  *JR* 17:181.

44  Ibid., 187.

45  Ibid., 188.

46  Ibid.

47  This divide between inclusive and exclusive approaches to colonial encounter has been observed and discussed elsewhere and in other contexts. For example, Deborah Doxtator, "Inclusive and Exclusive Perceptions of Difference: Native and Euro-Based Concepts of Time, History and Change," in *Decentring the Renaissance: Canada and Europe in Multi-disciplinary Perspective,* ed. Carolyn Podruchny and Germaine Warkentin (Toronto: University of Toronto Press, 2001), 33–47; James Ronda, "'We Are Well As We Are': An Indian Critique of Seventeenth-Century Christian Missions," *William and Mary Quarterly,* 3rd ser., 34, 1 (1977): 66–82; and Erik Seeman, *Death in the New World: Cross-Cultural Encounters, 1492–1800* (Philadelphia: University of Pennsylvania Press, 2010), 11.

48  Max One-Onti Gros-Louis, "Anonwentsa: La Rencontre: Mémoire présenté à la commission de consultation sur les practiques d'accommodement reliées aux différences culturelles," Quebec, 30–31 October, 2007, accessed 3 November 2008, http://www.accommodements. qc.ca/documentation/index-en.html. This website was taken down in October 2012. The documents and reports relating to the commission were transferred to the Bibliothèque et archives nationales de Québec, where they are available for consultation. Fonds Commission de consultation sur les pratiques d'accommodement reliées aux différences culturelles (CCPARDC), 1995–2008, cote E186. Annabelle Nicoud, "Le site internet de la commission Bouchard-Taylor renaît," *La Presse,* 17 October 2012.

# 2

# Managing Alliance, Negotiating Christianity: Haudenosaunee Uses of Anglicanism in Northeastern North America, 1760s–1830s

*Elizabeth Elbourne*

Throughout the eighteenth century, Christianity was a political football in Haudenosaunee territory in northeastern North America. Among the Six Nations, some, particularly Kanien'kehá:ka (Mohawk) concentrated in the settlements of Canajoharie and Tionondoroge (Fort Hunter) in what is now New York State, used Anglicanism to broker ties with the British, even as many other Haudenosaunee evinced suspicion of Christianity.[1] This chapter argues that Anglicanism, like Christianity in general, was a source of both power and danger in several ways, ranging from its potentially corrosive impact on Indigenous societies to its political implications. The danger and the power were intimately linked. Christianity needed to be managed in order for it to be harnessed effectively. Both the agents of the British administration and key Haudenosaunee figures attempted to do this. Echoing Timothy Pearson's emphasis on the importance of ritual elsewhere in this volume, and his argument that many Haudenosaunee sought to use ritual to strengthen community unity, I suggest here that liturgy, ritual, and biblical translation all provided ways to tap into Christianity's sacred power while keeping at a distance its more dangerous effects. There was not agreement, however, on how or whether to use these routes. By the early nineteenth century, Anglicanism became harder to manage after many of the Six Nations migrated to Upper Canada, and education came more firmly under settler and church control.

Throughout, the limitations to my argument are significant. In particular, the limited nature of the sources (many generated by white military officers) and the difficulty of knowing what many people were experiencing intellectually and emotionally (or truly grasping the dynamics of internal debate) impose humility on the researcher, even if it is revealing that military and diplomatic sources say something about aspects of religious practice. In this sense, this chapter reflects what Carmen Lansdowne describes in this volume as the "absences that break your heart." At the same time, Lansdowne's findings about the importance of Indigenous priests echo what seems to have been an eighteenth-century Haudenosaunee reality as well as, broadly speaking, an African one: local agents were more responsible for whatever happened to Christian missions than were European missionaries, even if the words of these agents are hard to determine. Other authors in this collection also suggest themes that resonate with my own work. Cecilia Morgan and Jean-François Bélisle and Nicole St-Onge remind us that Christianity is a transnational phenomenon and that Indigenous people sometimes acted as transnational agents. Several authors, such as Tasha Beeds and Amanda Fehr, offer intimate and fine-grained portraits of individuals who negotiated Indigenous and Christian identities: my own work suggests that this was a possible but fraught negotiation in the late-eighteenth-century Haudenosaunee world, as identities were in the process of being defined against one another in violent environments. It seems to me that the history of Christianity lies in the tensions and spaces between the local and the global, the intimate and the transnational. Siphiwe Dube captures the moral ambiguities of a colonial religion that was necessarily Janus-faced. Where this chapter perhaps differs in emphasis from some others in this volume is in stressing Christianity as an *imperial* as well as a colonial religion, linked to imperial metropoles as well as to settler domination, and sometimes enabling Indigenous interlocutors to speak over the heads of settlers. This was, to return to the main theme of the essay, a dangerous but potentially powerful opportunity.

## Anglicanism and Alliance Politics

By the 1760s, reinforcing Anglicanism as much as possible among the Six Nations, and in particular among the Mohawk near whom he lived in what is now upper-state New York, was an important aspect of British Superintendent of Indian Affairs Sir William Johnson's policy of attempted conciliation of the Indigenous peoples of northeastern North America. It was, however, a nervous plan. "Pray make my compliments to Doctor Ogilvie and Family and ask him whether he has any prayer Books left for ye Indians, as they now want them very much," Johnson wrote in 1761 to his agent in Montreal, Daniel Claus (also his future son-in-law), who had been placed in charge of diplomatic relationships with the Indigenous peoples of the newly conquered Canada. In the same letter, however, Johnson added that he had had a meeting with Six Nations deputies and that they were "full of their old fears again that the English would fall upon & destroy them."[2] As Claus and Johnson organized the acquisition and correction of Mohawk-language prayer books, they also discussed with growing urgency the danger posed by the disaffection of the Indian nations. Johnson was certain, for example, that apparent British moves to settle Niagara would "confirm all the Nations in the opinion they long have had of our design of rooting them out of their Country," adding "[what] the consequence will be, time only will shew, but I must avow I dread it."[3]

Johnson was of course prescient: by 1763, Pontiac's war would be in full swing.[4] Neolin and other prophets roused the nations to action against the British, reflecting long-standing Amerindian uses of prophecy and ritual at times of conflict to purify and unify communities and to ensure military success.[5] One of Neolin's key claims, typical of late-eighteenth-century nativist movements, was the need to cast out Christian practices in order to restore strength to Indigenous communities. Many of the traditionally British-aligned Six Nations remained largely neutral or even actively pro-British, however. In the wake of the war and the negotiation of the Proclamation Line in 1763, Johnson's Indian department had a freer rein from the British military to pursue alliance policies that included personal diplomacy, occasional sexual interaction, the maintenance of gift-giving, and the promotion of Christianity in general and Anglicanism in particular.

Johnson continued to call for missionaries, and to promote the prayer book. In 1763, as the war came to a head, he urged the Reverend Henry Barclay to hurry up and finish revising his updated version of the "Indian Book of Common prayer" (eventually published in 1769) as it was "a Work very much wanted, & greatly inquired after by the Indians": "I am of opinion that this Edition will conduce to incline the Christian Indians to the Established Church, which will have a better effect on them than what I see arises from their inclination to the Presbyterian as all those Inds [Indians] who are Instructed by the Dissenting Ministers (who are the only Clergy in these parts) have imbibed an air of the most Ecclesiastical cant." In the surviving draft version of this letter, Sir William added, but crossed out, "and are in short intermixed with the greatest Distortion of the features & zealous Belchings of the Spirit, resembling the most bigoted Puritans."[6] By the late 1760s, the tension between dissent and Anglicanism had gone beyond conflict over "Belchings of the Spirit," as Anglicanism came to represent elite authority and royal alliance to Patriot dissidents, particularly in the New York region, where Johnson was one of a small number of Anglican landowners who dominated the countryside.[7] Johnson had begun by encouraging the Christianization efforts of Presbyterian missionary Samuel Kirkland among the Oneida and Seneca, as well as the school for Indigenous boys run by fervent Congregationalist minister Eleazor Wheelock, but by the end of the decade he had broken with Kirkland, withdrawn boys from Eleazor's school, and had an Anglican chapel built at Fort Hunter, in the heart of Kanien'kehá:ka territory.[8]

In the late 1760s, Johnson, now appointed a corresponding member of the Society for the Propagation for the Gospel, agitated for, and offered to help fund, a network of missionaries and schoolmasters among the Haudenosaunee. Johnson claimed that creating a "regular system" of "proper Missionaries & Schools in most of their towns" was "the only effectual means of converting & reducing them to order." He opposed boarding schools such as Wheelock's: "A few stragling [sic] missions or schools out of their Country will never answer the end proposed, the more distant Indians being extremely averse to sending their Children abroad for Instruction, and if they did, they are too apt to relapse afterwards of which I have seen examples amongst the best of them sufficient to justify my opinion."[9] In this sense one might see Haudenosaunee people attempting to manage Christianity, keeping missionaries (and Haudenosaunee children) close to hand rather than sending their children away to missionary-run schools.

Johnson and his clerical ally in North America, Reverend Charles Inglis (later bishop of Nova Scotia), argued in correspondence with the Society that conversion would lead the Haudenosaunee to ally with the British. As Inglis put it bluntly, "the most effectual method of securing their Friendship & making them serviceable to the state, is to make them Christians."[10] At the same time, Johnson, Inglis, and other elite Anglicans were increasingly concerned about the hegemony of Protestant dissent in northeastern North America and the political implications of dissenters' attacks on the established church, in an environment in which the authority of the state was tightly tied to church authority. Johnson and Inglis were seemingly as concerned about converting settlers as they were about converting Indigenous peoples to Anglicanism. Johnson was also desirous of creating an American episcopate as a bulwark against dissent. Dissenters could generate their own American priesthood; under an episcopal structure, on the other hand, would-be clergy had to sail back to Britain to be ordained by a bishop. Johnson even offered to create the seat for an American episcopate on land recently purchased from the Haudenosaunee, near his own estate at Johnstown.[11] If it had been realized, this would have been a remarkable confluence of religious, political, and military power for Johnson.

The fact that Johnson's own Irish family had until recently been Catholic, and therefore subject to discrimination under British law and ineligible to hold government office, only underscores the political ramifications of religious practice in the British imperial sphere. As Fintan O'Toole points out, prominent male members of the Johnson family, including Johnson's uncle, admiral Peter Warren, converted to Anglicanism in order to be eligible for careers in the British Empire.[12] Anglicanism was thus for the Irish Johnson not only a sign of alliance and imperial loyalty but also, arguably, a sign of the contextual reinvention of the self in response to political circumstances. The fervent promotion of Christianity did not prevent Johnson from ignoring some Christian strictures; he had a number of children outside the bonds of "Christian marriage," for example, including at least eight children with his Kanien'kehá:ka partner Mary Brant (Konwatsi'tsiaienni). Anglicanism was also a key route to advancement in the British military. It was not for nothing that John Stuart, who had been an SPG missionary to the Mohawk before the American Revolution, later opened a new church in Upper Canada after the turmoil of the Revolution in the military barracks in Kingston, or indeed that William Johnson constructed a church and a fort together in Mohawk territory.[13]

This combination of the promotion of Christianity with efforts to win the military allegiances of Indigenous peoples was longstanding. Johnson was most directly imitating the French, and continued to worry about French influence via Catholicism.[14] Haudenosaunee uses of Christianity were often linked to diplomatic and military policy on their side as well. French and Indigenous soldiers sometimes exchanged cultural signs of allegiance, thereby helping create linkages among fictive kin, as Indigenous soldiers had themselves baptized with French sponsors, or French soldiers adopted Indian tattoos, as Arnaud Balvay argues.[15] As early as 1710, a delegation of Kanien'kehá:ka to London brokered an alliance with the British and presented themselves as "four kings," requested missionaries, and garnered a gift of communion silver from Queen Anne that would continue to play an important role in Kanien'kehá:ka politics well into the nineteenth century.[16] In 1776, Joseph Brant ostentatiously espoused Anglicanism and freemasonry when negotiating with the British in London.

Given the stakes, however (as well as the longstanding Six Nations policy of hedging bets when dealing with European powers), it is perhaps not surprising that adherence to some form of Christianity remained a minority position among the Six Nations as a whole, well into the nineteenth century. In 1822, a delegation on behalf of the Six Nations to Britain could affirm, for example, that of the Six Nations the Mohawk were "chiefly Christian," the Oneida "partly Christian," while the Seneca, Cayuga, Onondaga, and Delawares were "not Christians."[17] The Kanien'kehá:ka were further divided among themselves, between the dominantly Catholic communities whose territories lay within the boundaries of New France (following seventeenth-century mass migration to the outer limits of hunting grounds in New France) and the dominantly Protestant communities whose lands would eventually be encompassed by New York. A significant portion of the Six Nations based in the nascent United States, including the majority of the Kanien'kehá:ka, would move to Upper Canada, founding the Grand River and the Bay of Quinte settlements, in the wake of the ethnic cleansing of the American Revolution. Nonetheless, the political importance of Anglicanism was disproportionate, given the importance of the Mohawk-British alliance.

Early Protestant missionary activity in Iroquoia had been relatively sporadic.[18] In 1704, the Society for the Propagation of the Gospel sent its first Anglican missionaries to the Iroquois, the Reverends Thoroughgood Moore and Charles Smith. The Mohawk refused to say whether or not they would accept Moore living among them, and Moore abandoned the mission after eight months. He concluded that the Mohawk were hostile because "I was an Englishman, to whom they bear no good will, but rather an Aversion, having a Common Saying among them that an English man is not good." This was, he claimed, because English settlers take their land without purchase, had built a fort at Albany, and had been misrepresented by the Dutch.[19] William Andrews worked as an SPG missionary in Tiononderoge from 1712 to 1719, but left claiming, as Daniel Richter records, that despite the fact that many sought baptism, the approximately 360 residents of the village were heathens, "and Heathens they will still be."[20]

Richter argues convincingly, however, that the Haudenosaunee did not entirely reject the mission but, rather, insisted that it exist on their terms, and that it build up rather than destroy community strength. They did not see "Christian" practices as incompatible with existing practices, and continued to do things such as consult shamans; they did not accept missionary ideas about guilt and repentance, but they did maintain Christianity internally, through Haudenosaunee agents. When SPG missionaries returned in the late 1720s, they encountered a group of fifty-odd Kanien'kehá:ka who were instructed in Christianity and discovered that many people had had themselves and their children baptized.[21] Anglican missionaries continued to have a thin presence on the ground in the mid- to late eighteenth century (the Reverend Barclay decamped to New York, for example, leaving a Mohawk reader in his place), but communities at the two principal towns of Canajoharie and Tiononderoge maintained Anglican practice, including church attendance.

In 1769, under his renewed plans for Anglican missions, Johnson appointed a schoolmaster, Colin McLeland, to run a school for children at Fort Hunter. McLeland soon had thirty pupils. A second schoolmaster was installed at Johnstown.[22] In 1770, Johnson and nine Haudenosaunee men staged a small ceremony for visiting Anglican priests Charles Inglis and Myles Cooper, then the president of King's College, New York (later Columbia). The aim of this ceremony was to persuade the SPG to send a missionary to the Mohawk; the event raises tantalizing questions about participants' aims and their degree of agency. Inglis and Cooper reported to London that they had taken a "journey of between two and three hundred miles, to pay a visit to Sir William Johnson in the Mohawks country," and that the day after they arrived they had been surprised by a "formal Delegation of Indians from the lower Mohawk Castle," including four "principal men in their nation." Tellingly, the group was ushered into the "apartment where Councils &c, are generally holden" and business only proceeded after the "customary" compliments had been exchanged, presumably the formal ceremonies and words with which Amerindian diplomatic meetings opened. Speaking through an interpreter, the "chief sachem" stated that the Mohawk were grateful for former missionaries but regretted that their teachers had had cause to leave them almost as soon as they had learned the language and thereby become capable of being more useful to the people; they regretted even more that they had been "so much neglected" for the past several years, "notwithstanding Sir William's repeated applications, and the promises they received, by his means, of speedy and effectual supply." Most of all, however:

> their amazement was increased at ye Information they had but lately received of the Government's Indulgence of a Missionary to a Tribe of their popish Brethren, who had all along, till the Conclusion of the late war, been intemperate Enemies to the Crown and People of Great Britain; whilst they themselves, who had ever been our unshaken Friends, in Times of the greatest Danger and Distress, and had shed the finest blood in their nation in our Cause, and for our Defence, should in their opinion be so undeservedly left to wander out of the way; and have the mortification to find, that all their applications for a clergyman had hitherto been rejected.

They stated that they had the means to provide a house and glebe for a missionary, "where they hoped a good man, who was interested in the welfare of their souls, might be induced to end his Days, with much Advantage to Them, and satisfaction to Himself." At the conclusion of this statement, they delivered a wampum belt to Inglis and Cooper, which the pair in turn sent to London.[23] This act mirrored the dispatch of a wampum belt to the archbishop of Canterbury in the aftermath of the 1710 visit of the Four Kings and the sealing of an alliance with the Anglican church.[24] Inglis and Cooper then gave a wampum belt in return to the Mohawk, with which Johnson had furnished them in advance. Later in the visit, a child was brought to them from Fort Hunter. One of the priests baptized the child, and the other stood as sponsor.

The diplomatic rituals underscore the way in which imperial alliances were brokered through shared religious practice. Johnson himself implied that religious allegiance was tied to land claims. He suggested to the SPG that the interest of the dissenters from densely populated New England in converting Indians lay in gaining access to Amerindian lands: "many of these [religious] Schemes which had their birth in N England have soon appeared calculated with a View to forming Settlements so obnoxious to the Indians who have repeatedly declared their aversion to those who acted on such interested principles."[25] Allegiance to Anglicanism, in contrast, might potentially be seen as a way of holding the British to the continent-wide land deals brokered in 1763 (the Proclamation Line) and in 1768 (the controversial Fort Stanwix treaty, in which Six Nations negotiators ceded land occupied by other groups but that had been claimed by the Six Nations through conquest, while arguably protecting core Haudenosaunee territory). On both of those occasions, Johnson had led the British negotiating team.

The SPG finally appointed John Stuart as a missionary. Stuart lived in Fort Hunter and travelled once a week to Canajoharie, some thirty miles away; he commented frequently that the Canajoharie community resented not having its own missionary. Nonetheless, Stuart was remained relatively hands-off, if only because communication with community members was difficult. He found Mohawk a difficult language to master, and the Mohawk did not, he reported, speak English. He could not find a translator until he was able to work for a while with the young Joseph Brant (Thayendanegea), later a key Haudenosaunee political figure who had been educated at Dr. Wheelock's school. Stuart in fact maintained a "white" English-speaking congregation in Fort Hunter and another "Indian" one to whom he struggled to read the service in Mohawk.

At the local level, Haudenosaunee Christian practitioners seem to have valued Christian ritual while resisting the behavioural precepts of the church. Stuart was soon fretting that the Kanien'kehá:ka had adopted Anglican rituals but not Anglican prescriptions for pious behaviour. In 1774 he complained that he had visited the inhabitants of Canajoharie and found their situation "really deplorable; For Drunkenness & Vice of every kind prevails amongst them to such a Degree, that several Times I have not found a sufficient Number of them duly qualified, to whom I cou'd administer the Sacrament. However, they have Prayers read in their Church every Sunday, by an Indian of that Village, at which they generally attend."[26] The majority of Mohawk attended Anglican Church services every Sunday, knew the responses and participated in ritual solemnly. "They attend divine Service constantly," Stuart wrote about the Tiononderoge community in 1772, "& make the Responses with the greatest Regularity and seeming Devotion and indeed their whole Deportment in Church is such as is but rarely seen in religious Assemblies that have been better instructed."[27]

Struggles over communion are telling. "Let their common Behaviour be what it will, they are desirous, in general, to partake of the Holy Communion," Stuart observed of residents of Canajoharie in the same year. Stuart tried to discipline this small congregation through excluding those from communion who were "notorious drunkards" or "vicious in their behaviour," but he clearly met resistance. "To refuse them," he commented, "reduces them to a kind of Dispair [sic] and often urges them to commit worse crimes than before; for they are pointed at as bad Persons, unfit for Society – my method hitherto has been, to admit the sober & to reject the notoriously vicious, altho I have been the object of their Resentment for this conduct, and have narrowly escaped the Effects of it."[28]

The Presbyterian missionary Samuel Kirkland had similar comments about the Oneida village of Oquaga, where there was a virulent struggle between a minority Presbyterian faction and a dominant Anglican faction (including Joseph Brant and his father-in-law, Isaac Dekayenensere). "Most of the town," Kirkland complained on 9 March 1773,

> had conceived a notion that an external good behaviour, with learning the Decalogue as to repeat it without Book was all the divine law intended or required, and that such a sort of obedience entitled [sic] to "*eternal life*" ... It seemed that they had no other idea of repentance than mere oral confession, that baptism or mere external sprinkling was all the regeneration held forth in the Scriptures and absolutely entitled to "eternal life," especially if the baptized person dies in infancy. Moreover that a feast was an essential part of the ordinance, and they accordingly practice feasting at baptisms, and for the most part dance and frolic the whole night.[29]

These are snapshots from a distance, but they suggest community efforts to use some of the ritual power of Christianity, including the protection implicit in the baptism of children, while maintaining internal control and minimizing missionary interference.

## Text and Power

The dangers of Christianity did not come from alliance politics alone, however. Many worried that Christian rituals and texts had sacred power that could be damaging or efficacious, regardless of whether a person had a Christian identity. Nativists argued that Christian practices had weakened Indian societies from within and needed to be rejected (albeit paradoxically sometimes appealing to Christian ideas of a jealous male deity who demanded exclusive worship).[30] This might, however, imply that Christianity had a dangerous independent power.

In the 1760s, for example, Samuel Kirkland recorded the views of some Oneida that Christianity damaged communities from within.[31] "Brothers, it is time we were rouzed up," the orator Captain Onoonghwandekha warned an emergency council meeting among the Seneca in 1765, called to determine whether the newly arrived Kirkland should be held responsible for the sudden death of a man in the house in which he was lodging. For Onoonghwandekha (in Kirkland's English rendition and with his emendations), "the white people's *Book,* which they call *Hawenigo hoyattonshah* or *Kayatlonshahdogeaghte* ie in Eng [sic] *God's Book* or the *Holy Book*" was "never made for Indians." He contrasted the written book of the white people with the oral "book" that "our great Superintendent Thaonghyawagon" had written in the heads and minds of Indians, expressed in "ancient usages and rites." To "attend to the Book which was made solely for White people" was dangerous: "How many remnants of tribes to the *East* are so reduced, that they *pound* sticks to make brooms, to buy a loaf of Bread or it may be a shirt. The warriors which they boasted of, before these foreigners, the white people, crossed the great Lake, where are they now? Why their grandsons are all become *mere women!*" Only in rejecting Christianity would the Seneca remain true men. Only thus, in addition, would they avoid punishment from their own God.[32] The debate (in which this proved to be a minority perspective) occasioned a wide-ranging discussion of causality and the meaning of suffering. Opponents claimed that, on the contrary, misfortune was not a punishment for collective sin.

In 1772, Oneida complaints about the exclusionary nature of evangelical Protestantism clearly had different implications but still drew on similar concerns about the corrosion of community strength. On this occasion, Kirkland heard from Tagawaron, an orator speaking for sachems and warriors of the towns of old Onoide and Kanonwaroharie, who complained about the divisive nature of evangelical Protestantism, in contrast to both Anglicanism and Catholicism. The orator accused the whites of telling the Oneida "two different Commands" as though "God had two minds." According to Kirkland, the sachems and warriors preferred the "old" (Catholicism and Anglicanism) because Jesuits and Anglicans were "very fond" of baptizing both children and adults as desired. If any adult wished to "be made holy," then "he must look out a Man" from among the people, "to give him a N[ame], learn the Lords prayer, creed, & 10 Comd & confess [his] Sins & then he was baptized without any objections, & a bottle or two [of] Rum given by the God-father to drink [his] health." In contrast, Kirkland refused to baptize at will, shut up the "way to Heavn" or made it "narrow," and frightened candidates into recidivism by a long and severe examination.[33]

One of the striking things about both debates is how much they turned around texts and the power of texts: in the one case, the biblical text was in itself a source of danger; in the other, learning key texts (the Lord's Prayer, the creed, and the Ten Commandments) gave the postulant access to the power of baptism, whatever his personal behaviour. It might be suggested that a critical route to the control of Christianity was through liturgy, public prayer, and ritual, in all of which the Six Nations maintained a strong interest throughout the late eighteenth century: these were ways to tap into the power of Christianity that did not require regular mediation by white priests and could potentially coexist with other forms of access to sacred power. They also permitted the promotion of a corporate religiosity, in contrast to the decentralized, and thus potentially more divisive, individualism promoted by much evangelical theology.[34]

Arguably, Anglicanism lent itself well to the control of texts. Mohawk prayer books and catechisms were circulating well before the Bible was first translated into Mohawk (although prayers and creeds were probably also memorized). William Andrews first published parts of the Book of Common Prayer in Mohawk in 1715, while Daniel Claus observed in 1761 that there were already several manuscript versions of the catechism in Mohawk in circulation.[35] Claus doubtless drew on such documents when, in the early 1780s while acting as military superintendent of the Canadian Indians during the war, he wrote a primer and catechism for children in Mohawk (continuing the military promotion of Anglicanism), as well as further revising the prayer book and circulating it among refugees.[36] Aaron Hill wrote to Claus in 1782 that his translation was invaluable: "Brother, we render you our highest Thanks and most heartily salute you as many of us are Christians & proselytes, it is entirely owing to you that Christianity is upheld amongst us ... the Good Spirit from above must have inspired you to compose the little Books of Instruction, we are now all supplied with new Books, was it not for [your?] being alive, we should be miserable, as we know of no person whatsoever in the Indian Service able to undertake the Task."[37]

The sachem and schoolteacher Paulus Sahonwagy provides an example of a Kanien'kehá:ka Anglican agent who worked for many years among the community using these types of resources. He was first employed by the SPG as a "reader" in the 1750s. He taught more than forty children a day at Canajoharie by 1755, and read prayers and led services in the absence of the white minister; he also fought on the British side in the Seven Years' War and saw his salary suspended in 1759 after several complaints that he spent too much time on war parties to teach the children properly.[38] He was part of a Mohawk faction that bitterly opposed the land grabbing of George Klock, an important dispute over land that ultimately segued into open warfare during the Revolution and provided further motivation for the Kanien'kehá:ka alliance with William Johnson. In 1774 Stuart reported that the Canajoharie Mohawk complained bitterly about their lack of a minister and the lack of books in Mohawk but had appointed "one from amongst themselves to perform Divine Service on Sundays" and requested a salary for him; the following year, Stuart reported paying "five pounds to Paulus at Canajoharie."³⁹ Sahonwagy was still teaching the refugee Haudenosaunee in Niagara during the Revolution. He also appears in a footnote to Claus's third edition of the Mohawk prayer book, described as "the Mohawk Clerk and School-Master" who was "present at the correction of every proof sheet to approve of their being properly placed, &c."⁴⁰

In 1785, after the British betrayal of Haudenosaunee lands and the exodus of many to Upper Canada, Sahonwagy informed Claus that the English teacher at Grand River had quit and offered himself as a replacement: "The reason why the children here are strong in doing that which is not right is because there is no Indian teacher." Proposing that, at the urging of many, he resume his former work as teacher, despite what he described as the deplorable indifference of the chiefs, Sahonwagy told Claus: "It sickens me to see the children going wrong. Some are saying that an English-speaking man is coming to teach, now that is not comforting, if he does not understand our language he cannot restrain them from doing wrong."⁴¹ It seems possible that control of Anglican liturgy and teaching continued to enable men such as Sahonwagy to develop local versions of Christianity, to maintain military alliances and possibly to challenge the authority of particular elites.

During the Revolution, refugee Mohawk asked Claus to request a missionary from the SPG to replace Stuart, now imprisoned by the Americans. Although an ordained person was needed to perform sacraments, Claus's letter indicates that some community members had clearly been maintaining Anglican practice and religious education on their own, and that two Mohawk men had been running a school in New York. In the 1790s, Anglicans at Grand River still found themselves without an ordained minister, since Stuart, now a member of the loyalist diaspora in Upper Canada, was still employed by the SPG – but in Kingston, two hundred miles from Grand River. When he did manage to visit Grand River, he was presented with numerous children for baptism.⁴² Settlers in the Niagara region continued to urge Stuart to move there. Stuart acknowledged the appeal of "the neighbourhood of my old Parishioners the Mohawks, who are very importunate in their Intreaties for my Removal," although he ultimately decided he could not afford to leave the flourishing farm at Kingston that supported his eight children in the absence (he claimed) of an adequate salary.⁴³ Even this refusal is interesting, because in his musing on the topic of where he should live, Stuart presented the Mohawk as parishioners on a par with his Kingston flock, rather than as heathen in need of conversion. In 1821, John Brant reported to the New England Company in London, as he negotiated for money for a school, that "the children read and write in the Indian Language – and the Indians of the Six Nations have a primer and a prayer Book together with the Services for Marriage Baptism and Burial of the Dead."⁴⁴

## Community and Commemoration

Oral evidence from a variety of sources, most of it collected in the late nineteenth century, may tell us more about late-nineteenth-century views of Anglicanism than early-nineteenth-century views. Nonetheless, stories do suggestively imply that key religious symbols were used as tokens of community identity as well as signs of alliance with the British and thus, perhaps, reminders of obligation.

Queen Anne's silverware, donated by the queen in 1710, was particularly freighted with significance. Possibly the silver communion vessels were taken by members of the Six Nations who wanted a relationship with the imperial centre as both seal and symbol of a verbal agreement, consonant with the exchange of wampum belts in order to confirm and commemorate agreements between different parties. This is also in line with the exchange of gifts that typically sealed diplomatic alliances. The material objects that marked such exchanges had particular political value – perhaps especially objects such as communion vessels, which were used to enact ceremonies on a regular cyclical basis.

Some stories claimed that the Kanien'kehá:ka had brought the communion silver with them on their exodus; others stated (more accurately) that they had buried it before leaving.[45] After the Haudenosaunee exodus, the communion vessels were divided in 1788 between those establishing a new settlement at Grand River under Joseph Brant's leadership and those moving to Tyendinaga; they are still owned by the respective churches.[46] The move of some of the Six Nations to the Bay of Quinte under John Deserontyon was sealed, so stories said, by the use of Queen Anne's silver. In the early twentieth century, the Reverend A.H. Creegan interviewed Sampson Green, the great-grandson of a "white girl" who was with the Mohawk at the age of fifteen when they moved to the Bay of Quinte and later married into the community. Green recounted that

> her story was that when the little band landed on the shore of their new home, they upturned a canoe, covered it with the communion cloth, and placed all the pieces of the old Queen Anne communion set in plain view of all the people, that then the chief said prayers and they sang a hymn. Afterwards they planted a cross and a flagstaff on the spot. Many of the older residents remember the flagstaff.[47]

The landing is annually commemorated at the Bay of Quinte, and, in 2014, Queen Anne's silver was brought out for the 230th commemoration.[48] In 2012, the website of the Tyendinaga Mohawk Territory stated that the "Queen Anne

Silver embodies the relationship between the Mohawks and the British Crown," and that Christ Church, built in 1843 to replace the original chapel, was "an embodiment of the relationship between the Mohawks of the Bay of Quinte and the Anglican Church."[49] Although this text is no longer on the website and therefore cannot be said to reflect current views, it nonetheless arguably reflects one particular interpretation of the political meaning of the communion silver and the role of objects as bearers of memory and reminders of obligation.

As I have discussed in more detail elsewhere, there were numerous stories among both whites and Kanien'kehá:ka in the late nineteenth century about the Mohawk returning to recapture stolen church bells or, in one version, carrying a church bell into exile.[50] Nineteenth-century inhabitants of the former site of Canajoharie told a story that the Kanien'kehá:ka returned to steal the church bell, either during the Revolution or (less plausibly) after the arrival of Dutch settlers; they almost got away with the bell, but its clapper came undone and betrayed them.[51] In the collection *Captive Histories*, Taiaiake Alfred discusses an eerily parallel late nineteenth-century Kahnawake oral tradition that the Canadian Kanien'kehá:ka participated in a French-Indian raid of Deerfield, Massachusetts in 1704 in order to recapture a bell that the Jesuits had given the community and that the English settlers had supposedly stolen before it could be installed.[52] In all these stories, the bell became a symbol of community identity, to be defended against enemies.

In 1879, George Rokwaho Loft, the grandson of Karonyagigone (Big Clear Sky), who had, Loft said, served as the pilot on the Kanien'kehá:ka trek from the Mohawk Valley to Lachine, told historian Lyman Draper a story about fidelity that combined the idea of sacrifice and exodus with the image of a church bell:

> On some occasion – it would seem about 1775 – Washington spoke beautifully – saying "stay with me – you did not cause the war – it was the result of differences between me and the British – you stay and share with me – if I prosper, you shall prosper – be one with us." But the Mohawks said among themselves, "We have pledged our faith with the British Father and we must keep it: We will go over the Lake to Canada" – and so left the Mohawk country. They brought their old church bell with them – an evidence of their devotion to their religious teachings, for it must have cost them much toil and labour; and it is now in the church near Mill Point.[53]

It seems unlikely that the Mohawk did in fact take the bell with them: other stories tell of children too enfeebled by hunger to walk and being carried by their parents, of Americans who pursued the party and killed and wounded men or captured women, of people carrying bags of parched corn on their shoulders and shooting birds to make a thin gruel to be shared among starving families. Whatever the truth, the bell and the silverware again served as images of identity and resistance – and, in the context of the 1870s, arguably as tokens of political claims against the British.

The symbolism of alliance, sealed by sacred objects, could work in the opposite direction as well. Back in New York, after the bitter frontier warfare of the Revolution, rebels made a point of desecrating the symbols of Mohawk Anglicanism, in the context of wider attacks on Anglicanism. At least some New York Patriot Congregationalists and Presbyterians detested the Anglicanism of Tory elites and possibly saw Indigenous Anglicanism as another sign of a sinister alliance between many Amerindian warriors and the British. Stuart had continued to hold services for the Mohawk in the church at Fort Hunter after the Declaration of Independence, despite the fact that this had become (he claimed) an act of high treason. After the Kanien'kehá:ka left, however, and Stuart made a prisoner of war "as soon as my Protectors were fled," rebels plundered the Mohawk church and stole the pulpit cloth; "it was afterwards imployed as a Tavern," Stuart complained in 1781, "the Barrel of Rum placed in the Reading Desk – the succeeding Season it was used for a Stable."[54]

## Anglicanism in Upper Canada

In contrast, in the immediate aftermath of the Six Nations exile to Upper Canada, Christianity in general and Anglicanism in particular remained a potential means for Six Nations elites to access power brokered by the white loyalist military and fur trade elites who would make up the so-called family compact. Fur traders and military men occasionally still had long-term sexual alliances with Six Nations and Anishinaabe women, reflecting the customs of the (dominantly Scottish) men in the fur trade. Christianity (like freemasonry) could still function as a means to generate elite complicity in this context. As settler society overwhelmed Indigenous societies in terms of numbers, however, and these types of alliances ceased to be as economically or politically useful by the turn of the century, Indigenous groups became more vulnerable to coercion, including coercion condoned or carried out by the church.

All of Molly Brant's daughters with William Johnson married prominent white settlers in the late eighteenth century, and Molly Brant was herself an ostentatious Anglican. She was the only woman to be listed as a donor on the founding charter of the first Anglican church in Cataraqui (Kingston), the town where she spent the final years of her life and where John Stuart was minister from 1785 until his death in 1811.[55] In the late eighteenth century, travel writer

John C. Ogden portrayed Brant as "an Indian woman who sat in an honourable place among the English" and appeared "very devout during divine service and very attentive to the sermon."[56] The description of course implies a spatial separation between "English" and Indigenous groups in church, which is revealing in itself. Brant, however, still indicated her Kanien'kehá:ka allegiances through her Haudenosaunee-style clothing, which she wore even while also performing the allegiance implicit in Anglicanism. As Ogden put it succinctly, "she retains the habit of her country women and is a Protestant."[57]

In the 1870s, Mrs. Catherine Hill, Joseph Brant's granddaughter, recalled that after the early death of one of Molly Brant's daughters, Molly had refused to allow her daughter's widower, a man called Lemoine, to marry another one of her daughters:

> she [Molly] & Mrs. Ferguson [a third sister] were both opposed to the match for ill treatment, & also opposed him from the Episcopal stand-point of impropriety of marrying a deceased wife's sister. Miss. [Susan] Johnson was not herself disinclined. Lemoine came to Col. Ferguson's to see Susan – apparently in desperation – she was in a room above, confined; & Lemoine plead to see her for the last time, knowing the mother's & sister's decided opposition – Molly was inclined to gratify his wishes, but Mrs. Ferguson was unyielding, when he blew his brains out in the parlor with a pistol – & informant, Mrs Hill, was pointed out the spot on the wall where the bullet penetrated.[58]

The main interest of this story probably does not lie in the fact that Molly Brant opposed remarriage to a deceased wife's sister. Nonetheless, it is noteworthy that adherence to this (disputed) precept was a sign of Anglican orthodoxy. It is also striking that the daughters of Molly Brant and William Johnson were desirable marriage partners for members of the Anglican elite.

By the 1810s, however, Euro-Canadian elites had less need of Six Nations allies, a process accelerated by the restoration of diplomatic calm in the aftermath of the War of 1812, and the end of the Napoleonic wars.[59] The declining influence of the Brant family at a high political level reflected this. On a different scale, so, too, did the changing political weight of religious activity. Consider, for example, the translation career of the Brant family. Joseph Brant is not usually primarily associated with Christian missionary activity. He was, nonetheless, as we have seen, employed as a language assistant to John Stuart in the early 1770s. In particular he worked with Stuart in translating prayers, parts of the Bible, a short history of the Bible, and a catechism.[60] Brant thus filled a role familiar from many other missions: the linguist and interpreter who shadowed the "pioneer" missionary and, often, helped to create written versions of oral languages and craft translations of sacred texts, even though this work was rarely acknowledged by missionary publicity machines.

Unlike most translators, however, Brant escaped the control of his missionary employer in spectacular fashion, and then used translation work as a route to power and influence. Under usual missionary circumstances, the white missionary would have claimed the credit for the translation; however, Stuart's role was eradicated from the title page. After various peregrinations, the Gospel of St. Mark was finally published in London in 1787, added to a new edition of the Book of Common Prayer. The translation was attributed on the cover page to "Capt. Joseph Brant, An Indian of the Mohawk Nation." The preface by Charles Inglis, now bishop of Nova Scotia, extolled Brant in particular and the Mohawk in general as exemplary Christians, describing Brant as "a man of good abilities, who was educated at one of the American Colleges." The Gospel of St. Mark would "probably be the more acceptable to the Indians for being translated by a person who is of their own nation and kindred." In a postwar context in which the British military had been criticized extensively for using Indian warriors against white settlers, the preface was at pains to point out that "the Mohawks are a respectable nation" as well as being faithful alliance partners and potential agents of mission themselves.[61] These gospel-translating, mission-loving Mohawk were, in sum, exemplary Christian loyalists, in contrast to American rebels, and not at all the "merciless Indian savages" unleashed on virtuous settlers, as described by the Declaration of Independence. It is worth noting that, if a critical memoir by Anglican priest John Strachan (later bishop of Toronto) is to be believed, Brant's faith was supposedly shaken on the first of his two diplomatic visits to Britain, and (Strachan claimed) Brant's ensuing loss of respect for the British government and political system was an important motivation for his later political work trying to unite Indigenous peoples and make them independent of Britain.[62]

Be this as it may, Six Nations elites continued to translate the Bible. Joseph's protégé and adoptive nephew John Norton translated the Gospel of St. John into Mohawk for the British and Foreign Bible Society in 1804, a project memorialized in a window in the 1843 chapel built by the community at the Bay of Quinte. For his part, Henry Aaron Hill, or Kenwendeshon, who married Joseph Brant's daughter Christina and was a member of the powerful Hill family, translated the Gospel of Luke in 1828, as well as hymns and, eventually, many other scriptures. Hill also worked as an Anglican catechist at Grand River.[63] As a token of the declining power of the Mohawk intermediary, however, by the time Hill's last translations were published in the 1830s, according to Richard Ruggle, his contribution was not always highlighted and his name had been edged off the title page. His translation work was now encouraged by the Methodists, who at this stage were challenging Anglican hegemony at Grand River. After 1828 the Methodists followed the Anglicans in losing interest in promoting biblical translation, and further work was sponsored by the Young Men's Bible Society of New York.[64] Brant's daughter Elizabeth Kerr helped Hill translate parts of the Bible into English and presented copies of her work to Queen Victoria: this might be seen as an (ultimately unsuccessful) attempt to revive the flagging relationship between Six Nations and Anglican elites through Bible translation.

The conflict and ambivalence regarding Christianity observable even in Strachan's account of the life of Joseph Brant was consistently in evidence throughout the Grand River community and echoed, it seems to me, profound and important discussions about identity and how best to react to the colonial situation, particularly as controversy mounted about Brant's strategies (continuing to the present day, as Rick Monture has recently explored eloquently).[65] The community remained religiously diverse, and religious practice continued to have political implications throughout the early nineteenth century. Most famously, a challenge to Joseph Brant's authority spearheaded by Red Jacket and other Seneca dissidents in 1805 was accompanied by challenges to Anglicanism and other forms of Christianity by adherents of longhouse practice.[66] Even within the realm of Christian practice, political challenge was echoed by religious challenge. When brothers Aaron and Isaac Hill quarreled first with John Deserontyon at the Bay of Quinte and then with Joseph Brant at Grand River, they argued for different forms of Christianity. They also objected to Deserontyon's and Brant's spending habits. Eleanor Herrington reported in her 1922 study that Deserontyon had denounced the religious (or possibly irreligious) activities of the Hill brothers at a council formed to deal with the fact that Isaac and his supporters had killed two men in a violent confrontation.[67] Deserontyon claimed that Isaac Hill had opened a tavern at the Bay of Quinte with the sign of the devil, and that "since Captain Isaac's party has been formed the door of the church has been locked." At Grand River, the church had also been shut because of Isaac Hill. One issue seems to have been the divergence from the standard Anglican liturgy. "Captain Isaac with his people got tired of reading the same prayers over and over in the church," testified Deserontyon, "and in the council said they would make new prayers of their own, which surprised me much, knowing when the minister heard it he would throw us all away."[68]

Conflict among the Six Nations in Upper Canada over religion, politics, and identity might be symbolized by the divergent political views of two of Joseph Brant's sons. Isaac Brant, Joseph's eldest son by his first wife, was clearly very angry. He became very critical of his father, and eventually joined a faction at Grand River that strongly opposed him. According to John Strachan, citing Stuart, Isaac was "remarked for a ferocious and unfriendly temper, sometimes maliciously and wantonly shooting horses belonging to white people."[69] In 1795, Isaac Brant killed a white settler at Grand River named Lowell, a recent deserter from the American army, opening the thorny issue of whether Six Nations law or Euro-Canadian law should prevail in his punishment. While the case was still being debated, Isaac confronted and attacked his father, and then died some days later of a blow inflicted by Joseph.[70]

In contrast, John Brant (or Ahyouweighs or Tekarihogen), born in 1794 to Brant's third wife, a year before Isaac's death, worked politically as both "chief" and Christian gentleman (although he was certainly not uncritical of colonial policy, as illustrated by his bitter comments about land loss to the Colonial Office in 1822 and his anger in the 1830s at the flooding of Grand River land to construct a canal).[71] He took a leading role in the War of 1812, made a diplomatic trip to Britain to discuss land issues, became Indian Superintendent at Grand River, and just before his death won election to the Legislative Assembly. His legislative victory was overturned when the votes of Six Nations electors were rejected on the grounds that they were leaseholders.

Brant promoted education and Christianization at Grand River. While in London in 1822, he approached the New England Company to seek money for a schoolmaster, hoping to revive a school that had floundered in 1812. As the New England Company minutes recorded, "Mr. Brandt recommends plain reading and writing and account and thinks the Government allowance (about £25 per annum & two Rations) not sufficient."[72] Brant promoted local schools taught by Haudenosaunee: he asked for a schoolmaster to replace the "worn out" schoolmaster at the English School at Mohawk Town but stated that "a Native would be preferred," as there were "few white people living with them and those Old." Community reluctance to send children to distant schools was described by the Reverend Stewart of Upper Canada, who also spoke to the New England Company in 1820: "Children would not go to a School more than Two Miles distant and Parents would not suffer their Children to go as Boarders to the Schoolmaster – that is a degree of Civilization above them."[73] It seems that the Six Nations continued to resist losing control of Christianity.

At the very end of his life, John Brant quarrelled with a new Anglican missionary, Robert Lugger of the New England Company, and sided with the Methodists at Grand River, in part over the loss of local control over the school founded by Lugger. This school would become the Mohawk Institute and would ultimately be turned into an Anglican residential school, despite Brant's original hopes for a non-residential school run by local people.[74] This story lies beyond the purview of the current chapter. It does, however, underscore how difficult the management of Anglicanism would become as Indigenous peoples were reconceptualized as wards of the state rather than crucial military allies.

## Notes

1 Since "Kanien'kehá:ka" (people of the flint) and "Mohawk" are both terms in current use, I use both in this chapter. The name "Mohawk" was deployed in English in the eighteenth century, and many historical documents reflect this usage. The word is, however, derived from a term used by the Narragansett meaning "man eaters." "Kanien'kehá:ka" is the term people used for themselves in their own language. Although my usage is not entirely consistent, I generally use "Mohawk" when referring to historical documents and European perspectives and "Kanien'kehá:ka" when reflecting on current issues or when speculating about Kanien'kehá:ka perspectives in the past.

2 Library and Archives Canada (LAC), Claus Papers, vol. 1, 22–28: William Johnson to Daniel Claus, Castle Cumberland, 10 March 1761.

3 LAC, Claus Papers, vol. 1, 48–50: Johnson to Claus, Castle Cumberland, 20 May 1761.

4 Gregory Dowd, *War under Heaven: Pontiac, the Indian Nations and the British Empire* (Baltimore: Johns Hopkins Press, 2002); Jon William Parmenter, "Pontiac's War: Forging New Links in the Anglo-Iroquois Covenant Chain, 1758–1766," *Ethnohistory* 44, 4 (Autumn 1997): 617–54.

5 Alfred A. Cave, "The Delaware Prophet Neolin: A Reappraisal," *Ethnohistory* 46, 2 (Spring 1999), 265–90; Gregory Dowd, *A Spirited Resistance: The North American Struggle for Unity, 1745–1815* (Baltimore: Johns Hopkins Press, 1993). Compare also Catherine Murton Stoehr, "Nativism's Bastard: Neolin, Tenskwatawa, and the Anishnabeg Methodist Movement," in *Lines Drawn upon the Water: First Nations and the Great Lakes Borders and Borderlands,* ed. Karl Hele (Waterloo, ON: Wilfred Laurier Press, 2008), 175–90.

6 Sir William Johnson to Henry Barclay [draft], Johnson Hall, 30 March 1763, in *The Papers of Sir William Johnson,* ed. Alexander Flick (Albany: University of the State of New York, 1925), 4:72.

7 On the politics of New York and antagonism between Anglicans and other Protestants, see Edward Countryman, *A People in Revolution: The American Revolution and Political Society in New York, 1760–1790* (Baltimore and London: Johns Hopkins University Press, 1981); Peter M. Doll, *Revolution, Religion and National Identity: Imperial Anglicanism in British North America, 1745–1795* (Cranbury, NJ: Associated University Presses, 2000), 155–209; Robert W. Venables, "Tryon County," in *The Other New York: The American Revolution beyond New York City, 1763–1787,* ed. Joseph Tiedeman and Eugene Fingerhut (Albany: State University of New York Press, 2005), 179–97.

8 Alan Taylor, *The Divided Ground: Indians, Settlers and the Northern Borderland of the American Revolution* (New York: Alfred A. Knopf, 2006); James Axtell, "Dr. Wheelock's Little Red Schoolhouse" in *The European and the Indian: Essays in the Ethnohistory of Colonial North America* (New York: Oxford University Press, 1981), 87–109.

9 Rhodes House, Oxford, United Society for the Propagation of the Gospel Papers, North America [henceforward USPG, NA], ser. B, vol. 2, f. 92: William Johnson to SPG, Johnson Hall, 26 April 1770. The Society for the Propagation of the Gospel in Foreign Parts (SPG) was renamed the United Society for the Propagation of the Gospel in 1965 following the incorporation of the Universities' Mission to Central Africa. In this chapter, I therefore refer not to the USPG archives but to the society itself as the SPG.

10 USPG, NA, ser. B, vol. 2: Inglis to SPG, New York, 8 March 1770.

11  USPG, NA, ser. B, vol. 2, f. 89: William Johnson to SPG, Johnson Hall, 11 December 1768.
12  Fintan O'Toole, *White Savage: William Johnson and the Invention of America* (Albany: State University of New York Press, 2005).
13  Anglican Diocesan Archives of Ontario (ADOA), Kingston, Ontario, John Stuart papers, "Correspondence with the Bishop of Nova Scotia, 1788–1801," 5a–d: John Stuart to Charles Inglis, 5 March 1790.
14  E.g., USPG, NA, ser. B, vol. 2: William Johnson to SPG, Johnson Hall, 8 October 1766.
15  Arnaud Balvay, *L'Epée et la plume: Amérindiens et soldats des troupes de la marine en Louisiane et au Pays d'en Haut* (Quebec: Les Presses de l'Université Laval, 2006).
16  Eric Hinderaker, "The 'Four Indian Kings' and the Imaginative Construction of the First British Empire," *William and Mary Quarterly*, 3rd ser. 53 (1996), 487–526.
17  London Metropolitan Archives, Company for the Propagation of the Gospel in New England: MS 7920, Minute Book, 8 November 1816–11 May 1830, Minutes of the Indian Committee, 11 April 1822.
18  Daniel Richter, "'Some of them ... would always have a minister with them': Mohawk Protestantism, 1683–1719," *American Indian Quarterly* 4 (Fall 1992), 471–84; Denys Delâge, "Les Iroquois chrétiens des 'réductions,' 1667–1770: I, Migration et rapports avec les Français," *Recherches Amérindiennes au Québec*, vol. 21, 1–2 (1991), 59–70.
19  USPG, NA, ser. A, vol. 2, f. 122: Rev. Thoroughgood Moore to the SPG, New York, 13 November 1705, reproduced in John Wolfe Lydekker, *The Faithful Mohawks* (Cambridge: Cambridge University Press, 1938), 21–23.
20  Richter, "Some of them ..."; quotation from William Andrews to SPG Secretary, 17 April 1718, USPG, NA, ser. A, vol. 13, p. 319.
21  Richter, "Some of them ..."
22  USPG, NA, ser. B, vol. 2, f. 90: William Johnson to SPG, Johnson Hall, December 1769.
23  USPG, NA, ser. B, vol. 2: Charles Inglis to SPG, New York, 12 June 1770.
24  Troy Bickham, "Hendrik/Tiyanoga/Theyanoguen (1680–1755): Iroquois Emissary to England," in *The Human Tradition in the Atlantic World, 1500–1850*, ed. Karen Racine and Beatriz Mamigonian (Rowman and Littlefield, 2010), 76.
25  USPG, NA, ser B, vol. 2: William Johnson to SPG, Johnson Hall, 8 October 1766.
26  USPG, NA, ser. B, vol. 2, f. 201: John Stuart to SPG, Fort Hunter, Tryon County, 9 August 1774; reproduced in Lydekker, *Faithful Mohawks*, 135–36.
27  USPG, NA, ser. B, vol. 2, f. 198: John Stuart to SPG, Fort Hunter, Tryon County, 8 January 1772.
28  SPG, NA, ser. B, vol. 2, f. 199: John Stuart to SPG, Fort Hunter, Tryon County, 20 July 1772.
29  Walter Pilkington, ed., *The Journals of Samuel Kirkland, 18th-Century Missionary to the Iroquois, Government Agent, Father of Hamilton College* (Clinton, NY: Hamilton College, 1980), 80.
30  As Cave argues in "The Delaware Prophet Neolin." On the emergence of a white– "Indian" binary, including different religious paths, see Nancy Shoemaker, *A Strange Likeness: Becoming Red and White in Eighteenth-Century North America* (New York: Oxford University Press, 2006).
31  I discuss these examples and Kirkland's interaction with the Six Nations further in Elizabeth Elbourne, "Christian Soldiers, Christian Allies: Coercion and Conversion in Southern Africa and Northeastern America at the Turn of the Nineteenth Century," in *Beyond Conversion and Syncretism: Indigenous Encounters with Missionary Christianity, 1800–2000*, ed. David Lindenfeld and Miles Richardson (New York: Berghahn Books, 2012). I make a broad argument for the importance of the military context for understanding Christianity on imperial frontiers and the value of looking at "military" and "religious" history in concert. The omnipresence of the military was a key factor making Christian alliance

risky as well as potentially fruitful, and my argument in this volume builds on this earlier discussion.

32 Pilkington, *Journals of Samuel Kirkland*, 23–24.

33 Ibid., 73–74 (2 March 1772).

34 I am indebted to the anonymous reviewer of this volume for this argument about evangelical decentralized individualism.

35 Library and Archives Canada (LAC), Claus Papers, vol. 1: Daniel Claus to William Johnson, 18 March 1761, 34–35.

36 Daniel Claus, *A Primer, for the use of the Mohawk children, to acquire the spelling, reading and writing of their own ... Waerighwaghsawe Iksaongoenwa: Tsiwaondad-derighhonny Kaghyadoghsera ...* (Montreal: Fleury Mesplet, 1781).

37 LAC, USPG papers, ser. C, Canada (pre-diocesan), Box 1: Aaron Hill to Daniel Claus, Niagara, 1 September 1782, Mohawk original and English translation enclosed in Claus to SPG, 9 October 1782.

38 Gus Richardson, "Sahonwagy," *Canadian Dictionary of Biography Online* (2000), http://www.biographi.ca/en/bio/sahonwagy_4E.html.

39 USPG, NA, ser. B, vol 2: John Stuart to SPG, Fort Hunter, Tryon County, 19 February 1774, and Stuart to SPG, Philadelphia, 17 October 1775.

40 "Advertisement," in *The Order for Morning and Evening Prayer, and Administration of the Sacraments and some other offices of the Church of England ... Ne Yakawea Niyadewighniserage Yondereanayendakhkwa Orhoenk éne, neoni Yogarask-ha Oghseragwégouh ...* 3rd ed., revised with corrections and additions by Daniel Claus, 1780.

41 LAC, Claus Papers, vol. 4, p. 79: Paulus Sa hon wag y to Daniel Claus, Grand River, 7 August 1785 [Mohawk version]; translation from the Mohawk (cited above), vol. 23, 24–25.

42 ADOA, Stuart Papers, "Correspondence, Bishop of Nova Scotia, 1788–1801": John Stuart to Charles Inglis, 6 July 1788.

43 ADOA, Stuart Papers, "Correspondence, Bishop of Nova Scotia, 1788–1801": Stuart to Charles Inglis, 5 March 1790 (5a–d).

44 London Metropolitan Archives, Company for the Propagation of the Gospel in New England: MS 7920, Minute Book, 8 November 1816–11 May 1830, Minutes of the Indian Committee, 11 April 1822.

45 E.g., Draper Papers, ser. F, vol. 1, 140ff: Thomas Pilkin to Lyman Draper, 13 March 1878.

46 Information about the division of Queen Anne's silver is from the website maintained by the Mohawk of the Bay of Quinte/Kenhteke/Kanyen'kehà:ka, www.mbq-tmt.org. See also M. Eleanor Herrington, "Captain John Deserontyou and the Mohawk Settlement at Deseronto," Bulletin of the Departments of History and Political and Economic Science in Queen's University, Kingston, Ontario, Canada, 41 (November 1921), 8; C.M. Johnson, Deserontyon (Odeserundiye), John (Captain John), *Dictionary of Canadian Biography Online*, http://www.biographi.ca/en/bio/deserontyon_john_5E.html.

47 Herrington, "Captain John Deserontyou," 8.

48 Meghan Balogh, "Mohawks Mark 230th Anniversary of Ancestral Landing," *Napanee Guide*, 2 June 2014.

49 Elizabeth II presented the community with a new silver chalice in 1984 as a replacement for a piece of the collection that had gone missing after the American Revolution.

50 Elbourne, "Christian Soldiers, Christian Allies."

51 W.L. Greene to Lyman Draper, Danube, New York, 4 January 1878, Draper Papers, ser. F, vol. 2, 43ff; Nathaniel Benton, *History of Herkimer County* (New York: J. Munsell, 1856).

52 Mrs. E.A. Smith, "The Story of the Bell, 1882," and Taiaiake Alfred, "A Different View: A Descendant Recounts the 1774 Attack, 1995" in *Captive Histories: English, French and*

*Native Narratives of the 1704 Deerfield Raid,* ed. Evan Haefeli and Kevin Sweeney (Amherst and Boston: Massachusetts University Press, 2006), 213–20, 244–52.

53  Draper Papers, ser. F (Brant Papers), vol. 13. This narrative comes from notes that Draper made while collecting oral history among the Ontario Six Nations in the late 1870s, and is headed "from George Rokwaho Loft, born at Bay Quinte, Sept. 4, 1815."

54  USPG, NA, ser. B, vol. 2: John Stuart to SPG, Montreal, 13 October 1781; Lydekker, *Faithful Mohawks,* 164–65.

55  Lois M. Feister and Bonnie Pulis, "Molly Brant: Her Domestic and Political Roles in Eighteenth-Century New York," in *Northeastern Indian Lives, 1632–1816,* ed. Robert Steven Grumet (University of Massachusetts Press, 1996), 317.

56  John C. Ogden, *A Tour through Upper and Lower Canada,* 2nd ed. (Wilmington: Bonsal and Niles, 1800), 60.

57  Ibid., 61.

58  Draper Papers, Ser. F, vol. 13, 93.

59  Carl Benn, *The Iroquois in the War of 1812* (Toronto: University of Toronto Press, 1998).

60  N.N. [John Strachan], "The Life of Captain Brant," in James Strachan, *A Visit to the Province of Upper Canada* (Aberdeen: D. Chalmers and Co., 1820), 152–53.

61  Anon. [Charles Inglis], "Preface," *The Book of Common Prayer, and Administration of the Sacraments, and other Rites and Ceremonies of the Church ...* (London: C. Buckton, 1787), i–iii.

62  N.N. [John Strachan], "The Life of Captain Brant," 164–65.

63  Richard E. Ruggle, "Kenwendeshon," *Canadian Dictionary of Biography Online,* http://www.biographi.ca/en/bio/kenwendeshon_6E.html.

64  Ruggle, "Kenwendeshon."

65  Rick Monture, *We Share Our Matters: Two Centuries of Writing and Resistance at Six Nations of the Grand River* (Winnipeg: University of Manitoba Press, 2014), esp. 29–61.

66  William Stone, *Life and Times of Red Jacket* (New York: Wiley and Putnam, 1841); Christopher Densmore, *Red Jacket: Iroquois Diplomat and Orator* (Syracuse, NY: Syracuse University Press, 1999).

67  These men were Deserontyon's brother-in-law and the brother-in-law's son.

68  Herrington, *Captain John Deserontyou,* 14.

69  "Life of Captain Brant," 167.

70  Taylor, *Divided Ground,* 327–28; Draper Papers, ser. F, vol. 13, f. 21.

71  E.g., Hamilton Public Library, John Brant letterbook, 63: John Brant to Colonel Givins, Brantford, 5 December 1831.

72  LMA, New England Company papers: MS 7920, vol. 2, "At an interview held the 11th day of May 1822."

73  LMA, New England Company papers, MS 7923, *Estates Committee and Indian Committees minute book, 1807–1822,* Indian Committee, 26 October 1820.

74  Charles M. Johnston, "The Six Nations in the Grand River Valley, 1784–1847," in *Aboriginal Ontario: Historical Perspectives on the First Nations,* ed. Edward Rogers and Donald B. Smith (Toronto: Dundurn Press, 1994), 177–78.

# 3

# A Subversive Sincerity:
# The I:yem Memorial, Catholicism, and
# Political Opportunity in S'olh Téméxw

*Amanda Fehr*

> *The cross bears the inscription: "Eayem Memorial 1938 AD,*
> *Erected by the Stalo Indians. In memory of many hundreds of our*
> *forefathers buried here, this is one of our six ancient cemeteries within*
> *our five mile Native fishing grounds which we inherited from our*
> *ancestors. R.I.P."*
>
> – CHILLIWACK PROGRESS, 17 AUGUST 1938[1]

THE I:YEM MEMORIAL, erected by the Stó:lō Coast Salish in southwestern British Columbia, incorporated and blended aspects of Roman Catholicism with an articulation of a distinct Stó:lō identity and assertion of rights. In this chapter, I challenge binaries between Indigenous and Christian as well as the spiritual and the political, and I pay attention to ideas of symbolism and performance. I struggle with limited sources and employ a methodological approach that I call ethnohistory. While I focus on the politics within a particular First Nation rather than the political or military alliances forged between Indigenous people and newcomers, the themes of colonialism, conflict, and Indigenous peoples' ability to find innovative ways to deal with a dynamic cultural and political environment – themes common in other chapters – are also addressed here.

S'olh Téméxw, the territory of the Stó:lō,[2] has been described as being "as much a mythological universe as a biological world," where people simultaneously walk "through both spiritual and physical realms."[3] This has always been a place of transformation and change, where, originating with the arrival of Xexá:ls, or the transformers, at or near the beginning of time, attempts have been made to make things permanent or, literally, right. Communities were linked to particular ancestors who, through the acts of the transformers, were turned into resources or features of the landscape. For some people, the plural Xexá:ls becomes the singular Xa:ls, with certain elders speaking of the "little Christ," or Jesus, battling powerful medicine men in the Fraser Canyon.[4]

A part of S'olh Téméxw located in the Fraser Canyon four kilometres north of Yale, I:yem was historically economically, politically, and spiritually significant to the Stó:lō.[5] This particular place also serves as an example of how Stó:lō places were affected by colonialism, and how Stó:lō people interpreted and participated in their changing world. The cemetery at I:yem contains three or four large box graves moved from earlier burial sites that were disturbed when the Canadian Pacific Railway (CPR) cut through the region in the early 1880s. As the majority of Stó:lō people had migrated downriver into the Fraser Valley, in 1938 I:yem was no longer a permanent village site, home to some of the most powerful and wealthy people in the canyon, but rather a place that was used only seasonally by certain families with fishing spots there.[6] By 1938, the Oblates of Mary Immaculate had been active in S'olh Téméxw for nearly one hundred years.[7] Both church and state were advocates for the 1885 amendment to the Indian Act, prohibiting religious and political ceremonies such as the potlatch and winter dance of the Coast Salish.[8] These restrictions, combined with later amendments of 1914, 1918, and 1927, made any gathering organized by Aboriginal people themselves, or discussions of land claims outside of the church, essentially illegal.[9] It was in this context of religious restrictions and a will to commemorate their ancestors that brothers-in-law Chief Isaac James of Ruby Creek and Dennis Siya:mia Peters[10] declared their ancestors buried in the canyon as Stó:lō and honoured them with a large, white granite cross atop two concrete blocks, with an accompanying bronze plaque that identified the I:yem memorial, the cemetery, and the five-mile Native fishing grounds.

The memorial symbolized a traditional claim to the territory while preserving distinct Indigenous histories and identities at a time when the Indian Act prohibited Indigenous people from using the courts for land claims and banned older Coast Salish ceremonies designed to publicly regulate the passing on of history and property. It would have been politically savvy to protect the territory from outsiders, such as provincial and federal governments, and from other Aboriginal groups by erecting a monument in the form of a Christian cross detailing the Stó:lō's traditional rights to the Fraser Canyon. A Christian guise enabled the memorial's creators to raise funds to publicly articulate their rights and claims to territory, outside of the courtroom and the longhouse. There were further strategic benefits in the form the memorial took, as the symbol of the cross would have been meaningful to most non-Natives at the time, ensuring that the sacred space it signified was protected from further destruction. I argue here that limitations inherent in separating the memorial text from the cross it was attached to become apparent, as a focus on the political and pragmatic dismisses any sincere spiritual expressions of Christianity and ignores the potential spiritual power of Christianity from the perspective of the

Stó:lō who erected the memorial.[11] Arguably, the memorial's cross could also be considered a part of a deliberate assertion of Stó:lō identity in 1938. Appreciating both the politically subversive and spiritually significant messages and form of the I:yem memorial, this chapter considers the political and spiritual ramifications of the erection and dedication of the memorial in 1938 as an entrée to explore how the memorial's creators, and some of their contemporaries, saw Christianity, politics, and Stó:lō identity interacting in their world. Following a brief historiographical discussion and outline of my method and theoretical approach, I take a close look at the memorial's creators, Isaac James and Dennis S. Peters, before returning to the dedication of the monument at I:yem to consider some of its broader implications.

The period during which the memorial was constructed remains largely unstudied by scholars of both religion/encounters and Stó:lō history, and has even been called "passive" by political scientist Paul Tennant in his study of BC Aboriginal politics.[12] The I:yem memorial, built during this period by Indigenous people affiliated with the Catholic Church, challenges this generalization, drawing attention to the use of religion in alternative and innovative expressions of political identities and claims to territory made outside of courts or longhouses. My argument and approach has been influenced by ethnohistorian Keith Thor Carlson's detailed discussion of shifting Stó:lō collective identities, where he draws attention to the role of church and state in dividing Stó:lō communities in the nineteenth century, as well as the ability of Stó:lō people to use colonial institutions to remain a distinct community.[13] Of particular interest is his analysis of missionaries and the anti-potlatch law. Carlson pays attention to the role of the Catholic Church, more specifically the Oblates of Mary Immaculate in the region, looking at denominational conflicts and the recognition of some individuals as chiefs by the missionaries.[14] It is not surprising that, more recently, these "church chiefs" are at times dismissed as acting in their own self-interest, or that the seemingly Christian aspects of their lives are downplayed.[15] My discussion of I:yem shows how, in the 1930s, seemingly Christian elements became the innovative means for the Stó:lō to articulate their own identity as Stó:lō and to define their claim to the Fraser Canyon in the wake of restrictions imposed during the nineteenth century.

In this chapter I shift my focus from Indigenous–newcomer history (or missionary encounters) to Stó:lō history – interpreting the way Stó:lō people themselves have historicized events that could be associated with spirituality and Christianity. Here I take the ethnohistorical approach described by Carlson, whereby scholars "explore not only the story of Natives in newcomer history, but also the saga of newcomers in multiple Aboriginal histories," requiring "the construction of new chronologies and interpretive frameworks that go beyond the story of Aboriginal people in Canadian history; stories that are sensitive to, but not necessarily centred on, the role and place of colonialism within Aboriginal history."[16] It is not my intention to dismiss the consequences of a history of intense missionization and the power dynamics entailed but rather to recognize the validity of exploring how some Stó:lō people in the early twentieth century interpreted their world, and to create an academic space to consider their professed beliefs. Taking care not to reduce everything to either spirituality or Indigeneity, I focus on Stó:lō histories in order to explore differences and diversity within them, highlighting the multifaceted and shifting natures of individual and collective identities.[17] I see this attempt to engage with Stó:lō perspectives in order to complicate our understanding of their histories as decolonizing.[18] While my approach and analysis are inspired and informed by interviews that I conducted with community members during the joint University of Saskatchewan/University of Victoria Ethnohistory field schools in 2007 and 2009, this reconstruction is based almost entirely upon petitions to the government, newspaper articles, field notes of earlier ethnographers, and recorded oral histories from the Stó:lō Nation Archives.[19]

Framing this study as a Stó:lō history raises questions about the applicability of the terms "encounter" and "exchange" for this study, and more generally for discussing Indigenous histories of Christianity. This collection seeks to engage Aboriginal perspectives, and other contributors are critical of binaries between Aboriginal people and newcomers in the literature; however, these very binaries are maintained in the exploration of encounters and exchange between Indigenous perspectives and what are depicted as alien systems of belief.[20] While I agree with the underlying ideas explored by other authors who use these terms, I question ideas of exchange and encounter in my case study of some Stó:lō leaders. Ideas of encounter and exchange are arguably appropriate in contexts such as early religious encounters between missionaries and Indigenous peoples, however; I hesitate to apply them to my own case study of Stó:lō people, whose ancestors included prophets who taught aspects of Catholicism prior to the arrival of the first missionaries and who themselves constructed a memorial in the shape of a cross another hundred years later.[21] Much of my own terminology is less than ideal; a more satisfying lexicon remains elusive.[22] Nonetheless I try to be as specific as possible (while leaving room for ambiguity) and pay attention to individual and community particularities in an effort to explore the entangled nature of political and religious expression in S'olh Téméxw.

Questions of representation are closely related to those of terminology, as the individuals I focus on simultaneously dominate the source base and are marginalized within it.[23] In part because of the limitations of the sources, the disciplinary approach and focus of the historian further shapes the depiction of the historical actors. For my own study, I question how various components of individuals' lives and identities may in fact fit together; I attempt to focus on more than one particular aspect in my depiction of them and their histories.

I now consider the two Stó:lō men responsible for creating the I:yem memorial in 1938, and what their lives tell us about the intersections among politics, religious belief, and status during this time of change in Stó:lō society. Brothers-in-law Chief Isaac James of the Yale Reserve at Ruby Creek and Dennis Siya:mia Peters were fairly representative of Stó:lō political leadership during the late nineteenth century and the first half of the twentieth. Both Peters and James were involved in politics, were signatories of earlier petitions, and had personal connections to, and rights to fish at, I:yem; however, the two men also differed in several ways, especially in terms of their status and how they were regarded by some of their contemporaries. Like the late nineteenth-century Stó:lō leaders that have come to be described as "church chiefs," James was recognized as a siyá:m, which typically referred to a respected leader and/or someone who was knowledgeable or wealthy,[24] as well as an elected chief under the Indian Act, who had church- and state-sponsored authority to speak for his community. Peters was a more ambiguous figure, drawing attention to differences within Stó:lō society in the early twentieth century, and what it may have meant to be a Stó:lō political leader at that time.

This was a hierarchical society, where "children were taught who social equals were and who inferiors were."[25] Among the Stó:lō, people of high status (Smela:lh or "worthy") were and are recognized to this day as those who know their history, whereas lower-status people (S'texem or "worthless") are described as those who have lost or forgotten their history.[26] Through knowing one's history and genealogy it was/is possible to gain access and ownership rights to particular fishing spots, such as those at I:yem. Colonialism brought demographic changes, as well as the interference of the church and state, which could result in increased social mobility for people who had been of lower status.[27] While some Stó:lō leaders in the early twentieth century were able to draw on old and new forms of authority, questions remained over whose claims to high status and authority were more legitimate, and some claims (such as Peters') were more controversial at the time. The status of these individuals is further complicated today, as community members' interpretations of the past are shaped, in part, by their use of history in establishing their own status, as well as current ideas of tradition and Stó:lō-ness that seem to privilege what is now seen as Stó:lō political activism over Christian "church chiefs."

In 1938 Dennis S. Peters' family fishing spot at I:yem was disputed and his hereditary name, "Siya:mia," was contested within his family, likely related to some of the changes in Stó:lō society outlined above.[28] Even Peters' descendants have depicted him as being a less spiritual, less culturally knowledgeable person than Isaac James; his incredible breadth of knowledge with regard to Aboriginal rights and the land question may have come at the expense of other types of knowledge.[29] It is unclear if this gap in his knowledge was a result of his time at residential school and/or due to his own views and values about what was important. Alternatively, as a member of another family hinted, Peters did not have a high status and lacked the knowledge of some of his contemporaries. Tillie Gutierrez explained to me in 2007, "Dennis Peters – he didn't have too much ... His song recorded by Oliver Wells, when the University people used to come up there and ask him to sing, and drum and sing – and he didn't really know any songs, so he asked my granddad."[30] Nonetheless, Peters is publicly remembered as a "leading member of the Stahlo Tribes"[31] and a "protest leader from the Hope Band."[32] Examples like these begin to complicate the view of Peters as a Stó:lō political leader, highlighting variations within Stó:lō society and suggesting that he may have had a different understanding of what it meant to be Stó:lō than others. Even though a surface view of James and Peters would suggest they were both elite males, their positions in society were more nuanced and have been underexplored by anthropologists concerned with traditional leadership.

Prior to his partnership with James, Peters worked extensively with his cousin Pierre Ayessick, seemingly an earlier example of the higher status of the latter adding legitimacy to the knowledge and work of the former. Ayessick[33] has been described by anthropologist Wilson Duff as coming from what for generations was regarded as the highest-ranking family in Hope, and Carlson notes that several elders today remember Ayessick as one of the prominent church chiefs of the late nineteenth century who helped to articulate a Stó:lō tribal identity.[34] One of Dennis Peters' descendants has explained this relationship, dismissing Ayessick (and by association Isaac James) as being "the church chief and Dennis the political chief, probably more of a siyá:m."[35] While this split seems reflective of current Stó:lō and academic views of the various roles these men filled in their community, I hesitate to completely dismiss the importance of the apparently well-respected church chiefs in shaping a Stó:lō political agenda at this time, especially as it is clear that Peters needed the authority of James within his own community. Considering the relationship between people like Peters and Ayessick or James allows for a more complex view of Stó:lō society and the relationship between politics and Christianity at the time.

In addition to being a high-class siyá:m and elected chief, Isaac James was also believed to have special powers. Though he reportedly would not say what these powers were, his brother-in-law and Wilson Duff's Yale informant, Patrick

Charlie, who himself claimed to be spiritually powerful,[36] knew that James had power by the way that he acted.[37] Patrick Charlie even provided Duff with an example of Isaac James foreseeing the future, explaining that James had predicted how younger people would alter a church plan that the two men had made together. Such an unexpected relationship between special powers and the construction of a church helps to indicate what it meant for some Stó:lō to be spiritually powerful around the time the monument was created, further situating the memorial as something that may itself have been a product of James's spiritual powers and that could have been considered spiritually powerful in its own right. James was also a caretaker of the spiritually powerful canyon cemeteries, drawing attention to the memorial as something that would have been understood as more than a strategic political statement and highlighting the potentially different perspectives of the memorial's creators. Even though James's spiritual powers have been noted in the ethnographic record, and Peters is depicted in the oral histories as someone whose preoccupation with the land question may have been at the expense of other forms of knowledge, it is significant that they worked together to create the memorial at I:yem. We must then consider how seemingly separate categories of Stó:lō identity could fit together and inform one another. Regardless of Peters' role, be it as a traditional siyá:m or a more ambiguous figure, he worked closely with individuals who are at times dismissed as being "church chiefs" but seem to have been well respected at the time. Like the political and religious aspects of the memorial, the various categories scholars have used to assess Stó:lō leaders in the past were often entangled.[38]

Dennis S. Peters' relationship with the Roman Catholic Church was complicated, and some care must be taken to distinguish between Church doctrine and the beliefs of those affiliated with the Church. I have been unable to find much information about Peters' relationship with the Church, other than the fact that he was Catholic and that a high requiem mass was held at his death in 1944, that much of his work was done with the support of Stó:lō leaders closely affiliated with the Catholic Church, and that in 1938 he was involved in making the first public articulation of Stó:lō identity on a seemingly Christian cross.[39] Recognizing that the memorial creators were members of the Roman Catholic Church, I do not assume that those who built the memorial shared all values held by Roman Catholic missionaries. A belief in God or the power of the cross did not necessarily entail complete compliance with mission doctrine. Although Peters and his family identified as Catholic, he did not support Catholic missionary schools. In fact, his 1922 petition on behalf of Ayessick, who is depicted as having a close relationship with Roman Catholic missionaries, specified that the Stó:lō did not want churches "to have any control" over their education.[40]

The involvement of Dennis S. Peters and his family in the Native Brotherhood of BC, a political advocacy group, further complicates our understanding of their relationship with the Catholic Church, drawing attention to the various relationships between politics and belief, as the memorial's creators worked with both Catholic and Protestant allies.[41] According to Paul Tennant, the Protestant leanings of the Native Brotherhood was considered problematic by the Catholic missionaries and many Catholic Aboriginal people, who viewed the Brotherhood's position against residential schools as an attack on their beliefs and institutions.[42] Conversely, I suggest that Indigenous identities, beliefs, and politics were often more nuanced. Such attitudes towards church-run residential schools and involvement in the Native Brotherhood demonstrate complexity and consistency while showcasing the problems of strict dichotomies between Christian and non-Christian, Protestant and Catholic, or spiritual and political. They also serve as a caution against dismissing the so-called church chiefs or their supporters as less authentic Stó:lō who conformed to missionary ideals, or dismissing Catholic Church–affiliated people of the era as politically inactive. Challenging strict dichotomies, the creators of the I:yem memorial used English text and a Christian cross, and asserted broad traditional Aboriginal rights to the canyon and a specifically, albeit particular, Stó:lō identity.

The memorial at I:yem can be seen as the culmination of Dennis S. Peters' career of making use of innovative means to advocate for Stó:lō interests, most notably the interests of those with hereditary rights to continue fishing in the canyon. Prior to 1927, Peters made use of the courts and petitioned the government on multiple occasions, often on behalf of high-status Stó:lō leaders. Even while writing petitions advocating Stó:lō political, economic, and spiritual interests in the five-mile canyon fishery, the creators of the memorial at I:yem and their associates were also signatories of petitions both against and in support of the potlatch – suggesting they held different understandings of being Stó:lō from what one might assume. The first petition requesting that the Indian Act be further amended to prevent "potlatches, dances, and other pagan ceremonies," recirculated in 1915 but likely written earlier,[43] includes the signatures of Pierre Ayessick, Dennis Peters, Isaac James, and Captain Charlie.[44] The petitioners were concerned that the increasing number of downriver Indians participating in "a regrettable superstitious practice," was to the "detriment of civilization and progress amongst them."[45] More particularly, they seemed to object to what they saw as the "pagan," spiritual elements of these practices, especially the winter dance (Smilha dancing) that more recent scholars associate with traditional forms of Stó:lō governance. I am less comfortable interpreting this petition than those protesting the closing of the fishery, drawing attention to my own biases and assumptions of how change should occur within existing cultural parameters. Indeed, I initially questioned if this was the product of missionary influence or pressure, or perhaps an effort to be politically strategic and demonstrate "progress" and "civilization" to outsiders. Yet it would be problematic to unquestionably accept those petitions and statements that seem to correspond to more recent Stó:lō attitudes while rejecting those that do not. And, as has already been demonstrated, these men were comfortable going against the wishes of the Church regarding other issues. This petition, ambiguous though it may be, provides insights into the values of the memorial's creators, while drawing attention to various beliefs within Stó:lō society at this time, as it is unlikely that the large numbers of Stó:lō continuing to practise winter dancing saw themselves as "pagan." Those who built the memorial shared family connections, and likely shared a definition of what it meant to be Stó:lō that differed from that of some of the very people they identified as Stó:lō.[46]

A 1922 petition asking that the Indian Act be amended to allow potlatching in a particular form further complicates the memorialists' views towards potlatching and winter dancing. Isaac James,[47] who likely signed the earlier petition against the potlatch, as well as Chief Harry Stewart, who spoke at the dedication of the I:yem memorial, had their names added to this petition, which was drawn up by a lawyer on behalf of the Indians of BC. Surprisingly, these two petitions are more complementary than contradictory, as the very particular definition of the potlatch in the later petition is quite different from the "pagan superstitions" critiqued in the former. Emphasizing that the "potlatch was not a religious institution, nor a heathenish rite, but was the machinery through which the organisation of the Indians was perfected,"[48] the signatories were not protesting the banning of dances. These petitions regarding the potlatch help to situate the beliefs of the creators of the memorial who viewed a specific form of the potlatch necessary, but were opposed to "heathenish rites." The attitudes towards winter dancing and "pagan practices" in these petitions suggest that a Christian cross would not be seen as an inappropriate symbol for people advocating conversion and "civilization." Furthermore, it is necessary to consider what exactly Stó:lō spiritual beliefs at this time could have included from the perspective of leaders who petitioned against so-called pagan practices.[49]

Fishing rights were central to the earlier petitions that Peters was involved with, and rearticulated in the 1938 memorial. In fact, his contemporaries advocated the legalization of the potlatch largely because of its role in regulating rights to canyon fishing spots. While one could read these petitions as preserving economic and political rights at the expense of religious ones, it is necessary to consider the meaning of the fishery, and recognize that this went far beyond economics. In the 1922 petition, Peters gave testimony on behalf of his cousin Chief Pierre of Hope, Edmund Lorenzetto of Ohamil, and others who were demanding that the three-year closure of the fishery be lifted. This petition, which could be seen as an earlier, more detailed version of the message displayed on the I:yem memorial, indicates the meaning of the fishery. More to the point, as Dennis S. Peters explained, "we will never consider any amount of compensation nor substitution for the fish, we want the fish themselves."[50] Salmon were "more than food," and this was not simply an economic or political issue as most Stó:lō had found new economic opportunities downriver at this time. I will expand on this idea as I shift my discussion to the I:yem memorial itself, using it as a lens through which to better view the intersections of politics and belief for Peters, James, and some of their contemporaries.

My ethnohistorical reading of newspaper accounts of the dedication finds that Peters and James used the dedication of the I:yem memorial on Sunday, 14 August 1938, to effectively hold the type of potlatching ceremony outlined in the 1922 petition. They combined Christian symbols with a format similar to a potlatch to publicly mark I:yem as a Stó:lō place. As potlatches and even large meetings of Aboriginal people for political purposes were illegal at this time, the dedication provided a reminder of the relationship between those who lived and were buried in the canyon and their descendants now living further downriver, just as the witnesses of the last potlatches were passing away. Although arguably there was little conflict between the use of a Christian cross and a proclamation of Stó:lō identity to the people at the time, the ceremony itself would have been recognizable to the Stó:lō.

As the title of this chapter suggests, subversive or political elements of this monument and event should not negate the monument's spiritual aspects. The cross itself and prayers at the dedication marked the continued role of I:yem as a spiritually powerful place. Archbishop Duke congratulated the Stó:lō for their "faith in the teaching of Jesus Christ concerning the resurrection of the body."[51] This is the only direct reference to faith and belief in sources relating to the memorial. Notwithstanding the assumptions and potential bias in such a statement, it is still worth considering, as a faith in Jesus Christ is noted with more skepticism in the ethnographic record and in later oral histories. It should also be noted that many of the Stó:lō people in this region who attended the dedication identified themselves as Catholic, and were some of the Church's most faithful. In this way, it is perhaps the seemingly Christian elements of the dedication that would have been the most recognizable to some members of the Stó:lō audience. In 1914, in response to questions by the Royal Commissioner, the chief at Yale reported that the members of his band were Roman Catholic, attending daily prayers even though the priest visited only three times a year.[52] While such a political self-identification was possibly strategic, it would be limiting to completely dismiss the chief's assertion as simply that, especially when his statement about the beliefs of band members are considered with other ethnographic and oral sources.

As I have already suggested, the fishery was much more than an economic industry. The cross and the prayers at the dedication marked the continued role of I:yem as a spiritually powerful place, where the "little Christ" had walked and where ancestors were buried. During the ceremony, the archbishop acknowledged the Stó:lō's "gratitude to God for his providential care in the harvest of Fraser river salmon which through the years has supplied you so bountifully with food."[53] This invocation of God in relation to salmon complements Stó:lō accounts from the time period of their sacred first salmon ceremony (though the first salmon ceremony usually took place in the spring), such as that by Harry Joseph, Chief of the Seabird Island Reserve, speaking of a ceremony that took place just up the river from I:yem.[54] Joseph explained, "the man who had caught the fish stood in the middle of the house, made a speech, and prayed. He tells them that God (Chichelh Siyá:m) made these fish to feed us, and we should thank Him."[55] When fish are seen as sacred gifts from God, or as ancestors, then the memorial is not just a political statement.[56] The meaning of fish and the fishery draws attention to some of the ways that the political and spiritual were intertwined. Although anthropologist Wilson Duff was concerned that this account and the ceremony in general had been influenced by Christianity, they provide insights into Stó:lō beliefs around the time the memorial was created, and into how Archbishop Duke's prayer may have been understood by those gathered at I:yem. These beliefs are further contextualized with other accounts of Coast Salish memorials in the form of crosses and stories of Chichelh Siyá:m (often defined as "the Lord Above," "God," "the Creator," or "the Great First") in the ethnographic record that help to elucidate how people at the time viewed Christianity and what cross, god, and prayers could have meant in 1938.

A more general look at the beliefs of James's and Peters' contemporary, Bob Joe, helps to situate the memorial at I:yem and the beliefs of some Stó:lō people in the early twentieth century. Joe (whose memories of the I:yem memorial provide an important ethnographic source) discussed the Great Almighty and the I:yem memorial with local amateur ethnographer Oliver Wells in 1962, explaining, "Chichelh Siyam [sic] ... that's the Great Almighty ... Before the coming of the white man, they believed in the great man ... Long before the white race come to this country. And as far as that Bible was concerned, there's two or three in there, they worked pretty close to the Bible yeah."[57] This account helps to contextualize Joe's explanation of the memorial at I:yem, suggesting that his failure to mention the cross was not because of an opposition to it. In fact, he likely saw it as simply Stó:lō rather than a foreign symbol, as he explains that the Stó:lō believed in the Great Almighty prior to the arrival of newcomers and missionaries. Broadly speaking, this aspect of Joe's beliefs draws attention to the narrow way that some of the principal ethnographic informants have been depicted in published sources. It is significant that both the main political leaders and ethnographic informants in the early twentieth century had beliefs that are not often discussed – especially since these are the very people who were actively defining what it meant, and means, to be Stó:lō. It is ironic that outsiders excluded aspects of their informants' lives that did not fit with their ideas of unchanging Indigenous identities and that it is these outsider ideals that have continued to be adapted when defining Stó:lō people today. I should clarify here that my intention in noting these aspects of Joe's beliefs are not to negate the value of Joe's testimony or dismiss it as "tainted," but to suggest that he had a more nuanced and complex understanding of what it meant to be Stó:lō than is often recognized, and that scholars have a responsibility to address the aspects of his life that he considered important, even when they challenge our expectations. The fact that Bob Joe is not alone in his beliefs indicates the broader significance of the I:yem memorial in 1938 among the Stó:lō and further suggests how the memorial's creators and their peers may have understood their world.[58]

Stories of God or Jesus acting within S'olh Téméxw continued to be told by the grandchildren of the generation that erected the cross at I:yem, though these stories are often still glossed over by scholars. Like other women of her generation, Stó:lō elder Matilda Gutierrez, identified by her tribal elders as a person who would be charged with the responsibility for future intergenerational transmissions of legendary stories, referred to Jesus Christ as an actor in these stories and a protector of the Stó:lō people.[59] Moreover, other elders of Mrs. Gutierrez's generation typically used the singular "Xa:ls" or spoke of the "little Christ," God's servant, or Jesus travelling down the Fraser Canyon.[60]

These accounts help to situate the possible beliefs of Isaac James, Dennis S. Peters, and their contemporaries, suggesting further how the form of the I:yem memorial was meaningful at the time. Stó:lō people in 1938 would not have had to justify the beliefs or symbols they likely took for granted. They did not explain how the cross, which later generations might associate with colonial institutions did, in fact, fit with their definitions of Stó:lō identity. Yet the fact that such unsolicited stories were frequently told by the Stó:lō themselves hints at their importance. There is also a considerable amount of agency and power in these accounts of Chichelh Siyá:m and appearances of Jesus in S'olh Téméxw. Beyond claims to land and fish are claims to direct access to the Divine, who appeared to Stó:lō prophets and has walked along their river.

It is worth noting a failed attempt to build a similar memorial, or "big cross," in Stó:lō territory downriver from I:yem at the Tzeachten reserve in the Fraser

Valley. Chief William Hall,[61] who was a government-appointed chief rather than a hereditary chief, wrote in his journal of an effort in 1930 to get a "Big Cross" to mark the dead that had been moved to a new cemetery from the graveyard at the neighbouring reserve of Yakweakwioose.[62] Heated debate took place, not over the use of a cross but over which ancestors and denominations would be recognized. After several meetings, Chief Hall declared the effort "a failure," as only one person had donated money. He also noted that Bob Joe was involved in this effort and was angry and hurt when it failed.[63] This example is relevant to my case study of I:yem for two reasons. First, it draws attention to the broader trend of marking disturbed cemeteries with monuments. Disruption of Indigenous cemeteries by factors associated with colonialism occurred throughout BC, with some earlier instances outside of the Fraser Canyon of memorial crosses being constructed to mark relocated cemeteries.[64] Perhaps, then, the selection of the cross at I:yem was essentially a non-issue, as it was the accepted marker in Indigenous cemeteries at the time, as other burial grounds used before and after contact were marked with crosses. To this end, erecting a cross in a graveyard may not have been seen as problematic, or even noteworthy. Second, the example of a failed memorial draws attention to the challenges inherent in creating a monument like that at I:yem, suggesting that the I:yem memorial's very existence, which would have also required fundraising and thus some broader community support, demonstrates that its format and message were palatable to others at the time.

Such an articulation of Indigenous identity and territory was more broadly practised in the Coast Salish world. The Spintlum memorial, located eighty-seven kilometres upriver from I:yem in the town of Lytton, was erected on 16 April 1927 to preserve the memory of Chief David Spintlum (1812–1887) of the Nlaka'pamux and to make a claim to the territory. The extent to which these events are related is unclear; nonetheless, they suggest that the I:yem memorial was erected during a period when Indigenous people along the Fraser River were exploring innovative ways to define and assert themselves using what outsiders might see as Christian symbols to make claims outside of courtrooms or more traditional arenas in a period that is usually considered to be politically passive.

Since 1938, the meaning of the I:yem memorial and its form has changed. Seventy years after its creation, in October 2008, some members of the Yale First Nation used a backhoe to push the I:yem memorial into the Fraser Canyon, making their own claim to the territory, in which their ancestors also fished and were buried, and which is legally defined as Yale Indian Reserve 22.[65] Overlapping land claims and disputes over who should have control over the five-mile canyon fishery demonstrate the shifting meaning of the I:yem memorial, suggesting that a cross no longer had the power to protect the location as a sacred space. This is not to imply that other people were not upset by the destruction at I:yem. The leaders of those who are politically aligned with the Stó:lō Nation and Tribal Council, and who consider themselves Stó:lō, called the removal of a cemetery monument a "desecration" of their ancestors. In contrast, Robert Hope, the chief of the Yale First Nation, called the removal of the monument an effort to protect his ancestors from Stó:lō trespassers.[66] In the process, the memorial cross (which had been missing its plaque for years) was broken in the fall to the bottom of the rocky canyon, providing a powerful image of the shifting relationships between religious expressions and contemporary political claims and disputes over the still important canyon fishery.

While events such as the dedication of the I:yem memorial contain seemingly obvious elements of exchange, I question if that is the best lens of interpretation, especially when we attempt to engage with the views of the memorial's creators and some of their contemporaries in 1938. What an outsider (such as I) may view initially as foreign ideas, forms, and practices may be understood quite differently by insiders. Any "outsider" analysis, like those of earlier salvage ethnographers, is to some extent an attempt to identify the foreign influences while risking dismissing Stó:lō stories of their own encounters with God. I do not want to downplay the significance of change over time, or how individuals in 1938 were shaped by the near century of intensive colonization and missionization that had already taken place. At the same time, I do not wish to dismiss other motives that the creators of the memorial may have had, such as subversively using a Christian ceremony to bring together a large group of Stó:lō people to reassert and claim their rights to the canyon, in a time when potlatches and court claims were illegal. The memorial and its apparent elements of exchange fit with what it meant to be Stó:lō in 1938, though this identity may have had different meanings at other times, and for people belonging to different segments of Stó:lō society. Differences should not negate the legitimacy of how some in 1938 articulated their identities as Stó:lō, or the need for scholars to engage with these perspectives in order to fully understand the complex multidimensional communities being studied – communities that included people of differing status, gender, education, families, and religious belief.

This exploration of how some Stó:lō people understood the I:yem memorial at the time of its creation draws attention to the tangle of politics and beliefs at the time, offering a glimpse of what it could have meant to be Stó:lō in 1938. While to an outsider the I:yem memorial may appear to be the product of religious exchange, this political statement was created by people who thanked God for their salmon and whose ancestors were buried where (they understood)

Jesus once walked. The more general challenge of this chapter, and indeed what I hope to be its larger contribution, is the call to consider both spiritual and political motives seriously, creating a space to recognize a variety of motives for the various Indigenous participants in the creation of the memorial. I have revealed the political nature of this event, held at a time when Indigenous Catholics are generally understood to have been passively quiescent. Accessing the beliefs of the memorial's creators has proved more challenging, but it is reasonable to conclude that for some Stó:lō, at the time the memorial was created, the cross was understood as one of the symbols of their identity. Regardless of where these beliefs came from, it is necessary to recognize them as legitimate if we are to understand men like Isaac James, Dennis S. Peters, and their contemporaries, and what it may have meant for the Stó:lō to walk in both "spiritual and political realms" in 1938.

## Notes

1 "Stallo Tribe Erects Cross to Ancestors," *Chilliwack Progress,* 17 August 1938. Copy of article courtesy of Mabel Nichols. The terms "Eayem" and "Stalo" are inscribed on the memorial; throughout the rest of the chapter these terms appear in the form standardized in Keith Thor Carlson, ed., *A Stó:lō-Coast Salish Historical Atlas* (Vancouver: Douglas and McIntyre, 2002), unless quoting directly from an earlier source.

2 The term "Stó:lō," meaning either "river" or "people of the river," sits better with some contemporary Aboriginal political and cultural leaders than others. Most scholars agree that "Stó:lō" refers to a group of Aboriginal people of the Lower Fraser watershed in southwestern British Columbia, living in more than two dozen bands, or First Nations. They share a similar culture, the Halq'emélem language, and social affiliation.

3 Albert (Sonny) McHalsie, David M. Schaepe, and Keith Thor Carlson, "Making the World Right through Transformations," in Carlson, *A Stó:lō-Coast Salish Historical Atlas,* 6.

4 For example, as Agnes Kelly explained, "God didn't like this (the world at this time) so he sent Xa:ls (the "little Christ") down to make things right." Agnes Kelly, interview with Gordon Mohs, July 1986, copies at Stó:lō Nation Archives (SNA).

5 Wilson Duff, *The Upper Stalo Indians of the Fraser Valley British Columbia,* Anthropology in British Columbia Memoir No. 1 (Victoria: British Columbia Provincial Museum, 1952), 30; Albert (Sonny) McHalsie, "Halq'emélem Place Names in Stó:lō Territory," in Carlson, *A Stó:lō-Coast Salish Historical Atlas,* 142.

6 Wilson Duff, *The Upper Stalo.*

7 The Oblates arrived in Stó:lō territory in the 1840s, establishing a permanent mission along the Fraser River, St. Mary's, in 1859.

8 Potlatch can include a variety of different gatherings centred on the exchange of wealth. It is typically a public ceremony where names and associated rights to resources are passed on. Historian Keith Thor Carlson has emphasized the disastrous effects that the federal government's 1885 Indian Act amendment banning the potlatch had on the Fraser River fishery, arguing that "without large-scale potlatch naming ceremonies families could not as effectively communicate (and thereby re-assert) their claims to hereditary property." Keith Thor Carlson, "Innovation, Tradition, Colonialism and Aboriginal Fishing Conflicts

in the Lower Fraser Canyon," in *New Histories for Old: Changing Perspectives on Canada's Native Pasts*, ed. Ted Binnema and Susan Neylan (Vancouver: UBC Press, 2007), 159. See also Douglas C. Harris, *Fish Law and Colonialism: The Legal Capture of Salmon in British Columbia* (Toronto: University of Toronto Press, 2001), 5.

9   Paul Tennant, *Aboriginal Peoples and Politics: The Indian Land Question in British Columbia, 1849-1989* (Vancouver: UBC Press, 1990), 101–12.

10   Dennis Peters was married to Suzanne Charlie, and Isaac James was married to Cecilia Charlie.

11   The author's earlier research focused on the political significance of the memorial, issues of Stó:lō collective identity, and ideas of place making. This research is expanded here to take into consideration both political and spiritual motivations. See Amanda Fehr, "The Relationships of Place: A Study of Change and Continuity in Stó:lō Understandings of I:yem" (master's thesis, University of Saskatchewan, 2008). See also Amanda Fehr, "Relationships: A Study of Memory, Change, and Identity at a Place Called I:yem," *University of the Fraser Valley Research Review,* online journal (April 2009).

12   Tennant, *Aboriginal Peoples and Politics*, 82.

13   Keith Thor Carlson, *The Power of Place, the Problem of Time: Aboriginal Identity and Historical Consciousness in the Cauldron of Colonialism* (Toronto: University of Toronto Press, 2010).

14   Ibid., 194–200.

15   This was also apparent in interviews I conducted for earlier research. See Fehr, "The Relationships of Place."

16   Carlson, *The Power of Place*, 29.

17   By focusing on Indigeneity, I mean using "Indigenous" as the primary category of analysis. As Keith Thor Carlson has noted, "Too often the racial and or/ethnic issues of Aboriginal-newcomer history work to obscure important class and/or status and gender issues within Indigenous society." Carlson, *The Power of Place*, 29. While the analysis does not focus explicitly on class or gender as primary categories of analysis, it echoes Carlson's call to pay attention to differences within Aboriginal society and histories.

18   My interpretation of a decolonizing approach is one that challenges expectations and shares Denise Nadeau's goal to "disrupt ... stereotypical and colonial understandings of Indigenous Peoples" (see Chapter 8 in this collection). While my work is informed by Linda Tuhiwai Smith's *Decolonizing Methodologies,* I am also critical of scholarship (including that of Smith) that dismisses Christian influences as merely the *effects* of colonialism. Linda Tuhiwai Smith, *Decolonizing Methodologies: Research and Indigenous Peoples* (New York: Zed Books, 1999); M. Battiste, "The Decolonization of Aboriginal Education: Dialogue, Reflection and Action in Canada," in *Educational Theories and Practices from the Majority World,* ed. Pierre R. Dasen and Abdeljalil Akkari (New Delhi, India: Sage, 2008), 168–95; Paul Nadasdy, *Hunters and Bureaucrats: Power, Knowledge, and Aboriginal-State Relations in the Southwest Yukon* (Vancouver: UBC Press, 2003); Donald Fixico, *The American Indian Mind in a Linear World: American Indian Studies and Traditional Knowledge* (London: Routledge, 2003).

19   As an outsider, I was introduced to Stó:lō history and communities at the 2007 University of Saskatchewan/University of Victoria Ethnohistory Field School, where I interviewed community members about the I:yem memorial. In an effort to follow up on a story about Jesus that respected elder Tillie Gutierrez shared with me, I conducted some interviews with other community members on Christianity/spirituality under the auspices of the 2009 field school.

20   See, for example, Elbourne and Pearson's chapters in this volume.

21 See Keith Thor Carlson, "Prophesy," in Carlson, *A Stó:lō-Coast Salish Historical Atlas*, 154–61.
22 "Encounter" and "exchange" are not the only problematic terms in this collection or my own work. "Religion," "spirituality," and "Christian" are also loaded terms that need to be used with caution. In this chapter I attempt, where possible, to use the words that historical actors used. I use the term "spirituality" to be as inclusive as possible.
23 That is, while these individuals provide us with a significant source base (in their own petitions and writings as well as in the ethnographic record), these sources tend to highlight one aspect of these individuals' identities.
24 Mrs. Vincent Peters, Marian Smith Field Notes, Unpublished (summer 1945), RAI, MS 268: 4 (13), Microfilm copy, BC Archives.
25 Duff, *The Upper Stalo*, 80.
26 Carlson, "Reflections on Indigenous History and Memory: Reconstructing and Reconsidering Contact," in John Lutz, ed., *Myth and Memory: Stories of Indigenous-European Contact* (Vancouver: UBC Press, 2007), 48–49. See also Wayne Suttles, "Private Knowledge, Morality, and Social Class among the Coast Salish," *American Anthropologist* 60, 3 (June 1958): 501.
27 This was a result of marriages between high- and low-status individuals, legal prohibitions against the public passing on of names and property (leading to disputing claims), and new forms of authority (such as literacy or being a state- or church-appointed chief). See Carlson, *The Power of Place*, 135. See also Suttles, "Private Knowledge."
28 The name Siya:mia is derived from the word siyá:m (which can be translated as a "wealthy and respected leader"). It can also refer to someone who is rich, or even to God. See Peter Dennis Peters, interview with Sonny McHalsie, Randel Paul, and Richard Daly, 21 September 1988, SNA Oral History Collection, PPD-i-1, 36.
29 Peters, Interview with Sonny McHalsie et al., 1988, SNA, 23.
30 Gutierrez, Interview with Amanda Fehr, May 2007, SNA. Gutierrez also noted that Ed Lorenzetto, Harry Joseph, and Patrick Charlie came to ask her grandfather for information when being interviewed by Wilson Duff. She said he wouldn't tell them very much, except for Ed, her cousin.
31 Obituary of Dennis S. Peters, courtesy of Alice Marwood, Stó:lō Nation genealogist.
32 Reuben M. Ware, *Five Issues Five Battlegrounds: An Introduction to Indian Fishing in B.C. 1850–1930* (Chilliwack, BC: Coqualeetza Education Training Centre for Stó:lōNation, 1983), 31.
33 Pierre Ayessick (1854–1934) was baptized in 1864. His daughter, Adeline Lorenzetto, was married to Wilson Duff's principal Stó:lō informant, Ed Lorenzetto. There are significant overlaps between those seeking to define modern political identities through petitions and memorials and those speaking to anthropologists such as Smith, Duff, and Wells about "traditional" Stó:lō culture and beliefs.
34 Carlson, *The Power of Place*, 235; Duff, *The Upper Stalo*.
35 McHalsie, interview with Amanda Fehr, 24 June 2007, SNA.
36 According to Wilson Duff, Patrick Charlie had a "strange reputation among the Indians – who were not sure whether to regard him as a man who retains memories from a past life or as a little funny in the head ... The old people had been impressed but PC's generation expresses some scepticism." Duff, *The Upper Stalo*, 9. However, Patrick Charlie was also Catholic, the son of Captain Charlie, and made his "living working for the railroads" (ibid.).
37 Patrick Charlie, Wilson Duff, Unpublished Field Notes, Notebook #1, 1950.
38 This relates to Cecilia Morgan's discussion of entanglement in this collection.

39  The challenge of discerning belief from the use of religious symbols is also addressed in Elbourne's discussion of Joseph Brant.

40  Testimony of Dennis S. Peters on behalf of Chief Pierre, Edward Lorenzetto, and others, as quoted in Carlson, *A Stó:lō-Coast Salish Historical Atlas*, 187.

41  Oscar Peters was the chief of the Hope Band and served as a vice president of the Native Brotherhood. See Peter Dennis Peters, interview with Larry Commodore, 21 July 1985, Stó:lō Tribal Council Oral History, copies available at SNA, 85-SR4; Tennant, *Aboriginal Peoples and Politics*, 127. The organization received support from several Aboriginal people of the area, many of whom have already been referred to above. "Endorsements and Contentions of the Harrison, Yale and Chilliwack Valley Districts of the Native brotherhood," Letter to Mr. G. Williams, Native Brotherhood of BC, Chief John Ohamil, Chief Michael Peters, Chief Harry J. Peters, Acting Chief Willie George, and Chief Peter Pete. LAC, C-11-2 vol. 11299.

42  Tennant, *Aboriginal Peoples and Politics*, 119.

43  I am not certain that the "Dennis Peters" and "Isaac James" here are the same as those involved in the establishment of the I:yem memorial. Peters was born in 1871 and James in 1875 (or 1884), so it is definitely possible that these are the same individuals. Even if they are not, their association with Pierre Ayessick and Captain Charlie make this petition relevant to my discussion here. 1915 Petition Supporting the Banning of the Potlatch, RG 10 vol. 3629, file 6244-3, LAC, as quoted in Carlson, ed., *A Stó:lō-Coast Salish Historical Atlas*, 183.

44  Captain Charlie (1841–1923) was baptized in 1866. His son, Patrick Charlie, was Wilson Duff's primary informant from Yale. His name on this petition seems contradictory, as he himself was involved in a large potlatch around 1890 where he passed his name and associated fishing rights to a site across the river from I:yem to his son Patrick Charlie. Carlson, "Innovation, Tradition, Colonialism and Aboriginal Fishing Conflicts in the Lower Fraser Canyon," 149.

45  1915 Petition Supporting the Banning of the Potlatch, RG 10 vol. 3629, file 6244-3.

46  Here my findings are similar to those of Leslie Robertson and the Kwagu'ł Gixsam Clan in *Standing Up with Ga'axsta'las: Jane Constance Cook and the Politics of Memory, Church and Custom* (Vancouver: UBC Press, 2012).

47  The petition is signed by Isaac James, Chief of Skoalo; Isaac James was the chief of Ruby Creek or Skwhalook.

48  "1922 (February) Petition to the Superintendent General of Indian Affairs from Various BC Indian Tribes Protesting the Banning of the Potlatch," RG 10 vol. 3630 file 6244-4 LAC, as quoted in Carlson, ed., *A Stó:lō-Coast Salish Historical Atlas*, 187.

49  Leslie Robertson's recent work with the Kwagu'ł Gixsam Clan is an excellent example of scholarship that reconsiders an Aboriginal leader who supported the banning of the potlatch. Like Robertson, I am suggesting the need to complicate the historical narrative by re-examining the various motivations of these historical actors on their own terms.

50  Testimony of Dennis S. Peters on behalf of Chief Pierre, Edward Lorenzetto, and others, as quoted in Carlson, *A Stó:lō-Coast Salish Historical Atlas*, 187.

51  "Indian Memorial Is Blessed by Archbishop," *BC Catholic*, 20 August 1938. Clipping courtesy of Anthea Seles, records manager/archivist/privacy coordinator at the Archdiocese of Vancouver.

52  Royal Commission on Indian Affairs for the Province of British Columbia, Meeting with the Yale band or Tribe of Indians, at Yale, BC, on Thursday, 19 November 1914.

53  "Indian Memorial Is Blessed by Archbishop," *B.C. Catholic*, 20 August 1938. Clipping courtesy of Anthea Seles.

54  Harry Joseph was 75 when he was interviewed by Wilson Duff in 1949.

55  Wilson Duff conducted fieldwork with the upper Stó:lō (Chilliwack to Yale) during the summers of 1949 and 1950. See Duff, *The Upper Stalo*, 7.

56  For a discussion of Stó:lō food and its potential spiritual significance, see Lesley Wiebe, "Food Talk," *University of the Fraser Valley Online Research Review*, http://journals.ufv. ca/rr/RR22/article-PDFs/8-wiebe.pdf.

57  "Bob Joe at Tzeachten February 8, 1962," in *Oliver Wells Interview Collection (1961–1968)*, transcript, SNA, 101.

58  See also anthropologist Diamond Jenness's work with Old Pierre in Jenness, *The Faith of a Coast Salish Indian* (Victoria: BC Provincial Museum, 1955). This work is based on fieldwork that Jenness conducted in 1936. Jenness burned his original field notes.

59  When I interviewed Mrs. Gutierrez in 2007 about the I:yem memorial, she shared some stories about Jesus that I was at first unable to appreciate in the context of my research. I later found that Jesus or the "little Christ" often came up in interviews that Mrs. Gutierrez granted, even when she testified for the famous Vanderpeet case.

60  Keith Thor Carlson, ed., *You Are Asked to Witness: The Stó:lō in Canada's Pacific Coast History* (Chilliwack: Stó:lō Heritage Trust, 1997), 39.

61  Chief Hall was sixty-eight years old in 1930.

62  Chief William Hall, personal journal, 1930, SNA.

63  Ibid.

64  Royal Commission on Indian Affairs for the Province of British Columbia, Meeting with the Mission Band of Indians on their Reserve, North Vancouver, 17 June 1913.

65  The Stó:lō political organizations claimed that Yale was a Stó:lō band, and those at Yale claimed they were a distinct First Nation.

66  See, for example, Paul J. Henderson, "Native Battle in Yale," *Chilliwack Times*, 4 November 2008, http://www.mail-archive.com/natnews-north@yahoogroups.com/msg06755.html.

# Part 2
# Individuals in Encounter

# 4

## "The Joy My Heart Has Experienced": Eliza Field Jones and the Transatlantic Missionary World, 1830s–40s

*Cecilia Morgan*

THE FIRST DAY OF JUNE, 1838, was Eliza Field Jones's thirty-fourth birthday. Spent at her family home in Lambeth, the day was a pleasant one: she took tea with Mrs. G., paid visits to friends, heard recitations performed by school children at Camberwell, and sat for her portrait. At the day's end, Eliza sat down to confide her thoughts to her diary. "Oh!" she wrote, "how much goodness and mercy have followed me since on the wide ocean seven years ago this day. I was passing thro' much affliction hitherto the Lord hath helped me, and by his grace I hope to spend the remnant of my days more than once to his praise and glory."[1] Two weeks later she paid more visits and walked home, very tired, and "much shocked with the wickedness we witnessed in the streets."[2] However, on the following day, a letter from her niece, Catherine Sunego, seems to have lifted her spirits, as it bore news "good and bad, God bless the Credit Indians, and Catherine, and make her a good girl."[3] While seemingly disconnected, these quotes represent the variegated strands of Eliza Field Jones's life at this particular moment: her happiness, both domestic and spiritual, since her marriage and emigration to the settler colony of Upper Canada; her evangelically inspired concern with public morality in her birthplace; and her links to those "Credit Indians" who had become her relatives through her marriage, particularly Catherine (of whom more later).

Eliza Field Jones (Carey) is known to historians of Upper Canada and to those who study nineteenth-century Indigenous history and the history of religion because of her marriage to Kahkewaquonaby/Peter Jones, the mixed-race Mississauga missionary. After meeting Jones and becoming engaged to him during his first tour to Britain in 1831, in 1833 Eliza travelled to New York City to marry him. She spent the rest of their time together working alongside her husband at the Credit Mission in Upper Canada and accompanying him on a number of his fundraising tours of Britain. Donald Smith's extensive research on Jones's life provides us with a clear outline of Eliza's marriage, which lasted until Jones's death in 1856 and produced four sons; their third son, Peter Edmund, was notable for carrying out his father's legacy of, in his biographer's words, "bridging two peoples."[4] Smith's biography of Jones has explored the close and loving relationship of the couple, Eliza's role in supporting Jones's missionary efforts, and her efforts in ensuring that Jones's memory was not forgotten within mid-nineteenth-century settler society.[5]

It is, of course, impossible to "uncouple" Eliza from her husband, his multiple communities and points of identification: her narrative is interwoven with his in both the formal and intimate domains of their lives. However, shifting our focus to concentrate more thoroughly on her suggests ways to add layers to our understanding of Indigenous-European religious encounters in Upper Canada's settler society and to global missionary and humanitarian projects. Eliza Field Jones's meeting with the Christian Welsh-Ojibwa man who would become her husband occurred because of her membership in a well-off, evangelical Protestant British family and took place at a time when women such as she were increasingly becoming drawn into the orbit of Christian missionary societies and movements. Thus, Eliza's "religious encounter" was one that took place within the walls of her family's middle-class home while also being part of a larger global phenomenon, that of the spread of nineteenth-century Christian missions. Moreover, as we shall see, her narrative shares many features of those of other British women involved in missions. On both counts, then, Eliza Field Jones helps us to tie Upper Canada and the Ojibwa encounter with Christianity to other such meetings and contexts.

While not unique in its general themes, Jones's life provides us with a more nuanced and layered history of such meetings, suggesting the intricacies of such convergences at the individual, "micro" level. Such intricacies have been explored recently by women's studies scholar Jennifer Lund, whose analysis of Eliza's diaries of her life with Jones at the Credit River and Munceytown missions, their life in Brantford, her widowhood, and subsequent (quite unhappy) marriage to John Carey suggest a woman whose life was profoundly altered by marriage and mission work.[6] As well, Eliza's *Memoir of Elizabeth Jones, a Little Indian Girl*, a narrative of her young niece's death at the Credit Mission; her correspondence with her husband during their time in Britain; and her letters from Nahnebahwequa/Catherine Sunego Sutton suggest complex constructions and performances of white womanhood.

To be sure, Eliza's spiritual and secular upbringing had educated her in the superiority of both Christian morality and British social and cultural practices, as she would have been exposed to lessons about white, middle-class British women's greater moral authority over working-class and Indigenous women. The former were charged with the responsibility of uplifting and teaching the latter the ways of Christian, "civilized" marriage and maternity, a responsibility to be performed with kindness, sympathy, and benevolence. However, as much as Eliza Field Jones believed she had much to offer her husband's Indigenous community, she also felt a need to learn from the Mississauga. To some extent these competing impulses can be seen in her published work, with its greater attention to individual histories and personal experiences than the genre of published missionary writings often displayed. Yet it is in her personal correspondence, with its glimpses of both her own subjectivity and her daily relationship with her husband, that Eliza Field Jones suggests that being the "white wife" of an Indigenous missionary involved more than providing moral and material guidance to her husband's community. It also meant supporting his community's political challenges to colonial authority, being told of white missionaries' deficiencies in their service to Indigenous communities, becoming aware of Mississauga women's cultural knowledge, and, above all, dealing with the daily rounds of married life, a life of details both delightful and mundane. Exploring Eliza Field Jones's life suggests that Indigenous–European religious encounters were not always predictable and did not automatically follow the prescriptive scripts of European dominance and Indigenous acquiescence often expected by missionaries and their secular contemporaries. Furthermore, as Jean-François Bélisle and Nicole St-Onge's exploration of Louis Riel's transnational context demonstrates, placing an individual's encounter with Christianity within its larger, global framework alerts us to the tension-laden but often creative strategies that men and women, Indigenous and non-Indigenous, brought to the "mixed blessings" of religious encounter.

## Upper Canadian Encounters

Eliza Field was born in Lambeth in 1804, the eldest child of wealthy factory owner Charles Field and Elizabeth Carter. Charles's religious beliefs, passed down to his daughter, emanated from the borough's evangelical Surrey Chapel, which had the largest evangelical congregation in London. As Smith points out, Eliza's childhood and young adulthood combined both middle-class security and privilege with a desire to serve God and help the poor. She attended a boarding school in nearby Peckham, where she studied landscape painting with a French drawing master and spent her holidays horseback riding and vacationing at the fashionable seaside resort of Brighton; she also helped at home with her younger siblings, taught Sunday school, and paid visits to the sick and poor members of her church.[7] In many ways, then, Eliza's upbringing and experiences resembled those of other young, middle-class women whose families had been swept up in the evangelical revival of the late eighteenth and early nineteenth centuries, one that was a key component of middle-class identity and drew upon the faith and labour of women and children.[8] By the 1820s, concern for both the poor "at home" and for those living without the benefit of Christianity overseas was a fundamental tenet of evangelicalism and, a number of historians argue, middle-class understandings of Britishness and empire.[9] Eliza also was exposed to the multiple facets of imperial expansion's manifestations in Britain, as she heard Rammohun Roy speak, listened to accounts of how the *Bounty* mutineers on Pitcairn Island went "from a sad race [to] a moral one," and attended an antislavery meeting ("I pray this wicked system may soon be totally abolished").[10]

Eliza Field met Peter Jones on 24 June 1831 at the Bristol home of their mutual friends James and Martha Woods, where Jones was recovering from a serious illness. Judging by her invitation that he visit her parents, Eliza was struck by the Mississauga Methodist missionary. Their friendship developed over the following months and culminated with his proposal to her in February 1832, an offer which Eliza, by then deeply committed to him, accepted with alacrity. However, as Smith points out, Charles Field was less enthusiastic about the match and changed his decision about it a number of times. Although Jones was a welcome guest in the Field household, Charles objected to him as a prospective son-in-law on a number of grounds: his financial insecurity, his Methodism (although evangelical, the Fields were still attached to the Anglican Church), and his familial background (his father had married two Indigenous women simultaneously).[11] Moreover, although it is not clear that Charles Field objected to Jones's Indigenous ancestry, others within the Field family and circle of friends certainly did.[12]

Charles Field's concerns also were exacerbated at the prospect of his daughter's transatlantic migration, one from which she might never return. To be sure, as Alison Twells argues, by the 1830s the missionary wife had become an accepted figure in religious discourse and practice.[13] Before her marriage, Eliza witnessed this first-hand when she met a "Miss White" who was going to marry "Mr. Mundy" and travel with him to Calcutta;[14] she also spent time reading a number of missionary wives' memoirs as a way of educating herself about her future duties.[15] However, not all missionary wives married Indigenous missionaries. As I have argued elsewhere, Eliza's brother-in-law's objections to the union hurt and infuriated Eliza; she also experienced great trepidation about her ability to meet the material and cultural challenges of life in an Upper Canadian mission village.[16] The Jones wedding, which took place in New York City, was greeted with hostility by at least one reporter, who described the couple as enacting Shakespeare's *Othello;* the article was subsequently picked up by a number of Upper Canadian newspapers.[17] And this was not the last of such attacks on the couple. While in Exeter in 1838, Eliza confided in her diary that she "felt very much depressed owing to some information from Mrs. Poole respecting some impressions that had been made about me from an evil minded person in Canada."[18] As Smith points out, Eliza and Peter were unable to escape the gaze of the prurient and the racist, a situation that she found excruciating and that he – while angered – attempted at times to defuse with humour.[19] Yet eventually Eliza's family accepted the couple's marriage, providing a home for them during Peter's British tours and funds for their house, Echo Villa, which they built in Brantford in 1851.[20]

Eliza's initial impressions of the Mississauga have been discussed by a number of historians: they ranged from discomfort with practices that offended her sense of propriety and space (men spitting or entering her cabin without knocking), concern over Indigenous children's supposed lack of cleanliness, and admiration for the children's progress in the village school.[21] Yet she also felt her lack of Ojibwa language most acutely, particularly when she attempted to communicate with Mississauga women. While Peter often addressed her with Ojibwa terms of endearment, taught her a number of words, and wrote parts of his letters to her in the language (suggesting, for example, that she ask Catherine Sunego to translate the letters for her), she does not seem to have ever become fluent in the language. (It is not clear why this is so: it may be that her Mississauga relatives forbore from teaching her as a means of retaining a degree of privacy and control.)[22] Her longing to speak the language may have stemmed from a number of motives: the desire to communicate at a more intimate level with her husband, whose fluency in English did not mean that he turned away from a language that was, quite literally, his mother tongue; an eagerness, perhaps, to understand her new in-laws more fully and also ensure that her children would be fluent; and a belief, common in missionary circles, that her work with the Mississauga, particularly women and children, could only be truly successful if she could speak to them in their own language. Eliza also assisted her husband in his translation of the Bible into Ojibwa, a practice that, by the 1830s, had become an "established missionary tradition," seen as a vital way of developing true Christianity.[23]

The figure of the Indigenous convert whose life provided object lessons for audiences "at home" and in the mission field also made frequent appearances in missionary literature, whether in children's books, obituaries, or reports and speeches aimed at fund raising.[24] Eliza's 1838 *Memoir of Elizabeth Jones: a Little Indian Girl, Who Lived at the River-Credit Mission, Upper Canada* was part of this didactic body of writing. Published in London by John Mason, the *Memoir* was part of a list that included the Reverend Robert Newstead's *Missionary Stories for Children and Young Persons, Notices Concerning Idolatry and Devil-Worship in Ceylon,* and *Anecdotes of the Superstitions of Bengal.* In many ways Eliza Field's account of her niece's life and tragic death shared the images and tropes of religious materials aimed at children. For one, Elizabeth Jones's un-timely and unexpected drowning was a lesson in the virtues of being prepared, at every turn of a young life, to meet one's saviour. "Perhaps some young persons may wonder," Eliza wrote, "what disease carried her away in the spring-time of life to an early grave."

> Well do I remember telling her one evening of the sudden death of a neighbour, and, endeavouring to improve the circumstance, remarked how necessary it was for young and old to be prepared for death, as we did not know if we should live to see another rising sun. She looked most earnestly at me and said, "Why, aunt, I am not ill!" But, dear children, without the withering blast of sickness, this sweet flower was transplanted in an instant to a more congenial clime, in the bloom of health, and with a buoyancy of spirits that had excited the remarks of those around her; illustrating in her own history that death has not always sickness for its harbinger.[25]

During her all-too-brief life, the "sweet flower" was a paragon of Christian child-hood: pious, generous, kind to servants, tidy, honest, and full of God's grace.[26] Despite the bone-chilling cold of an Upper Canadian winter, she insisted on saying her prayers outside of the warmth of her bed; she was a devoted church-goer; wanted nothing more than that other children be good; and displayed great distress when she succumbed to temptation and misbehaved.[27] In short, the "little Indian girl" was a paragon and, it seems, an archetype.

But was that all? Not quite. Eliza's account of Elizabeth Jones's life differs from some of the more formulaic treatment of "native" converts in Upper Canadian writings. This is not an anonymous figure or archetype who abjures her own community and family for the missionaries and fellow-converts, a common strategy in missionary accounts of "success" stories.[28] Elizabeth Jones, the reader is told at the start, had a lineage and an ancestry. She was a member of the well-known Jones family: "her father, Mr. John Jones, whose Indian name is Tyentenegen, is an Indian of the Oojebway nation, and brother to the Rev. Peter Jones, otherwise Kahkewaquonaby, known as a Missionary to many in this country as well as amongst his own people." Moreover, Elizabeth's mater-nal family would be known to a number of British readers. "The mother of Elizabeth, whose maiden name was Christiana Brant, was a granddaughter of the late famous Capt. Joseph Brant, a noted Chief and warrior of the Mohawk nation of Indians, who many years ago visited England, and niece of Mr. John Brant, also a Chief, who came over to this country about the year 1819 or 1820."[29]

Missionaries, then, were not the only ones with transatlantic connections. As well as her descent from Brant, Mrs. John Jones "was a woman of strong mind, fine understanding, and good judgment. She united to a most amiable disposition unassuming yet dignified manners; all who knew her loved and respected her." The home she and John had created in Upper Canada was "the abode of peace and comfort; the Ministers and others who visited the Mission, were not only delighted with the hospitality and kindness manifested, but most of all with that beautiful influence of real religion which shed so sweet a luster, and sanctified every other blessing, diffusing joy and happiness to all around."[30] Not only did Elizabeth have true Christian womanhood as a maternal example; she also had her grandmother, Mrs. Lucy Brant, "who also displayed in her life and conversation those active Christian graces which emphatically made her a mother in this little Israel ... Elizabeth was made an early partaker of divine grace."[31]

To be sure, Eliza was certainly not immune to the missionary impulse to equate Christianity with civilization. Christiana Jones was an example to those "Indian neighbours" who had not had her advantages; they looked up to her "for advice and instruction ... whatever she did or said was sure, if possible, to be imitated and remembered by the women in the village." Having just emerged from "the superstitious and long-rooted habits of their forefathers," the Brant-Jones household was a great influence over the other Mississauga.[32] Nevertheless, she acknowledged quite readily that when Christiana became ill after the birth of a son, "it was truly affecting to witness the anxiety and kindness of the Indian women. Some brought her tea made of herbs and roots to quench her burning thirst; others rested in an adjoining room, while one or more watched every word and motion."[33] Although their kindness and care could not save her – and her well-attended funeral was a testament to the power of Christianity to take away the Indians' supposed fear of death – nevertheless the portrait of Christiana's last hours that Eliza offered her readers was one in which Indigenous women comforted and cherished their dying sister, offering her both hymns and Indigenous medicine.[34]

Furthermore, while as the previous quotations suggest the *Memoir* takes for granted the binary between "saved and civilized" and "heathen and uncivilized," we hear little about the latter. Unlike articles published in, for example, *Christian Guardian,* which played on themes such as infanticide, Indian women's drudgery, polygamy, and matricide as features of "heathen" communities, such practices do not appear in the *Memoir.*[35] Certainly Eliza would have been conscious of the need to present the Credit village in the best possible light to encourage continued support from British evangelicals, themselves faced with pressure to save Indigenous people around the globe and, increasingly, the "heathen" on their doorsteps.[36] Yet there is little doubt that the village in which Elizabeth lived could have been anything other than conducive to her exemplary behaviour. Furthermore, in case any readers might have held lingering doubts about the Mississauga's capacity to achieve "civilization," Eliza pays tribute to her niece's intelligence and quickness of mind. In a few weeks the "little Indian girl" went from being able to spell three-letter words to reading stories, spelling three-syllable words, and learning her catechism and hymns.[37] There was a lesson beyond this individual case, Eliza insisted:

> In mentioning this, I do not wish to depreciate the merit of many of the other children, being fully aware that circumstances gave Elizabeth advantages which they did not possess: but her rapid improvement and desire of information will show what the capacities of Indian children are; and I think prove that they only need the same privileges and blessings that English children enjoy, to make them equally clever and useful members of society.[38]

If ever there was an argument for the liberal, humanitarian approach to the missionary cause, this was it.[39]

It is not just the impressive behaviour of the Credit Mississauga that differentiates the *Memoir* from similar texts. The setting in which Elizabeth lived – and in which Eliza Field, her aunt, found herself – was noteworthy for its beauty and peace. The road to the settlement "opens to the eye of the traveller a diversified scene of land and water, hill and dale, the cultivated farm, and the native forest." While the latter appeared to Eliza as "interminable," it offered a "fine back-ground to a country partially cultivated and settled" and "tall dark pines throw around their deep shadows, giving a sense of loneliness and a tone of pensive feeling. Glimpses are caught and lost at intervals of the beautiful lake, when suddenly it opens before you in unobscured loveliness, which may be enjoyed for some distance as you journey along its wooded banks." The village, with its log and frame houses, plots of cultivated land, chapel, schoolhouse, and "a lovely spot ... sacred to the memory of the dead" was in "park-like scenery."[40] Moreover, November, the month that Elizabeth drowned, "which in England is usually quite dreary, is quite otherwise in Canada." It was such a beautiful day that she decided to go for walk across the bridge through which she fell.[41] Although some writers might have depicted the river and forest as forbidding and dangerous, Eliza's account is free of any sense that the landscape was a harbinger of Elizabeth's death. The tragedy occurs because of a rotten board in the bridge, nothing more.[42]

Elizabeth is deeply mourned and missed, not least by the author, who was in England when her niece died. She had offered to take her and help care for her after her mother's death, but her brother-in-law did not wish to be parted from his daughter. Although couched in the language and genre of the missionary enterprise, the *Memoir* also has an intensely personal dimension to it. Eliza makes it clear that she had a relationship with Elizabeth Jones; although she does not identify herself directly as her aunt, it is clear she was her teacher, family friend, and potential guardian. (It is also likely that an evangelical readership would know of the "'English lady' who married 'an Indian,'" in Eliza's husband's words.[43]) The grief of Elizabeth's father, other family members, and friends, a grief that suffuses the text, is assuaged only by the knowledge that the girl's death is part of God's plan and Elizabeth is now reunited with her mother and late siblings. Eliza's intimate personal location within the community of Christian Ojibwa, then, helps to produce a missionary text that is more multilayered and complex than others produced about Upper Canadian religious encounters. Her affiliations helped to shape her tale of Elizabeth's life and death in ways that her religious audience, who in all likelihood expected a simple tale of "heathen conversion," might not have anticipated.

## Family Connections

Although Eliza may have skirted around her familial relationship to Elizabeth Jones, personal and intimate relationships with other members of the Mississauga underpin her private correspondence and diary entries. Her other niece, Catherine Sunego Sutton, spent time as a child with the Jones family; she was taught by Eliza while at the Credit River Mission and accompanied her aunt for part of her trip to Britain in 1837–38. While Catherine's marriage to William Sutton took her away from the Credit, a surviving letter from 1847 sent from the Saugeen community to Eliza suggests that the relationship continued to have spiritual and emotional resonance for her. She reminded her aunt – who was also her "dear sister" – of her great love for her and the intensity of Eliza's influence on Catherine, an influence that was both material and religious. Catherine dearly hoped to see Eliza soon and expressed sorrow for any naughty behaviour she'd exhibited as a child. Yet she also was not afraid to complain to Eliza about a new missionary in her community whose behaviour and speeches towards the Ojibwa had left her downcast and despairing. Her spiritual gloom, however, had been mitigated by the behaviour of one of the "Indian Brothers" in chapel, who had recited and sang (the latter "in Indian") in such a way that healed Catherine's soul and lifted her from despair. As well as matters of spiritual importance, Catherine also included news of her family: the arrival of presents for the children, the children's attendance at school, the baby's learning to talk, and deaths in both Upper Canada and Britain.[44]

Whatever correspondence took place from Eliza to Catherine has not, unfortunately, survived (or at least has not surfaced in archives). However,

Catherine's letter and Eliza's published and unpublished writings raise intriguing questions about the timbre of Eliza's relationship with her Mississauga family during the 1830s and '40s. Clearly Eliza saw these relationships as mediated primarily by their shared religious convictions. Her desire that her Indigenous family – both those related to her directly through Jones and the community at large – experience conversion and salvation of their immortal souls is a theme that runs throughout her diaries. Furthermore, despite their very different geographic, cultural, and material locations and relationships to colonial and imperial power, it was her desire for their spiritual transformation and enlightenment that linked Eliza's different "families," Indigenous and English, to each other through her.

Yet it is difficult to ignore the ways that this desire for spiritual transformation, one shared with other white women involved in the mission field, was in turn mediated by her marriage to Jones, a union that allowed an individual such as Catherine to see her as her "dear aunt" as well as a sister in Christ. Furthermore, while Eliza may have arrived in Upper Canada full of hope (albeit a hope laced with anxiety) at the thought of serving as a "missionary wife" and thus as a role model to Mississauga women and children, once in the colony she was not insensitive to the lessons that could be learned from her Indigenous relatives. Mississauga women's medicine and, in particular, support of each other in childbirth and other aspects of their lives struck her as sensible and seemly, perhaps reminding her of white evangelical women's communities of philanthropy and care she had experienced in London.[45] To be sure, as historians have noted, such changes in missionary attitudes towards Indigenous values and practices might occur because of direct encounters, moments when missionary representations and teachings were contradicted through lived experiences in the mission field.[46] However, unlike some missionaries, Eliza entered into the Mississauga community as both a "mission wife" *and* as the helpmeet of one of its most prominent, if at times controversial, representatives. In her case, the gendered dynamics of being a missionary wife were undeniably complicated by her love for her "dear Peter."

## Metropolitan Encounters

Eliza's entries for her 1838 and 1845 trips to Britain with her husband also bear witness to the depth of her commitment to Peter and the missionary enterprise; they also tell us much about the emotional timbre of the couple's relationship and the depth of the romantic and affective bond between them. Moreover, they also are striking for their quotidian quality, an "ordinariness" that suggests that, despite the weight and meaning of racial categories in the couple's life, it also was possible for Eliza to hold those categories at bay, or if not quite at bay then perhaps in suspension.

The couple was apart for portions of these trips, as Eliza stayed with her family in London while Peter toured cities in other parts of Britain. Excited to receive "a letter from my dear Peter" on 6 April, Eliza was even more pleased six days later when, "to the joy [of] my heart, after breakfast my dear Peter arrived very tired."[47] The next day he was off to Manchester, leaving Eliza to pray for his "safe passage."[48] While disappointed over the following week that no letter arrived from "my beloved husband," her spirits lifted at the later arrival of a "delightful letter from Peter."[49] The image of Eliza waiting anxiously for post or carriage to bring either a letter from her husband or Peter himself recurs throughout her diary; she felt his absence keenly, worried for his safety, and tracked his arrivals and departures with great care.[50] However, while she clearly missed her husband, hers was not a solitary or lonely existence. There were friends and family to visit and schools to inspect; as well, evangelical work could be temporarily put aside to take in the illuminations laid on for Queen Victoria's coronation and the ascent of a large balloon.[51] Once Peter came back to London, Eliza busied herself preparing him for an audience with the Queen and accompanied him to it; they also went out to enjoy the sights of London.[52] As she left for Upper Canada, having bid a very emotional farewell to her family, she was moved to write a lengthy passage in her diary:

> Bless the Lord my soul for all the blessings that have followed me since my residence in England, I have received innumerable mercies from thy hand. Oh Heavenly Father, much kindness from thy people and favor in their eyes, generally, many traveling mercies, and many spiritual privileges. My dear husband has been successful through the blessing of God in obtaining many privileges for the Indians.

She did not know if she would return to Britain but, Eliza trusted, God would prepare her for the future.[53] (The next day she might have hoped that such was his desire, as a bout of bad seasickness left her wishing to return to England for the winter).[54]

As a number of essays in this collection point out, religious belief and practice have not always been clearly delineated separate and distinct spheres of existence. For Eliza, the various aspects of her life, ones that ranged from keeping track of her spiritual state to helping Peter prepare for an audience with the Queen, were not disparate or hived into separate categories of public versus private, sacred versus secular. Instead, they were pieces that comprised a whole, governed as they were by her Heavenly Father and his wishes for her – whatever those might be.

Return to Britain she did in 1845, this time travelling from Lambeth to Glasgow "to meet my dear husband," who had gone on ahead to tour Scotland. Her journey was far from smooth, though. Upon disembarking from the steamer at Rothesay, Eliza walked around town searching for Peter, enduring the "extreme heat of the July sun" and being lumbered with her satchel and umbrella. Unfortunately she had missed her husband, who had gone to nearby Greenock thinking she would be there. "What to do I knew not," Eliza confided to her diary, "so away I went ... seeking a lodging for the night – Unfortunately it was their fair time and every bed in the place was engaged, I wandered around tired and dispirited from place to place, the tears chased down my cheeks, and I put up my veil to hide my face."[55] Fortunately the couple was reunited: "on Monday just after dinner my precious husband arrived delighted and surprised to see me."[56] If Eliza felt any irritation or upset with her "precious husband" for the mix-up, there is no trace of it in the diary.

Over the next few days, she heard Peter preach, attended a number of meetings, and then travelled with him about Scotland on the increasingly popular tourist route.[57] After Greenock they took a steamer up the Clyde River to Glasgow and then a train to Edinburgh, where they explored the Castle and Holyrood House.[58] The couple enjoyed themselves, as they dined with Dr. D. the "great astronomer," toured Nairn's museum and ruined thirteenth-century cathedral, feasted on local strawberries and gooseberries, took a coach ride to Inverness, and then toured Loch Lomond on a steamer.[59] Eliza was effusive in her praise of the area: "The ride was splendid, the lonely lake burst all at once on view," the village was "sweet, picturesque," and then "in a little boat for the Island of [?] from which there is a distant, grand, beautiful and enchanting view of mountains wild, cultivated plains, lake and island." However, a shadow had been cast over this loveliness: "here the villages seemed all in trouble on account of the sudden removal of their beloved pastor who was this day to be interred in the quiet and romantically situated burial ground after enjoying much pleasure in viewing the mighty works of the great Creator."[60]

Scotland was not all picturesque carriage rides and sublime boat trips, though. Eliza also heard her husband preach and was delighted at his reception in Edinburgh, for example, when he spoke at some length to a large gathering and "all seemed much pleased"; a public breakfast at Edinburgh's Royal Hotel in "my dear husband's" honour resulted in "several speeches, splendid breakfast, all delighted."[61] Moreover, as well as the satisfaction of seeing her husband praised for his endeavours, Eliza's time in Scotland was interspersed with other reminders of missionary enterprises, as she met other missionaries' wives and heard of their experiences in the Pacific and India mission fields.[62]

## Conclusion

Obviously Eliza Field Jones's life took on a distinct trajectory because of her encounter with "her dear Peter" in 1831. She moved back and forth across the Atlantic, created homes in a number of settings (the Credit, Munceytown, and Brantford), as well as maintaining physical links with her English family, these links facilitated by her husband's work within the missionary movement and advocacy for the Mississauga. Moreover, by marrying Jones, accepting his family (at least to some extent) as her own, and by having children with him, Eliza – whose religious upbringing had been deeply inflected and influenced by metaphors of the global missionary family – helped both to expand and, to some extent, reshape those relationships. Concepts of domesticity and the "family of man" had, I would argue, rather different valences when this level of intimacy was involved: sharing a bed, the raising of children, and tending to each other's illnesses and, in Eliza's case, tending to Peter's final days. Furthermore, for Eliza, the notion of home – a notion so dear to missionary rhetoric in its signification of domestic space, England, and the "heavenly home" – was multilayered. "Home" might encompass her London birthplace and natal family, the mission villages of Upper Canada, the Jones residence in Brantford, and, ultimately, paradise. While it could be found on both sides of the Atlantic, from the 1830s until Jones's death, "home" was, ultimately, wherever her "dear hubby," as Peter often called himself in his letters to her, might be found.[63] Although to no small extent Eliza's definitions of home were shaped by middle-class notions of wifely duty, Jones held similar concepts of "home," speaking often, and eloquently, of feeling truly "at home" whenever he was with his wife.[64]

This is not to argue that somehow Eliza and her "dear hubby" or "Kahkwe" (another name Jones used in his letters to her)[65] were able to transcend the powerful representations that surrounded missionary work *or* interracial unions: those images, however, did not entirely capture the timbre of their relationship. How, for example, do we understand Eliza's internalization of the powerful and popular images of middle-class white women's benevolence towards Indigenous peoples, a benevolence that worked because of the former's supposed racial superiority and distance from the latter?[66] While such images may have given her an initial framework in which to apprehend her "dear Peter," that framework may have been less useful when it came to searching for him in Rothesay or reading about his feet, blistered from tramping the streets of Glasgow.[67]

Eliza's movements back and forth across the Atlantic also gave her multiple lenses on her husband. In Upper Canada she witnessed the "good works" of the missions and saw first-hand evidence of the Mississauga's embrace of Christianity; living and working with Peter allowed her to deploy evangelicals' lessons of the transformation of subjectivities, particularly as they pertained to gender relations, at a more fundamental and embodied level than would have been the case from the vantage point of her Lambeth home. She also, though, experienced her husband's frustration with the colonial government and certain elements of settler society. During the 1830s and '40s, southern Upper Canada increasingly became a more difficult place to live for both the Mississauga and Indigenous people more generally. In 1837 the colonial government attempted to marginalize the Mississauga and deny them the means to thrive by trying to move them off their lands to a location less hospitable to agriculture. As well, an ongoing influx of settlers – many of them British – resulted in increased pressure on Indigenous people's lands and resources.[68] No doubt Eliza also felt the divisions within the Mississauga themselves: not everyone believed in Peter Jones's vision of Christianity and "civilization."[69] The "blessings" that Eliza's life with her husband brought her, while plentiful, must at times have seemed very mixed indeed.

Although Eliza's location within settler society may have been both promising and frustrating, in the metropolitan context of the 1830s and 1840s somewhat different possibilities existed. To be sure, Peter Jones was often a highly visible figure because of his intertwined religious and racial identity, the latter so visible to some audiences that he complained to both his brother and Eliza of being perceived not as an example of the Mississauga's achievements but as a colonial aberration, a racialized freak show.[70] Yet his heightened visibility meant that he enjoyed public acclaim and acknowledgment that, as we have seen, Eliza shared in vicariously. As well, the welcome afforded them by wealthy and/or prominent evangelicals and supporters of overseas missions gave her the opportunity to tour beautiful gardens, dine at country estates, and discuss matters both spiritual and intellectual.

Eliza's life also provides an interesting counterpoint to those of other missionary wives of the early to mid-nineteenth century. Like those in the West Indies, hers was a set of experiences "defined by the parameters of the male missionary experience," as she was expected to be – and clearly saw herself as – her husband's helpmeet. Nevertheless, the degree of romantic attachment in her marriage was certainly far more intense and long-lasting than those experienced by missionary wives in the Caribbean, whose marriages were motivated by economic and spiritual reasons.[71] Eliza also left a great deal more sources than did many of her counterparts. While her diaries may not gratify all of an early-twenty-first-century historian's inquisitiveness, the traces she left are very different from those fragments – brief obituaries, scant acknowledgements in missionary societies' reports – that leave us only scattered glimpses of many missionary wives' experiences.[72] Yet in other respects Eliza resembled missionary spouses in the Caribbean and Australia, whose work tended to revolve around teaching literacy in English, the scriptures, and European domestic skills to women and girls.[73] Mission work, Clare Midgley points out, allowed such women to demonstrate strength of spiritual character and move beyond family homes and national borders; however, missionary societies simultaneously disapproved of women preachers and forbade them to lead mission communities.[74]

Eliza also ensured that her husband's memory would not be lost, as she helped to assemble and publish his diaries (in 1861), edited his notes on the Ojibwa into *History of the Ojebway Indians* (1861), and spearheaded a campaign for a marble monument to him, erected in 1857 at the Brantford Public Cemetery.[75] In these efforts Eliza also resembled other missionary spouses, children, and British evangelicals who raised monuments or published biographies, hagiographies, and memoirs, all of which served to place evangelical religion and missionary endeavours at the heart of British middle-class culture.[76] However, Eliza carried out her work of memorializing Kahkewaquonaby/Peter Jones in the context of a settler society that might well have preferred to have forgotten about him and his particular vision for the Mississauga, a society in which racial categories were solidifying and unions such as the Jones marriage became increasingly difficult to replicate.

Eliza Field Jones's life suggests not only the "complex cultural traffic"[77] that existed between colonies and the metropole in the 1830s and '40s: it also demonstrates just how complex that traffic might become when crosscut with, in Saurabh Dube's phrase, the "evangelical entanglements" of those decades.[78] Like the histories of Louis Riel and Edward Ahenakew, explored elsewhere in this book, Eliza and Peter Jones's narratives demonstrate that religious encounters might run in a number of different directions and take on multiple, sometimes contradictory, meanings. Paying careful attention to the ways in which such encounters took place at the individual level provides clear evidence that we need to think most carefully about religion, gender, and race, to treat them not as static categories but as historically shaped and contingent – categories experienced, negotiated, and sometimes undermined by individuals.

Finally, Eliza Field Jones's life reminds us of the need to keep both local and global contexts in mind: not to privilege one over the other but, rather, to understand how these contexts interacted in dynamic and, at times, unexpected ways. Without the transnational and imperial missionary movement, it is quite likely that Eliza and Peter would not have met. Conversely, without the specificities of that local context in which that movement was enacted, and the individuals who did the enacting, the story of the "English lady" and the Anishinaabe missionary might have had a different ending.

### Notes

1  Eliza Field Jones Diary, 1 June 1838, Box 4, Peter Jones Fonds 17, ser. 2, Victoria University Library, Toronto.
2  Ibid., 17 June 1838.
3  Ibid., 18 June 1838.
4  A medical doctor, Peter Edmund Jones was also secretary of the Grand Indian Council of Ontario. Like his father, he married a white woman. His biographer suggests that Eliza was a stricter and "more Victorian" parent than her husband (Allan Sherwin, *Bridging Two Peoples: Chief Peter E. Jones, 1843–1909* [Waterloo, ON: Wilfrid Laurier University Press, 2012] 9).
5  Donald B. Smith, *Sacred Feathers: The Reverend Peter Jones (Kahkewquonaby) and the Mississauga Indians* (Toronto: University of Toronto Press, 1987).
6  Jennifer Lund, "Negotiating Race and Gender in the Diaries of Eliza Jones, British Wife of an Ojibwa Missionary in Upper Canada, 1823–1883" (PhD diss., York University, 2010). My analysis differs from Lund's primarily in its focus on the transatlantic and imperial ties that Eliza Field Jones's life represents.
7  Donald B. Smith, *Sacred Feathers,* 131–32.
8  Catherine Hall and Leonore Davidoff, *Family Fortunes: Men and Women of the English Middle Class, 1780–1850* (Chicago: University of Chicago Press, 1987); Susan Thorne, *Congregational Missions and the Making of an Imperial Culture in 19th-Century Britain* (Stanford: Stanford University Press, 1999): Alison Twells, *The Civilising Mission and the English Middle Class, 1792–1850: The "Heathen" at Home and Overseas* (London: Palgrave Macmillan, 2009); Clare Midgely, "Can Women Be Missionaries? Envisioning Female Agency in the Early Nineteenth-Century British Empire," *Journal of British Studies* 45 (April 2006): 335–58.
9  Twells, *The Civilising Mission,* chaps. 1–4.
10  Eliza Field Diary, 11, 14, and 17 June 1832.
11  Smith, *Sacred Feathers,* 135–40.
12  Ibid., 139–40.
13  Ibid., 116.
14  Eliza Field Diary, 24 April 1832.
15  Lund, "Negotiating Race and Gender," 24, 110–12.
16  Cecilia Morgan, "Creating Interracial Intimacies: British North America, Canada, and the Transatlantic World, 1830–1914," *Journal of the Canadian Historical Association/Revue en ligne de la SHC,* new series, 19, 2 (2008): 75–104; Smith, *Sacred Feathers,* 137–38. See also Ann Laura Stoler, ed., *Haunted by Empire: Geographies of Intimacy in North American History* (Durham: Duke University Press, 2006); Antoinette Burton and Tony Ballantyne, eds., *Moving Subjects: Gender, Mobility, and Intimacy in an Age of Empire* (Urbana: University of Illinois Press, 2011).
17  Ibid., 141–42.
18  Ibid., 142–43; Eliza Field Jones Diary, 10 April 1838.

19 Smith, *Sacred Feathers*, 142–43; Morgan, "Creating Interracial Intimacies."
20 Smith, *Sacred Feathers*, 213. For a very different familial reaction to a similarly mixed-race marriage, see Theresa Strouth Gaul, ed., *To Marry an Indian: The Marriage of Harriett Gold and Elias Boudinot through Their Letters, 1823–1839* (Chapel Hill: University of North Carolina Press, 2005).
21 Smith, *Sacred Feathers*, 146–47; also Morgan, "Creating Interracial Intimacies," 100–1.
22 Many thanks to Siphiwe Dube for his questions on this point.
23 Twells, *The Civilising Mission*, 137–38.
24 For work on Indigenous converts' representations, both in missionary literature and as exhibitions, see Allan Greer, *Mohawk Saint: Catherine Tekakwitha and the Jesuits* (Oxford: Oxford University Press, 2005); Cecilia Morgan, "Turning Strangers into Sisters? Missionaries and Colonization in Upper Canada," in *Sisters or Strangers? Immigrant, Ethnic, and Racialized Women in Canadian History*, ed. Marlene Epp, Franca Iacovetta, and Frances Swyripa (Toronto: University of Toronto Press, 2004), 23–48, 31–33; Elizabeth Elbourne, *Blood Ground: Colonialism, Missions, and the Contest for Christianity in the Cape Colony and Britain, 1799–1853* (Montreal/Kingston: McGill-Queen's University Press, 2002), 122–29; Hilary M. Carey, "Companions in the Wilderness? Missionary Wives in Colonial Australia, 1788–1900," *Journal of Religious History* 19, 2 (1995): 227–48, 240.
25 Elizabeth Jones, *Memoir of Elizabeth Jones: a Little Indian Girl, Who Lived at the River-Credit Mission, Upper Canada* (London: John Mason, 1838), 26–27.
26 Ibid., 14–16, 17.
27 Ibid., 18–21.
28 For Upper Canada, see Morgan, "Turning Strangers into Sisters," 28–34.
29 Jones, *Memoir*, 5–6.
30 Ibid., 6.
31 Ibid., 7.
32 Ibid., 6.
33 Ibid., 8–9.
34 Ibid., 9–10.
35 Morgan, "Turning Strangers into Sisters," 31–32.
36 Twells, *The Civilizing Mission*, chap. 5.
37 Jones, *Memoir*, 16–17.
38 Ibid., 17.
39 For discussion of liberalism and humanitarianism in the missionary movement, see Catherine Hall, *Civilizing Subjects: Metropole and Colony in the English Imagination 1830–1867* (Chicago: University of Chicago Press, 2002); also Twells, *The Civilising Mission*.
40 Jones, *Memoir*, 11–12.
41 Ibid., 28.
42 It is not clear if anyone was held responsible for the rotten board that caused Elizabeth's fall.
43 Morgan, "Creating Interracial Intimacies," 84.
44 Catherine Sutton to Eliza Jones, 25 March 1847, File 7, Box 5, Peter Jones Fonds 17, Ser 2. I discuss this letter in more detail in "'Write me. Write me': Native and Métis Letter-Writing across the British Empire, 1800–1870," in *Critical Perspectives on Colonialism: Writing the Empire from Below*, ed. Fiona Paisley and Kirsty Reid (New York: Routledge, 2014), 56.
45 Lund, "Negotiating Race and Gender," 7.
46 Myra Rutherdale makes this point in her *Women and the White Man's God: Gender and Race in the Canadian Mission Field* (Vancouver: UBC Press, 2002).
47 Eliza Field Jones Diary, 6, 12 April 1838.

48  Ibid., 14 April 1838.
49  Ibid., 17, 22 April 1838.
50  Ibid., 22 June and 2, 16 July 1838.
51  Ibid., 28 June and 2 July 1838.
52  Ibid., 21 July and 30 August 1838.
53  Ibid., 17, 18 September 1838.
54  Ibid., 19 September 1838.
55  Ibid., 18 July 1845.
56  Ibid., 20 July 1845.
57  Ibid., 21 July 1845. For tourism in Scotland, see Alistair J. Durie, *Scotland for the Holidays: Tourism in Scotland, c. 1780–1939* (Edinburgh: Tuckwell Press, 1999).
58  Eliza Field Jones Diary, 21, 25 July 1845.
59  Ibid., 9, 13, August and 1, 3 September 1845.
60  Ibid., 11 September 1845.
61  Ibid., 29 July and 4, 12 August 1845.
62  Ibid., 11, 26 August 1845.
63  For example, Peter Jones to Eliza Field Jones, 25 and 29 October 1845, Box 3, File 4, Peter Jones Letterbook, Peter Jones Fonds 17.
64  Morgan, "Creating Interracial Intimacies."
65  For example, Jones to Eliza Field Jones, 19 and 25 November 1845.
66  See Jane Haggis, "White Women and Colonialism: Towards a Non-Recuperative History," in *Gender and Imperialism,* ed. Clare Midgely (Manchester: Manchester University Press, 1999), 45–75; Antoinette Burton, *Burdens of History: British Feminists, Indian Women, and Imperial Culture, 1865–1915* (Chapel Hill: University of North Carolina Press, 1994); Peggy Pascoe, *Relations of Rescue: The Search for Female Moral Authority in the American West, 1874–1939* (New York: Oxford University Press, 1990); Fiona Paisley, *Loving Protection? Australian Feminism and Indigenous Women's Rights, 1919–1939* (Melbourne: Melbourne University Press, 2002); Anna Cole, Victoria Haskins, and Fiona Paisley, eds., *Uncommon Ground: White Women in Indigenous History* (Canberra: Indigenous Studies Press, 2005).
67  Peter Jones to Eliza Field Jones, 6 July 1845.
68  See Smith, *Sacred Feathers,* chap. 10; Peter S. Schmalz, *The Ojibwa of Southern Ontario* (Toronto: University of Toronto Press, 1991), chaps. 6 and 7; Theodore Binnema and Kevin Hutchings, "The Emigrant and the Noble Savage: Sir Francis Bond Head's Romantic Approach to Aboriginal Policy in Upper Canada, 1836–1838," *Journal of Canadian Studies/ Revue d'études canadiennes* 39, 1 (Winter 2005): 115–38.
69  Smith, *Sacred Feathers,* chap. 10.
70  Cecilia Morgan, "Missionaries and Celebrity within the Transatlantic World: The Ojibwa of Upper Canada, 1830–1860," in *Celebrity Colonialism: Fame, Power and Representation in Colonial and Postcolonial Cultures,* ed. Robert Clarke (Newcastle upon Tyne: Cambridge Scholars' Press, 2009), 15–36.
71  Patricia T. Rooke, "'Ordinary Events of Nature and Providence': Reconstructing Female Missionary Experience in the British West Indies, 1800–45," *Journal of Religious History* 19, 2 (December 1995): 204–26. Rooke acknowledges that some unions, such as that of the Knibbs and the Wrays, were shaped by domestic harmony and notions of companionate marriage. See also Hall, *Civilizing Subjects,* 94–100.
72  Rooke, "Ordinary Events of Nature and Providence," 204.
73  Carey, "Companions in the Wilderness," 232, 238.
74  Midgley, "Can Women Be Missionaries?" 357.
75  Smith, *Sacred Feathers,* 246–47.

76  Twells, *The Civilizing Mission,* 209.
77  Tony Ballantyne, "Religion, Difference, and the Limits of British Imperial History," *Victorian Studies* 47, 3 (Spring 2005): 446.
78  Saurabh Dube, "Conversion to Translation: Colonial Registers of a Vernacular Christianity," *South Atlantic Quarterly* 101, 4 (Fall 2002): 807–8. Dube's phrase seems particularly apt, not just for Eliza but for the Mississauga more generally.

# 5
## Between García Moreno and Chan Santa Cruz: Riel and the Métis Rebellions

*Jean-François Bélisle and Nicole St-Onge*

THROUGHOUT 2010, A SERIES of commemorations marked the 125th anniversary of the Northwest Rebellion and its military and judicial suppression. These commemorations spurred renewed discussion in popular and academic circles alike about the genesis, history, and current status of the "Métis Nation." Curiously absent from this discussion, however, was the figure of Louis Riel. Absent, too, were Riel's voluminous writings, his political philosophy, and his distinctive ecclesiology.

Riel and his writings have remained secondary, perhaps even marginal, topics of inquiry for academics. However, his symbolic presence has grown significantly in the country's popular imagination since 1980. Traditionally maligned in English Canada as a traitor to Confederation and eulogized in French Canada as a Catholic martyr, Riel has been variously recast as the revolutionary leader of a war of national or ethnic liberation, a founder of western Canada, and even one of the Fathers of Confederation.[1] Underlying the latter recasting were discursive processes similar to those that elevated Túpac Amaru II and Miguel Hidalgo y Costilla to the status of national heroes in Peru and Mexico, respectively, where, ironically, the historical roots of the state lay in the repression of Indigenous and mestizo resistance. This reassessment of Riel has abated in recent years as historians have increasingly turned their attention away from the man himself and towards works of discourse analysis. Informed by postcolonial theory, these studies situate the mythology of Riel within the context of a shifting and variegated Canadian identity.[2]

Whether focused on the actual historical figure or posthumous representations of the figure, the dominant texts of Riel historiography share a common conception of Riel's political role in resisting the colonialism of the Canadian state. This conception tends to marginalize – if not to suppress altogether – the religious content of Riel's thought. Indeed, it would be no exaggeration to posit a *malaise* vis-à-vis Riel's mysticism, a sense of profound unease resulting from hackneyed debate about his mental health. In this regard, Gregory Betts's

Foucauldian interpretation is particularly revealing as it treats the conceptualization of madness as a strategy of social control. According to Betts, "across all the uses and depictions of Louis Riel's insanity, two beliefs remain consistent: that insanity is morally repugnant, and that, had Riel been undeniably proven insane, it would undermine the moral integrity of his life and politics."[3] The latter contention is powerfully borne out by Maggie Siggins's biography, which places Riel and his activities squarely in the realm of politics, and refuses to address the possibility of Riel's mental illness. Siggins sees any discussion of mental health as a ploy to dismiss the legitimacy of Aboriginal struggles or a desire to perceive Riel as merely a prophetic figure rather than an effective leader – again diminishing the importance of his political agenda.[4]

This reference to a "prophetic figure" recalls the work of Thomas Flanagan, who first illuminated this dimension of Riel's life and thought.[5] In Flanagan's wake, Gilles Martel, Manfred Mossmann, and John Michael Bumsted draw inspiration from the burgeoning field of millenarian studies.[6] Their works situate Riel within a long tradition of socio-religious movements whose messianism was an "archaic" response to colonialism and its concomitant dissolution of Indigenous economic, political, and social orders.[7]

From this historiography there emerges a dichotomous portrait of Riel. On the one hand, there is the political Riel, the leader of the provisional government whose messianic discourse was either ignored or had little bearing on the resistance movement. On the other hand, there is the prophetic Riel, the mystic whose brand of messianism emerged from a unique combination of sociological factors,[8] but whose vision of a new "Catholic and Living Church of the New World" either had no political traction, or, according to Flanagan, brought about the categorical ruin of the Métis.[9] More recently, Jennifer Reid insists on the need to reintroduce a religious dimension to the study of the rebellions. She argues that religion can be a revealing element of the potential for dislocation that we see in the Métis worldview.[10] While she emphasizes the importance of religion as one of the central dimensions of Métis interrogation of the process of colonialism, she maintains in her analysis of Riel and the rebellions the traditional distinction between a religious discourse and a political one. Reid thus avoids the whole question of the political content in Riel's reinterpretation and redefinition of society in his creation of a new church.[11]

In this chapter, we propose a rereading of Riel and the rebellions and seek to re-examine the accepted dichotomous conception of the religious and the political. We want to emphasize a reading of the man, his writings, and events that realizes a melding of the religious and the political spheres within the Métis world. By 1885, this melding inevitably led to a double rupture from the two dominant forms of institutionalized power that held sway over the Métis:

the Catholic Church and the state. To repeat here Betts's expression, it is with the notion of a "double heresy" that both Riel's thoughts and the rebellions per se can be seen as a rupture with both the colonialism of the Canadian state (here conceptualized as the institutionalization of power over a particular space) and the spiritual and temporal powers asserted by the Catholic Church (especially within the context of its late-nineteenth-century ultramontane ecclesiology).[12]

We are inspired in our approach by numerous recent publications in the field of sociology of religion that, in this new "post-secular" era, have examined various contemporary state-building projects using methodologies that differ from those inspired by the theses of Durkheim and Weber, with their assumption of political rationality and their conception of the state as existing in a separate sphere from the religious.[13] These new approaches have led to a re-examination of the relationship between the religious and the political realms, especially in the nineteenth-century Catholic world, emphasizing the complex ties that exist between religion making and nation building.[14] Researchers such as José Casanova argue that there was an ongoing and dynamic process of mutual invention with the rise and consolidation of nation states occurring in tandem with a redefinition of the Church.[15] This perspective allows us to better situate historically the evolution of Riel's thinking. We also propose to situate Riel and the rebellions in light of a postcolonial reassessment of religion such as that found in Timothy Fitzgerald's writings, which not only question the Eurocentric character of the religious worldview imposed by colonialization but also make evident the essentially political content of various redefinitions of the religious.[16] It is true that writings dealing with millenarianism generally have emphasized the political content found in various incarnations of socioreligious movements,[17] but we propose to develop further this perspective by arguing that, in a postcolonial perspective, any refashioning of a political worldview is wedded to a similar development on a religious plane.[18]

Within this approach, Riel's second provisional government in 1885, the famous "Exovidat," is no mere organizational curiosity. Rather, it can be conceived as being the construction of an alternate model of both religious and political power (albeit in an embryonic state). Exovidat was the beginning of an institutional process that meant to put in place the basis of an original societal construction that we label the church-state.

We propose to try to understand the two rebellions and the elaboration of Exovidat within the context of Riel's own thoughts and within his appropriation of historical precedents that, in distinct ways, resonated deeply for him. On the basis of Riel's copious writings, we focus upon the link evident between the Métis leader's political-religious thoughts and the debates centred on the relations between Church and state that raged at that time in French Canada. To illustrate the profound impact that these debates had on Riel's thinking, we pay particular attention to the influence that Ecuadorian president Gabriel García Moreno had on contemporaneous French Canadian Catholic intellectuals. García Moreno's time in power and the regime he put in place were seen at the time as the most advanced ultramontane redefinition of a state in existence.[19] He became a veritable icon within French Canadian ultra-Catholic circles. Riel was inspired by García Moreno's myth-driven persona, which confirmed for him both the soundness of his ultramontane thinking and the viability of his utopian church-state.

After a short discussion on the mechanisms of appropriation of Riel's messianism by the Métis population during the rebellions, we finish our reconsideration of Riel's political and religious thinking by examining a historical parallel. The Mayan free state known as Cruzob, centred in the town of Chan Santa Cruz on the Yucatán peninsula, with its new church founded on the cult of the "Talking Cross," parallels in many regards the situation of the Métis. Cruzob represents one of the most sophisticated examples of an alternative project of reinvention of both the political and the religious on a hemispheric level. This example allows us to situate Riel's thinking and his role in the rebellions on a broader intellectual plane that goes beyond traditional analyses of the question of messianism. Messianism can thus come to be seen, to paraphrase Weber, as a process of re-enchantment of the world to the extent that the miraculous is conceived as the only answer possible in a context of profound crisis experienced by societies that see their economic, social, and political parameters violently challenged.

As Peter Beyer has demonstrated convincingly – although perhaps without enough emphasis on the potential for religious syncretism – Riel's millenarianism was founded essentially on the discourse of French Canadian ultramontanism.[20] More particularly, Riel drew on the ultra-Catholic strain of this discourse. During the latter half of the nineteenth century, French Canadian ultramontanism split into two divergent strains: the moderate and the intransigent, also known as neo-ultramontane.[21] While sharing the common objective of submitting the political realm to the clerical agenda, moderates sought to achieve this end through negotiation, ultra-Catholics through outright imposition.[22] Yet despite failing to garner consensus on method, the intransigents nevertheless succeeded in defining the terms of debate on the relationship between the religious and political spheres in the 1860s and 1870s.[23] Their discourse played a central role in the formulation of Riel's political thought, as revealed in the latter's correspondence with Bishop Ignace Bourget of Montreal, one of the chief proponents and theorists of the ultra-Catholic movement. In a letter that confirmed his mission from Riel's perspective,[24] Bourget suggested that religion would be the only way to save the Métis from their oppression.[25] This *catholicisme de combat* provided the raw materials that gradually coalesced into the politico-religious content of Riel's millenarianism.[26] Particularly formative was the utopian aspect of neo-ultramontanism, a vision of the "re-enchantment of the world." This vision lent coherence and direction to Riel's project of a "Catholic and Living Church of the New World."[27]

Amidst Riel's voluminous writings, there is a particular passage that illustrates each of these dimensions. Riel expresses his profound admiration for the icon of neo-ultramontanism, García Moreno, and lauds the Ecuadorian statesman as one of the greatest Christians in Latin American history. Riel even suggests that this distinction should be formalized by rechristening the South Pole *le pôle Moreno*.[28] Informing this prescription was Bourget's intensive publicity and sermonizing. Bourget had hailed García Moreno's administration (1859–65 and 1869–75) and constitution (1869) as models to be replicated in French Canada. These models had affirmed the supremacy of the religious sphere over the political. They had afforded an ultramontane formulation of national identity, defining Ecuadorians as "un peuple catholique," and thus binding faith and citizenship inextricably.[29] Equally critical to García Moreno's apotheosis was his foreign policy, which envisaged the restitution of the Papal States,[30] and his successful motion that Ecuador be consecrated to the Sacred Heart of Jesus, whose cult was quickly becoming the most politicized in the Catholic world.[31] Cast as the archetypal Christian statesman, García Moreno served as the living validation of Bourget's theocratic political project, laid out in the famous *Programme catholique* (1871).[32] In addition to serving as an institutional model, Ecuador seemed to confirm French Canada's own "civilizing mission" when it received, in the same year, the very first contingent of French Canadian missionaries to venture beyond North America.[33] Here, then, were the essential axes of Riel's politico-religious thought: the theocratic organization of the state; the notion of "un peuple catholique";[34] and a vision of the world based on the geopolitics of faith – a vision that would inspire Riel to reconceptualize the continent as the guardian of Métis autonomy.

After García Moreno's assassination in 1875 – the year that marked the beginning of Riel's mystic phase – he was eulogized by the ultra-Catholic press as the secular prophet of ultramontanism.[35] Circulated through an international network of writers and intellectuals,[36] the figure of García Moreno became widely popularized and came to occupy a prominent place in the politico-religious imaginary of the Catholic world. In Europe and the Americas alike, his name was synonymous with the ultra-Catholic political agenda.[37] Within a decade of his death, the Ecuadorian statesman had been elevated to the status of mythic hero – a modern-day Charlemagne or Saint Louis – through whom God had instituted a model regime.[38] This notion of the Man of Providence – which was by no means restricted to ultra-Catholic circles[39] – enabled adherents of ultramontanism to affirm that their political agenda was fully realizable, provided that it was implemented by "a perfect Christian, one who works, who sacrifices himself, and who prays."[40]

Although retaining its power to underscore the achievability of the ultramontane utopia when the active resistance began in 1885, this discourse was nevertheless marginalized by the evolution of the Catholic Church. Ironically, it was precisely at the time when the figure of García Moreno attained its widest renown, illustrated by the success of his biography written by R.P.A. Berthe,[41] that it began losing its political relevance as a symbol of rearguard support for the Vatican. In the 1880s, Pope Leo XIII advocated the normalization of relations between church and state in accordance with what was termed "liberal ultramontanism" – an ecclesiology holding that the complete autonomy of the Catholic Church be upheld together with its exclusive prerogatives in managing religious affairs, but urging national churches to remain formally neutral in political affairs.[42] Concurrently in French Canada, the Catholic Church began marginalizing the neo-ultramontanism discourse after having consolidated its position vis-à-vis the Quebec government's apparatus,[43] which had readily relinquished most of its responsibilities for social regulation.[44]

This change in perspective on the nature of relations between ecclesiastical and secular authorities on the part of the Catholic Church, both in French Canada and globally, meant that Riel's vision of an ultramontane utopia diverged ever more widely from accepted Church doctrine. Riel's message, still anchored in an intransigent form of neo-ultramontanism, was rapidly becoming anachronistic. French Canadian Church authorities came to perceive it as a deviant intellectual position rather than the logical if extreme conclusion of a once-accepted conservative Catholic way of thinking. This provoked a profound crisis in Riel's relationship with his Church. According to the logic of "recovering lost purity" – a logic underlying virtually all sectarian movements – the mission of the Roman Catholic Church (and its French Canadian subsidiary) was now compromised. For Riel, it could be restored and resumed only by a new "Catholic and Living Church of the New World." Serious interpretive problems beset any account of the transition from what was only a mystical interpretation of the world to Riel's brand of applied messianism within the rebellion. While there is historiographical consensus on the mobilizing character of Riel's prophetic discourse, there has been little or no satisfactory explanation of the process by which this discourse was received and internalized by the Métis.

According to the traditional interpretation, the Métis were simply deluded and duped. This perspective was adopted by many contemporaries, such as Father Piquet, who stated that Riel was "comme le serpent fascine l'oiseau [il] Riel fascinait le pauvre peuple Métis et l'attirait à lui pour en faire le jouet de ses ambitions."[45] Informing this interpretation was the timeworn dichotomy between "primitive" and "civilized": the Métis were either too naive or too irrational to recognize textbook symptoms of madness.[46] The current tendency, however, is to ascribe the acceptance of Riel's messianism to a form of religious syncretism that incorporated the miraculous and the transcendent into its worldview. A commonly cited example of this syncretism is the Métis belief that devotion to Saint Joseph could render them invincible.[47] An equally revealing aspect of Métis devotional life – one that is associated with the myth of García Moreno – was their collective consecration to the Sacred Heart. In addition to underscoring their status as "un peuple élu," this consecration had a miraculous dimension: it ensured that Métis political aspirations could be fulfilled through the patronage of the divine organ. Yet, while the consecration to the Sacred Heart clearly reveals a sacralization of the political sphere (according to a logic that resembled that of the ultra-Catholics), it reveals little about the way(s) in which the Métis integrated their belief in divine intervention into their daily lives and into their perceptions of the real world.

One angle from which to approach this problem is Gilles Martel's concept of "la conscience némésiaque" (from the Greek Νέμεσις, the spirit of retribution against hubris).[48] According to Martel, Métis religious culture was underpinned by notions of cosmic justice and especially by the idea that all misfortune had divine origin. Thus, within the Métis worldview, the only legitimate response to suffering was piety. Appropriating the traditional French Canadian self-image as a pious people afloat in a sea of impiety, Riel transposed the notion of a Catholic counterrevolution onto the Métis experience. He thereby produced a meaningful interpretation of local circumstances framed within the broader context of a beleaguered Church. In the same way that ultra-Catholics had framed their political project against a succession of revolutionary catastrophes, from the French Revolution as universal calamity and the Lower Canadian Rebellion as a local one, so too did Riel ascribe local meaning to remote cataclysm. His politico-religious discourse provided a framework for interpreting the many changes that shook the Métis world in the 1870s and early 1880s. Its counterrevolutionary content resonated with the Métis, who – through decades of exposure to the sermonizing of an ultramontane clergy – had absorbed elements of a worldview predicated on a "culture of traumatism."[49] Thus, a foundation had already been laid for the reception of Riel's message and for the realization of his politico-religious vision. In an epistemological sense, then, the Métis were poised to inaugurate a Christian fortress for the defence of the one true faith.

The pre-existence of this foundation underscores the importance of the Roman Catholic apostolate in the evolution of the Métis world.[50] Indeed, the Catholic Church – an empire of piety that had expanded in tandem with an empire of commerce over the course of the nineteenth century – was the institution with the strongest local presence and the greatest degree of popular acceptance. As the self-proclaimed protectors of the Métis, Catholic clergyman served as intermediaries between their *protégés* and all other forms of institutionalized power, whether governmental or commercial. Moreover, clerics inculcated patterns of thought and behaviour through their various education initiatives. They also imposed and enforced social norms through their monopoly over the performance of sacred rites and ceremonies. Accepted by Riel until his return to Batoche, this instrumentalization of the Métis faith was one of the most significant dimensions of the Métis world being questioned by the mid-1880s.

To an extent, the rebellion exacerbated a long-standing tension between institutional Catholicism and the experiential piety of the Métis. This tension received expression in the letters and journals of local clerics, who frequently censured the Métis for their alleged indifference to dogma and their inconsistency in outward devotion. In much the same way that the Métis provisional government took shape according to the organizational structure of the bison hunt (a point developed by Martel on the basis of James C. Scott's notion of "infrapolitics"),[51] Riel's new church developed through a process by which Métis experiential piety, which can be designated by the term "infrareligion" (that is, a process of religion making from below), came to florescence and overtly challenged the power of the clergy. Among the avowed justifications for this rupture was *la trahison des clercs* – a festering memory of betrayal that originated in the clergy's ambiguous role in the amnesty question and the marginalization of the Métis after the Manitoba Act of 1870. This sense of betrayal on the part of the Métis deepened in 1885 when the prelates and priests of western Canada refused to countenance the rebellion. The resultant hostility towards *la religion des clercs* facilitated Métis recognition of Riel as a prophet. It also informed their acceptance of his proclamation that "Rome has fallen" and the Exovidat's official ratification of the split with orthodoxy on 25 March 1885.[52] This split marked the symbolic beginning of a new church-state.

During its brief existence, the Exovidat took precocious measures to establish and consolidate alternative forms of power. These measures ranged from the passing of prodigious motions that redefined time and space, to the issuance of modest rules on daily living. Among its best-known initiatives was the creation of a calendar that fixed Saturday as the new Lord's Day and that designated new periods of fasting and abstinence. Each of the Exovidat's initiatives represented embryonic modalities of social regulation that can be associated with a dynamic of institutionalization of an alternative political regime and church.

Notwithstanding some obvious contextual differences, Riel's church-state project exhibited striking similarities to the most successful socio-religious movement of the late nineteenth century – the Mayan free state known as Cruzob on the Yucatán Peninsula.[53] Like the Métis, the Maya asserted themselves by force of arms. Unlike the Métis, however, the Maya managed to sustain their armed resistance over the course of a half-century. This protracted struggle – the so-called Caste War of Yucatán (1847–1901) – began in a context of waning state power as the Mexican government vied with regional elites for control of the peninsula. The struggle raged on until a unique geopolitical situation emerged – a kind of "middle ground" achieved through the tacit involvement of British Honduran authorities.[54] Overlapping chronologically with the Métis rebellions, the case of Cruzob is instructional in that it provides insights into the dynamic of institutionalization of a church-state model.

Beginning as a large-scale peasant uprising in defence of communal lands,[55] the Caste War was transformed into a "holy war" in 1850 when the prophet Juan de la Cruz foretold that a "Talking Cross" would reveal itself to the Maya. According to the prophet, the miraculous object would render them invisible in battle and lead them to victory against the Mexican forces.[56] While religious syncretism was arguably a more marked feature of the Mayan movement than it was of the Métis movement, both groups conceptualized themselves as inaugurators of a new phase of Christianity. Through the "Mayanization" of Catholicism, the "Cult of the Talking Cross" was to herald the coming of the Mayan Christ and hasten the departure of the Antichrist, whose reign had begun with the establishment of the colonial regime.[57] Thus, the "official" beginning of Cruzob was linked discursively to a new church and to a new dispensation of symbols. This new church – like that of the Métis at Batoche – quickly became a marker of group identity and cohesion.[58]

The infrapolitical dimension of religion is more readily discernible in the Mayan experience than in the Métis experience. Because political responsibility (vested in the *cacique*) and religious responsibility (vested in the *confraternity*) were traditionally linked in the communal universe of the Maya, the new form of political power was necessarily preconditioned to fuse with the new church. Reinforcing this tendency towards fusion was the principle that political legitimacy flowed directly from the "Talking Cross" in the form of spoken and written directives.[59] This principle of divine locution provided a means of implementing new political, military, social, and moral orientations that, in turn, became modalities of social regulation in Cruzob.

This principle also underlay an internal struggle for control of the locus of devotion – the church building was erected in 1858 to enshrine the "Talking Cross." From this struggle emerged a governing hierarchy exhibiting both military and religious dimensions. Although differing in obvious ways from the classical model of the state, the Cruzob hierarchy was nevertheless endowed with many – if not most – of the prerogatives that are customarily ascribed to the state. In addition to claiming a monopoly on the legitimate use of violence in the domestic context, Cruzob pursued its own foreign policy initiatives. For instance, it negotiated international treaties and forged lucrative trade relations with British Honduras (particularly in the wood industry). This participation in Atlantic commerce generated revenue for the waging of war. For its part, the Exovidat was animated by similar preoccupations with domestic and foreign policy, as well as the promotion of Métis commercial interests. It is therefore reasonable – although admittedly counterfactual – to suggest that the Exovidat would have succeeded in creating a political life as intense as that of the Maya free state if it had succeeded in institutionalizing its church-state model.

Examining possible parallels between the Cruzob on the one hand and Riel and the Métis rebellions on the other allows us to place the latter within a very long tradition of questioning of not only the process of colonization but also the process of postcolonial consolidation of the nation state on a hemispheric scale.[60] Although Riel's orientation towards ultramontanism has struck many authors as odd and incongruous, it was, in fact, a manifestation of diversity in the historical religious experience of colonized societies. In a general sense, its underlying logic resembled that of other socio-religious movements in the hemispheric context, as illustrated by the case of the Maya free state of Cruzob. In this way, the Métis rebellions insert themselves into a logic similar to that put forth in the Mesoamerican context, with the notions or concepts of *utopias indias* or the homologous *utopia andina* for the old Andean Inca space. Both these utopias are based on the idea that the rupture is conceived as a vast process of decolonization of the imagined space that is put in place by a radical reorganization in both a religious and political sense.[61] Among the most famous examples, the great revolt of Túpac Amaru has already been alluded to. Another striking example of such a radical moment of rupture and political-religious reconceptualization is the 1791–1804 Haitian revolution. There the fusion of the political and religious spheres was expressed, on a symbolic level, by the

voodoo ceremony of *Bois caïman,* marking the beginnings of the revolt and
where Toussaint L'Ouverture's image as revolutionary leader is inseparable from
that of a thaumaturge, who dominates the voodoo kingdom of Christophe
Henri in the north of the island for nearly twenty years.[62] This utopian content
is a constant in the vast majority of colonial resistance movements having a
millenarianist orientation.[63] Two other celebrated examples that are also contemporaneous with the Métis rebellions are the long-running traditions of resistance of *Yaquis, Mayos,* and *Tomochic* in northern Mexico,[64] and the famous
revolt of the *Canudos* in northeast Brazil, with its central mythical figure and
leader, Antonio Conselheiro.[65]

There are certain caveats to keep in mind, however, when examining and
interpreting messianic and millenarian movements. According to the traditional
conception, messianism is a phenomenon in which "pre-political peoples" – Eric
Hobsbawm's categorization – responded to crises by redefining their worlds
through utopian discourse.[66] The interpretive purchase of this conception is
somewhat limited. The historian is faced with phenomena that cannot simply
be reduced to explanatory frameworks that evoke only "native" universes or
worldviews. The messianic occurrences are too frequent and occur in too many
settings to be explained fully by the evocation of a blanket, nebulous, pre-political
native process.[67] Messianism is frequent, complex, and involves the reinvention
of self through the reinvention of a people's mental or "imagined" space. One
interesting example of this in our hemisphere is the case of Sandino, which had
both a Creole discourse and a spiritualism linked to an anti-imperialist agenda.[68]
Another, even more interesting, example is that of Jules-Paul Tardivel, who,
similar to Riel, elaborated his societal project of a theocracy, his "Republic of
New France," using a utopian ultramontanism that seemed not only desirable
but also achievable when it takes as its inspiration the mythic figure of García
Moreno.[69]

Beyond this re-questioning of both the essentially millenarian character of
Riel and the fact that millenarianism remains to this day the dominant interpretive approach to Riel's thoughts and his political and spiritual roles, the most
interesting element that can be taken from the above comparison of the Métis
rebellion centred at Batoche with the five decades of existence of the Cruzob
centred in Chan Santa Cruz concerns the Exovidat. The Exovidat proposed an
alternative conception of society for the Métis that was historically situated
within the realm of actual possibility. What we are seeing in both cases are
original forms of political and religious reinvention that are posited as viable
alternatives to the subaltern position imposed on a population by the postcolonial logic of the state and the Church. In both cases, we see some of the

most sophisticated attempts to fuse the dynamics of religion making with that of nation building in a perspective that was both simultaneously the sacralization of the political and the politicization of the religious.[70] This seemed eminently logical and possible to Riel as he based his thinking on a utopian ultramontanism that was eminently desirable and attainable.

As to questions concerning the viability of the Exovidat, one simply has to turn to the example of the half-century of existence of the Cruzob. Although both the societal models proposed in Batoche and in Chan Santa Cruz deviated sharply from traditional (occidental) views of the roles of Church and state, this does not mean that they were inherently flawed. The fall of the Cruzob was not linked to its fusing of the infrapolitical to a lived daily piety. Rather, it resulted from a changing regional geopolitical context linked to the normalization of relations between Mexico and Great Britain at the end of the nineteenth century.[71] The fall of the Cruzob can be tied directly to the disappearance of a middle ground following a vast and repressive campaign of regional pacification. In North America, the example of the rise and demise of a "Comanche Empire" seems a particularly relevant comparison.[72] There is a direct correlation between the possibility for autonomy in frontier regions and the elaboration of alternative constructs of society. There is also, more sadly, a correlation between the truly vast process – loosely coined "Indian Wars" – raging from the northern Plains to Patagonia, and the eventual disappearance of these last spaces of autonomy. This double correlation is the key element in explaining the messianic character of the rebellions. It gives meaning to what we term, to paraphrase Weber, the process of re-enchantment of the world. In societies experiencing profound crises, as their economic, social, and symbolic points of references are questioned, the miraculous becomes the only possible or imagined answer. In his writings and in the first tentative and tantalizing decisions of the Exovidat, Riel proposed a vast redefinition of the world, both temporal and imagined, that was constructed on the bases of a geopolitically reconfigured faith. In his view of the world, only these reconstructed physical and mental spaces could guarantee the survival of his people. This was especially true in the context of the northern Plains, given the truly enormous disparity in strength that existed between the colonial powers and the Métis by 1885.

## Notes

1  Douglas Owram, "The Myth of Louis Riel," *Canadian Historical Review* 43, 3 (1982): 315–36; and Desmond Morton, "Reflections on the Image of Louis Riel a Century After," in *Images of Louis Riel in Canadian Culture*, ed. Ramon Hathorn and Patrick Holland (Lewiston, NY: E. Mellen Press, 1992), 47–62.

2   See especially Ian Angus, "Louis Riel and English-Canadian Political Thought," *University of Toronto Quarterly* 74, 4 (Fall 2005): 884–94; and Jennifer Reid, *Louis Riel and the Creation of Modern Canada: Mythic Discourse and the Postcolonial State* (Albuquerque: University of New Mexico Press, 2008).

3   Gregory Betts, "Non Compos Mentis: A Meta-Historical Survey of the Historiographic Narratives of Louis Riel's 'Insanity,'" *International Journal of Canadian Studies* 38 (2008): 33.

4   Maggie Siggins, *Riel: A Life of Revolution* (Toronto: Harper-Collins, 1994).

5   Thomas Flanagan, *Louis "David" Riel: "Prophet of the New World"* (Toronto: University of Toronto Press, 1979).

6   Gilles Martel, *Le messianisme de Louis Riel* (Waterloo, ON: Wilfrid Laurier University Press, 1984); Manfred Mossman, "The Charismatic Pattern: Canada's Riel Rebellion of 1885 as a Millenarian Protest Movement," *Prairie Forum* 10 (1985): 307–25; and J.M. Bumsted, "The 'Mahdi' of Western Canada? Louis Riel and His Papers," *The Beaver*, August-September 1987, 47–54.

7   See, for instance, Vittorio Lanternari, *Les mouvements religieux des peuples opprimés* (Paris: Maspéro, 1962); and Michael Adas, *Prophets of Rebellion: Millenarian Protest Movements against the European Colonial Order* (Chapel Hill: University of North Carolina Press, 1979).

8   See, for instance, Gilles Martel, "L'idéologie messianique de Louis Riel et ses déterminants sociaux," *Transactions of the Royal Society of Canada* 5, 1 (1986): 229–38.

9   Thomas Flanagan, *Riel and the Rebellion: 1885 Reconsidered* (Saskatoon, SK: Western Producer Prairie Books, 1983).

10  Jennifer I.M. Reid, "'Faire Place à une Race Métisse': Colonial Crisis and the Vision of Louis Riel," in *Religion and Global Culture: New Terrain in the Study of Religion and the Work of Charles H. Long*, ed. Jennifer I.M. Reid (Lanham, MD: Lexington Books, 1992), 51–66; and Jennifer I.M. Reid, *Writing and Colonial Resistance: Mathias Carvalho's Louis Riel* (Aurora, CO: Davies Group, 2011).

11  Reid, *Louis Riel and the Creation of Modern Canada.*

12  Betts, "Non Compos Mentis," 28.

13  Derek Peterson and Darren Walhof, eds., *The Invention of Religion: Rethinking Belief in Politics and History* (Piscataway, NJ: Rutgers University Press, 2002).

14  Markus Dressler and Aryind Mandair, eds., *Secularism and Religion-Making (Reflection and Theory in the Study of Religion)* (New York: Oxford University Press, 2011).

15  José Casanova, "Globalizing Catholicism and the Return to a Universal Church," in *Transnational Religion and Fading States*, ed. Susanne H. Rudolph and James P. Piscatori (Boulder, CO: Westview Press, 1997), 121–42.

16  Timothy Fitzgerald, ed., *Religion and the Secular: Historical and Colonial Formations* (London: Equinox, 2007).

17  For a reflection on the relationship between utopia and ideology as two poles of the political imagination in a millenarian vision, see Pascal Bouvier, *Millénarisme, messianisme, fondamentalisme: Permanence d'un imaginaire politique* (Paris: L'Harmattan, 2008).

18  Purushottama Bilimoria and Andrew B. Irvine, eds., *Postcolonial Philosophy of Religion* (n.p.: Springer, 2009).

19  Marie-Danielle Demélas and Yves Saint-Geours, *Jérusalem et Babylone: Politique et religion en Amérique du Sud: L'Equateur, XVIIIᵉ–XIXᵉ siècles* (Paris, Editions Recherche sur les Civilisations, 1989); and Derek Williams, "Assembling the 'Empire of Morality': State Building Strategies in Catholic Ecuador, 1861–1875," *Journal of Historical Sociology* 14, 2 (2001): 149–74.

20 Peter Beyer, "The Religious Beliefs of Louis Riel: An Analysis Using the Sociological Theory of Niklas Luhmann" (PhD diss., University of Toronto, 1981).

21 The term "neo-ultramontanism" appeared in the 1860s to define the ultra-Catholics who promoted the creation of a Catholic party that would defend the pope's political agenda on a national basis. In French Canada, the expression *intransigeant* was used to define this political current. René Hardy, "Libéralisme Catholique et Ultramontanisme au Québec: Eléments de définitions," *Revue d'histoire de l'Amérique française* 25, 2 (1971): 247–51.

22 Nive Voisine and Jean Hamelin, *Les Ultramontains Canadiens-Français* (Montreal: Boréal Express, 1986).

23 Nadia F. Eid, *Le clergé et le pouvoir politique au Québec: Une analyse de l'idéologie ultramontaine au milieu du XIX^e siècle* (Montreal: Hurtubise HMH, 1978).

24 George F. Stanley, ed., *The Collected Writings of Louis Riel/Les écrits complets de Louis Riel*, vol. 2 (Edmonton: University of Alberta Press, 1985), 22.

25 Léon Pouliot, "Correspondance Louis Riel – Mgr Bourget," *Revue d'histoire de l'Amérique française* 15, 3 (1961): 442.

26 At first, ultramontane thinking reflected Riel's religious conservatism and his desire to see his faith fully conform to the religious and political teachings of the Catholic Church in its most orthodox nineteenth-century incarnation. Only later, as we approach 1885, did ultramontane ideology in its most extreme expression become one of the pillars of Riel's political thinking that saw the rise of a *catholicisme de combat* (a militant fighting Catholicism). It is in this context that we can understand Riel's admiration for García Moreno.

27 Thomas Flanagan, ed., *The Diaries of Louis Riel* (Edmonton: Hurtig Publishers, 1976), 57–88.

28 Stanley, *Collected Writings,* vol. 2, 51, 345, 490, 497.

29 Ignace Bourget, *Fin du voyage à Rome,* Fonds Lartigue-Bourget, folio 901.060, 1870, Archive de la Chancellerie de l'Archevêché de Montréal.

30 For instance, García Moreno had protested against the capture of Rome in letters to Victor Emmanuel II, to the chanceries of the major European powers, and to the governments of all the Latin American republics. These letters underscored a unity of purpose with Bourget, who had made a similar entreaty to Queen Victoria. See Ignace Bourget, *Requêtes à la Reine en faveur du pouvoir temporel des Papes,* Fonds Lartigue-Bourget, folio 901.060, 1871, Archive de la Chancellerie de l'Archevêché de Montréal.

31 Fulvio De Giorgi, "Forme Spirituali, Forme Simboliche, Forme Politiche: La Devozione al s. Cuore," *Rivista di storia della Chiesa in Italia* 48 (1994): 365–459; Miguel Rodriguez, "Du Voeu Royal au Voeu National," *Les Cahiers du Centre de Recherches Historiques* 21 (1998): 53–74; Raymond Jonas, *France and the Cult of the Sacred Heart: An Epic Tale for Modern Times* (Berkeley: University of California Press, 2000).

32 Adrien Thério, Donald Smith, and Patrick Imbert, eds., *Ignace Bourget, Écrivain* (Montreal: Editions Jumonville, 1975).

33 Henri Bourassa, *Le Canada apostolique: Revue des oeuvres de missions des communautés franco-canadiennes* (Montreal: Bibliothèque de l'Action Française, 1919).

34 Riel used this expression in a letter to Bourget, 6–7-XII-1875, *Écrits*, vol. 1, 476.

35 The foundational text of this movement was the eulogy by French journalist Louis Veuillot, one of the most prominent and outspoken adherents of ultramontanism in the nineteenth century: *L'Univers,* 27–28-IX-1875. Veuillot's text was reprinted and widely circulated in French Canada. See, for instance, *Le Collégien,* 1-X-1875.

36 Vincent Viaene, "The Roman Question: Catholic Mobilisation and Papal Diplomacy during the Pontificate of Pius IX (1846–1878)," in *Black International/L'Internationale noire,*

*1870–1878: The Holy See and Militant Catholicism in Europe/Le Saint-Siege et le catholicisme militant en Europe,* ed. Emiel Lamberts (Leuven: Leuven University Press, 2002), 135–78.

37  Peter H. Smith, "The Image of a Dictator: Gabriel García Moreno," *Hispanic American Historical Review* 45, 1 (1965): 1–24; Massimo Granata, "L'Intransigentismo Cattolico ed il Mito di García Moreno," *Bollettino dell'Archivio per la Storia del Movimento Sociale Cattolico in Italia* 19, 1 (1984): 49–77; Michel Lagrée, "García Moreno, la révolution et l'imaginaire catholique en France à la fin du XIXᵉ siècle," in *Religion et Révolution,* ed. J-C Martin (Paris: Anthropos, 1994), 203–13.

38  As an example of the universality of this image in the 1880s, it may be noted that Honoré Mercier was dubbed "le García Moreno canadien" following the resolution of the Jesuits' estates question in 1888–89. Mercier bore this moniker strategically (as, for instance, when he presented himself as the champion of French-Catholic rights in the Franco-American communities of New England and during a sojourn in Paris). See especially, Pierre Savard, *Jules-Paul Tardivel, la France et les États-Unis, 1851–1905* (Quebec City: Presses de l'Université Laval, 1967), 69; and Gilles Gallichan, *Honoré Mercier: La politique et la culture* (Sillery, QC: Septentrion, 1994), 53.

39  Raoul Girardet, *Mythes et mythologies politiques* (Paris: Seuil, 1986); Chiara Bottici, *A Philosophy of Political Myth* (New York: Cambridge University Press, 2007); and Didier Fischer, *L'Homme Providentiel: Un mythe politique en République de Thiers à de Gaulle* (Paris: L'Harmattan, 2009).

40  Quote by Jules-Paul Tardivel, renowned ultra-Catholic journalist of the late nineteenth century, to insist that French Canada could be saved only by "un homme providentiel" like Gabriel García Moreno. See *La Vérité,* 16-II-1884.

41  R.P.A. Berthe, *García Moreno: Président de l'Équateur, vengeur et martyr du droit chrétien (1821–1875)* (Paris: Retaux-Bray, 1887). After barely six months on the shelves, the first edition had sold five thousand copies.

42  José Casanova, "Globalizing Catholicism and the Return to a Universal Church," in *Transnational Religion and Fading States,* ed. Susanne Hoeber Rudolph and James P. Piscatori (Boulder, CO: Westview Press, 1997): 121–42.

43  An example of this marginalization of the neo-ultramontane political agenda was the unanimous reaction against the Tardivel's utopia of "République de Nouvelle-France." The reaction was not based only on the marginal interest in the idea of independence but also in the use of García Moreno's regime as a model. Jean-François Bélisle, "García Moreno de Carne y Hueso ou le caractère mythique du modèle d'homme d'état chrétien dans les milieux Ultramontains du Canada français," in *Constructions identitaires et pratiques sociales,* ed. Jean-Pierre Wallot (Ottawa: Presses de l'Université d'Ottawa, 2002): 344–58.

44  In addition to acquiring prerogatives in the fields of education, health care, and social work, the Catholic Church assumed the role of public censor through the Index Librorum Prohibitorum. Although it did not carry the force of law, the Index provided a means by which the institutional Church imposed and enforced social norms, which were generally accepted by the majority of the population. See Philippe Sylvain and Nive Voisine, *Histoire du Catholicisme Québécois: Réveil et consolation (1840–1898),* vol. 3 (Montreal: Boréal Express, 1991).

45  "Like a snake mesmerising a bird, Riel mesmerised the Metis. He lured them to him so they could become a toy to his ambitions." "Troisième lettre du frère Piquet," in *Le véritable Riel* (Montreal: Imprimerie générale, 1887), 29.

46  Flanagan, *Riel and the Rebellion.*

47  Flanagan, *Louis "David" Riel*, 155.
48  Martel, *Le messianisme de Louis Riel*, 6, 65, 115, 189.
49  Nadia F. Eid, *Le clergé et le pouvoir politique au Québec*, 156.
50  Raymond Huel, *Proclaiming the Gospel to the Indians and the Métis* (Edmonton: University of Alberta, 1996).
51  James C. Scott, *Domination and the Arts of Resistance: Hidden Transcripts* (New Haven: Yale University Press, 1990).
52  Flanagan, *Louis "David" Riel*, 158.
53  Laura Caso Barrera, "Símbolos Religiosos de Unificación Étnica: El Caso de los Métis (Canadá y los Mayas-Yucatecos)," in *Religiosidad y Resistencia Indígenas Hacia el Fin del Milenio*, ed. A. Barabas (Quito, EC: Ediciones Abya-Yala, 1994), 187–216.
54  Don E. Dumond, "The Talking Crosses of Yucatan: A New Look at Their History," *Ethnohistory* 32 (1985): 291–308.
55  Terry Rugeley, *Yucatán's Maya Peasantry and the Origins of the Caste War* (Austin: University of Texas Press, 1996).
56  Juan de la Cruz, "Proclamación de un Crucero (1850)," in *The Indian Christ, The Indian King: The Indigenous Substrate of Maya Myth and Ritual*, ed. Victoria Reifler Bricker (Austin: University of Texas Press, 1981), 104.
57  Jesús Lizama Quijano, "Las Señales del Fin del Mundo: Una Aproximación a la Tradición Profética de los Cruzoob," in *Religión Popular de la Reconstrucción Histórica al Análisis Antropológico*, ed. Genny Negroe Sierra and Francisco Fernández Repetto (Mérida: Universidad Autónoma de Yucatán, 2000), 140–56.
58  Quetzil E. Castañeda, "'We Are *Not* Indigenous!' An Introduction to the Maya Identity of Yucatan," *Journal of Latin American Anthropology* 9, 1 (2004): 36–63; and Wolfgang Gabbert, *Becoming Maya: Ethnicity and Social Inequality in Yucatan since 1500* (Tucson: University of Arizona Press, 2004).
59  Nelson Reed, *The Caste War of Yucatan* (Stanford: Stanford University Press, 1964), 196–98.
60  Steve J. Stern, ed., *Resistance, Rebellion, and Consciousness in the Andean Peasant World: 18th to 20th Centuries* (Madison: University of Wisconsin Press, 1987); and Friedrich Katz, ed., *Riot, Rebellion, and Revolution: Rural Social Conflict in Mexico* (Princeton, NJ: Princeton University Press, 1988).
61  Alicia Barabas, *Utopías Indias: Movimientos Sociorreligiosos en México* (Mexico City: Instituto Nacional de Antropología e Historia, 2002); and Alberto Flores Galindo and Manuel Burga, "Que es la Utopía Andina?" *Allpanchis* 20 (1982): 85–102.
62  Pierre Pluchon, *Vaudou, Sorciers, Empoisonneurs: De Saint-Domingue à Haïti* (Paris: Kathala, 1987).
63  Frank Graziano, *The Millennial New World* (New York: Oxford University Press, 1999).
64  Paul J. Vanderwood, *The Power of God against the Guns of Government: Religious Upheaval in Mexico at the Turn of the Nineteenth Century* (Stanford: Stanford University Press, 1998).
65  Robert M. Levine, *Vale of Tears: Revisiting the Canudos Massacre in Northeastern Brazil, 1893–1897* (Berkeley: University of California Press, 1995).
66  Eric J. Hobsbawm, *Primitive Rebels: Studies in Archaic Forms of Social Movement in the 19th and 20th Centuries* (Manchester: Manchester University Press, 1959).
67  Gary W. Trompf, "Millenarism: History, Sociology, and Cross-Cultural Analysis," *Journal of Religious History* 24, 1 (2000): 103–24.
68  Marco Aurelio Navarro-Génie, *Augusto "César" Sandino: Messiah of Light and Truth* (Syracuse, NY: Syracuse University Press, 2002). In this regard the parallel that Reid makes between Riel, Carvalho, and especially Marti is interesting. Reid, *Writing and Colonial*

*Resistance,* 57–76; Albert Braz, "Promised Land/Cursed Land: The peculiar Canada of Mathias Carvalho," *Interfaces Brasil/Canadá* 1, 1 (2001): 119–29.

69  Conceived largely in reaction to the hanging of Louis Riel, Tardivel uses the 1869 constitution of García Moreno as a source of inspiration to elaborate the institutional framework of the utopian French Canadian state. Pierre Savard, *Jules-Paul Tardivel: La France et les Etats-Unis, 1851–1905* (Quebec City: Presses de l'Université Laval, 1967). Faced with the marked lack of interest within Quebec society for his societal project, Tardivel conceived of the coming of his Catholic republic as an event occurring in a "distant" future. In 1895, Tardivel also published a futuristic novel that saw the founding of the "Republic of New France" as occurring in 1945. *Pour la Patrie: Roman du XXᵉ Siècle* (Montreal: Cadieux and Derome, 1895).

70  Renato Moro, "Religion and Politics in the Time of Secularisation: The Sacralisation of Politics and Politicisation of Religion," *Totalitarian Movements and Political Religions* 6, 1 (June 2005): 71–86.

71  Allen Wells and Gilbert M. Joseph, *Summer of Discontent, Seasons of Upheaval: Elite Politics and Rural Insurgency in Yucatan, 1876–1915* (Stanford: Stanford University Press, 1996), 44–46.

72  Pekka Hamalainen, *The Comanche Empire* (The Lamar Series in Western History) (New Haven, CT: Yale University Press, 2008).

# 6

# Rethinking Edward Ahenakew's Intellectual Legacy: Expressions of nêhiyawi-mâmitonêyihcikan (Cree Consciousness or Thinking)

*Tasha Beeds*

As ARTICULATED BY MANY Indigenous scholars, writers, storytellers, and kêhtê-ayak (Old Ones),[1] we must write and speak from our own places of being and experience. If we do so, we can ground our research in tâpwêwin (truth). The first words often given by nêhiyawak (Cree and Cree-Métis people)[2] and other Indigenous peoples articulate kinship and territory connections, placing introductions within the web of wâhkôtowin (kinship/ the way we are related to one another and the rest of Creation). As a woman of nêhiyaw Métis and mixed Caribbean ancestry, I was raised within the territories of my mother's people: kinêpiko-maskotêw (Snake Plains), atâhk-akohp (Star-Blanket/Sandy Lake First Nations), and nêwo-nâkiwin ([the] Fourth Stop – Mont Nebo). These are the territories of my maternal ancestors, the places where they walked, lived, loved, birthed, and died. nimosômak (my grandfathers) were men of the land and nôhkomak (my grandmothers) were keepers of it. Their bones rest under the prairie grass and their voices whisper with the wind through the poplars, jack pines, and maples. Following the trail of nêhiyaw Métis poet and writer Gregory Scofield in *Thunder through My Veins*, I "claim the rite" to the voices of my people – all of the grandmothers and grandfathers whom I embody.[3] When I entered the world, they entered it again through me. They are the ancestors who flow through my consciousness, who are beside me always, and whose spirits animate the territories I call home.

My scholarship emerges from this space of nêhiyawi-mâmitonêyihcikan (Cree consciousness) and, like other contributors to this volume, especially Carmen Lansdowne and Denise Nadeau, I consider my academic endeavours to be much more than an intellectual exercise. As a scholar, I believe that a crucial part of my responsibility is to contribute to the recovery of Indigenous intellectual, emotional, physical, and spiritual spaces, both within and outside of academia. In light of this responsibility, I consciously attempt to work "on the inside of language" as Kiowa writer Scott Momaday states:

There is nothing more powerful [than words]. When one ventures to speak, when he [or she][4] utters a prayer or tells a story, he [or she] is dealing with forces that are supernatural and irresistible. He [or she] assumes great risks and responsibilities. He [or she] is clear and deliberate in his [or her] mind and in his [or her] speech; he [or she] will be taken at his [or her] word ... To be careless in the presence of words, on the inside of language, is to violate a fundamental morality.[5]

I was raised to be aware of words and the spiritual power they carry when one is speaking and, by extension, when one is writing. As such, I approach my work in academia by carrying an awareness of my "word bundles"[6] as well as an awareness of the responsibilities I have to them and to the ancestral, territorial, and communal connections that inform my work.

As a child, I could feel my ancestors when I picked blueberries, saskatoons, and chokecherries with my aunties and mother, and when I rode in the back of the truck with nôhkom and nimosôm as we made our way to different reserves for feasts, ceremonies, and celebrations. I stepped in the same places as my ancestors did when I followed my uncle and cousins through the bush hunting deer and when we gathered at the lake to fish. I heard my ancestors when nimosôm and I sat back to back under the trees and he told me the stories of kistêsinâw/wîsahkêcâhk (Elder Brother/Sacred Being),[7] of the mêmêkwêsisak (Little People/Sacred Being), and of the wîtihkow (a Sacred Being of Cannibalistic Darkness). It was through nimosôm that I first came to know these spiritual beings that are housed in the âtayôhkêwina (sacred stories); at the time, I never realized what a gift he was giving me. Others from my community, like my teacher and mentor Maria Campbell, provided me with another level of understanding in regards to the âtayôhkêwina. From her, I also came to know the work of the late nêhiyaw Anglican Minister Edward Ahenakew. Because he was from atâhk-akohp, some of my family members had personally known him. In fact, one of his sisters, Flora, married into the Beeds family. I had heard of Edward Ahenakew growing up; I knew he was very well respected within nêhiyaw and Métis communities, but I never realized the legacy he left for nêhiyawak until I began to study his life and writing.

## A Life of Convergence

In the territories of Western Indigenous Nations, Edward Ahenakew was one of the first nêhiyaw people in the post-reserve era to bridge the Indigenous and non-Indigenous worlds in terms of language, spirituality, and politics. Born in 1885, he was an Anglican Minister and a nêhiyaw napêw (Cree man); he was also a leader of the people and of the church; he wrote and spoke both English and nêhiyawêwin (the Cree language); he was also a linguist, a writer, and an oral historian. Ahenakew was very well educated in both the Euro-Canadian school system and the nêhiyaw system. He was exposed to classical nêhiyaw ideas, philosophies, and language by the nêhiyaw kêhtê-ayak who surrounded him during his childhood and as an adult. He was also highly skilled and competent in the Euro-Canadian education system. In 1903, Ahenakew passed his junior matriculation exams and went on to teach at John Smith First Nations as well as Sturgeon Lake and Fort a la Corne.[8] He attended Wycliffe College in Toronto and then Emmanuel College in Saskatoon, where he received his degree in theology. He was ordained in 1912 as an Anglican Minister and served eight different First Nations communities.[9] After the 1918 flu epidemic, he enrolled in the Faculty of Medicine at the University of Alberta but had to leave due to physical illness and other circumstances. In 1920, he served as the first president of the League of Indians of Western Canada.[10] Ahenakew was made a canon of St. Alban's Cathedral in 1933 and received an honorary doctorate of divinity in 1947.[11] His accomplishments extended to the writing world when he published "Cree Trickster Tales," a section of the nêhiyaw spiritual narratives known as the âtayôhkêwina (sacred stories) in 1929 in the *Journal of American Folklore*. In 1938, he was instrumental in helping to create a Cree-English Dictionary.[12] He also wrote and distributed a publication called the *Cree Guide*, which was written primarily in syllabics, the nêhiyaw writing system.[13] Finally, the oral narratives with which he was entrusted by nêhiyaw leader kâ-pitikow (Thunderchild) were published posthumously in 1973 in a book titled *Voices of the Plains Cree*, edited by Ruth Buck. It is clear Ahenakew saw value in both nêhiyawêwin (the Cree language) and English.

In many ways, Ahenakew epitomized not only an era of transition but also one of intersection. Often, discourse about Indigenous and non-Indigenous societies and people focuses on the diametrical differences between them instead of the ways in which they exhibit similarities. Members of contemporary Indigenous intelligentsia, however, such as Anishinaabe scholar Dale Turner, are a part of a new generation of Indigenous people who examine manifestations of these points of convergence and the ways they overlap. For instance, Turner states: "As a matter of survival, Aboriginal intellectuals must engage the non-Aboriginal intellectual landscape from which their political rights and sovereignty are put to use in Aboriginal communities."[14] By engaging and seeing the ways Indigenous peoples have historically adapted "outsider" knowledge, we can also envision new means of bringing our traditional ways of knowing into contemporary situations. Edward Ahenakew exemplifies resiliency and adaptability in his engagement of the non-Indigenous intellectual landscape, although some scholars have argued he was inherently conflicted with his multiple and differing roles.

Often, Ahenakew's vital role in the preservation of nêhiyawiwin (Creeness) is not taken into account by many scholars simply because he was a Christian minister; others have missed key elements in regards to their analysis of Ahenakew's place in history by removing it from the paradigm of nêhiyaw culture. If one examines him in the context of nêhiyawi-mâmitonêyihcikan, like nêhiyaw scholar Winona Wheeler does, one can see how Ahenakew drew upon his nêhiyaw beliefs, wherein "conflict" is not a necessary outcome of the meeting of cultures. Because of his varying roles, it is clear Ahenakew achieved what nêhiyaw Métis scholar Joe Couture describes as a "pluridimensional state of being."[15] Instead of simply choosing one way or the other, Ahenakew achieved this state of being by becoming all that he was capable of becoming. Furthermore, because he was grounded in nêhiyawi-mâmitonêyihcikan through his early life experiences, his in-depth mentorship with kêhtê-ayak, such as kâ-pitikow, and through his knowledge of nêhiyaw oral histories, he was able to channel mamâhtâwisiwin into his writing. "mamâhtâwisiwin," as a noun, is the Great Mystery; as a verb, it is the process of tapping into the life force. It also denotes the spiritual power that stretches beyond our own historicity to other times and places. Ermine further concludes: "This Cree concept describes a capacity to be or do anything, to be creative."[16] Ahenakew was creative in his capacity to be and, like many others of his generation, looked for ways to move through a time of major upheaval in nêhiyaw culture and society in order to bring the past forward so that future generations could benefit.

## Edward Ahenakew's Transitioning of "ê-kî-mâyahkamikahk" (When/Where It Went Wrong)

Ahenakew was born during the 1885 Resistance, a time of great change for Indigenous peoples in their territories of western Canada. In nêhiyaw oral history, the Resistance is much more than an armed conflict between nêhiyaw Métis and Euro-Canadians. According to many nêhiyawak, this time period is known as ê-kî-mâyahkamikahk (when/where it went wrong). This is an era marked with pâstâhowin or the transgressions of nêhiyaw natural laws. By forcefully restructuring the land, Euro-Canadians negatively shifted the âtayôhkanak, the spiritual powers of the land. Indigenous people's place within the land, and within the realm of the âtayôhkanak, was also radically altered, thus negatively affecting the ties of wâhkôtowin. This is the era when Euro-Canadians attempted to control the land, the beings, and the people, violently disregarding nêhiyawak core values such as honour, humility, truth, and respect in the process.

The kêhtê-ayak who mark this time period with the heaviness of pâstâhowin do so because some of them were only one or two generations removed from the events, and they see their effects today, in the young people and in the environment. Often, these lived memories are shadowed with pain and sadness for nêhiyawak. For them, this time period was one of great suffering. As Noel Dyck states: "The events of 1885 sealed the fate of the reserve agricultural program and provided the pretext for the imposition of a repressive system of reserve administration that lasted until the middle of the twentieth century."[17] pîhtokahânapiwiyin (Poundmaker) "remarked that after the uprising '[being] Indian was like being in a cage ... There was no freedom for an Indian.' [pîhtokahânapiwiyin] Poundmaker was also referring to how this marginalization had become not only social, but with the arrival of the pass system, became physical as well."[18] Indigenous peoples were, as pîhtokahânapiwiyin remarked, physically confined and treated like animals by the Euro-Canadians of the day.

## Bearing ê-kîmâyahkamikahk: The Strength of Edward Ahenakew's ohkoma (Grandmother)

Ahenakew came into the world when it was shifting for his people, and his own narrative of his birth elucidates the hardship and difficulties the people faced and simultaneously honours the strength and determination of his ohkoma. The following narrative was included in a paper titled "Genealogical sketch of my family," which Ahenakew wrote in 1948. He states:[19]

Her name was Keeskanakwas (kîskanakwâs/Cut Sleeve), her Christian Name being Mary. As her husband, Ahenakew, was the brother of a chief, so was she the sister of one, of Chief Red Pheasant Kamekosit-Peyaao who had his hunting grounds in the Battleford country. When the Rebellion broke out, Cut Sleeve was visiting her daughter in that country. All the others of her sons and daughters were in the Prince Albert country. Anxious for them, she left Poundmaker's Reserve where her daughter lived, and started for Sandy Lake, some one hundred and fifty miles away. She was determined to travel over the Thickout Hills. The winter had ended but there was still snow on the ground and there was no road. More than that, she had little food, for her daughter's house had been broken into and ransacked. Snaring a rabbit when she could and eating withered rosehips and shrivelled berries, she was able to keep alive and to go a few miles each day. She mended her moccasins until they could no longer be mended, and then she made others for her feet from pieces of her blanket. Growing steadily weaker, she could travel only a few miles each day, and it was more than a month before she reached Sandy Lake. Fortunately the band had returned from the neutral encampment at Prince Albert. But when she came within sight of her son's camp, it seemed deserted. She crawled towards it, for her stumbling weakness, her worn feet made walking too painful. And at the door to the *teepee,* she found that still more effort was required of her. My mother was quite alone, and it was the hour of my birth.

Had she not come, had she not found still the strength to help, I might not be here to write this today.[20]

Ahenakew encompasses a great deal in this small narrative. He outlines nêhiyaw band territories, his kinship ties, and the prominence of his ohkoma kîskanak-wâs's family while also establishing the influence of Christianity. He also brings the abstraction of the "Rebellion" to a personal level. Much of the documented record about the 1885 Resistance and the surrounding events was recorded through the lens of Euro-Canadian eyes with little acknowledgment, if any, of how the daily lives of Indigenous people were impacted.

In his birth narrative, Ahenakew speaks of how his ohkoma was "anxious" for her family; he captures her love, concern, and fear for her sons and daughters. The troubles have already impacted pîhtokahânapiwiyin and his people, as kîskanakwâs's daughter's home has been ransacked of food. Without stating so outright, the narrative establishes the sense of danger present for Indigenous people and paints a changing landscape where food is no longer plentiful. The inclusion of the place name "Thickout Hills," where kîskanakwâs is "determined" to go, also articulates the difficult terrain she must move through to reach atâhk-akohp. Despite these obstacles, kîskanakwâs walks 150 miles to ensure that her family is safe. At the end of the narrative, Ahenakew honours his ohkoma with his life. He is here because of her strength and courage, and his gift "of writing" is directly connected to her. His gift of writing also allows us, as a new generation of nêhiyawak, to understand the 1885 Resistance from a nêhiyaw perspective. It also allows us to honour those nêhiyaw women who were so often left out of the historical narratives.

The story of Ahenakew's ohkoma and his birth are part of the key to understanding him, not just as an educated Anglican clergyman but also as a nêhiyaw napêw. When I visited Maria Campbell in the summer of 2009 at Gabriel's Crossing, she told me of how, as little as one generation ago, Indigenous women placed the placenta of childbirth in the earth so that the child born would always find his or her way home. Through this ceremony, the connection nêhiyawak have to kikâwinâw-askiy (Our Mother – Earth/Land) is honoured, maintained, and ensured by nêhiyaw women. In his birth narrative, Ahenakew tells us his ohkoma's Christian name, Mary, but it is her nêhiyaw name that he uses. Although influenced by Christianity and educated in the Euro-Canadian system, one can see by his writings that Ahenakew was bound to his people and his territory through the presence and actions of his kêhtê-ayak. Furthermore, as Stan Cuthand notes in the introduction of *Voices of the Plains Cree,* after his birth Ahenakew "was sickly and frail"; subsequently, Ahenakew's mother, Ellen Ermine Skin, "made a solemn vow. If he lived, she would present him to the

Church for the ministry."[21] Pragmatically, by presenting him to the Church, his mother was ensuring that if he did live he would have an education and a chance at life. Her generation was experiencing, first hand, the changes that were coming inevitably to nêhiyawak. Like the ancestors before them, they always looked ahead to ensure the well-being of future generations. As the treaties indicate, education was a part of that planning. On a spiritual level, her vow shows syncretism wherein a belief in the Creator crosses cultures. Many nêhiyawak, including my own mosôm, said that praying in a church or a field, in English or in nêhiyawêwin, was the same: Creator hears all prayers wherever you say them. Furthermore, incorporating elements of Christianity into their spiritual practices and beliefs would not have been something nêhiyawak had never done before. For instance, they brought in other Indigenous cultural spiritual practices from other Indigenous peoples like the Anishinaabe. Regardless of cultural differences, Ahenakew's mother was presenting her son to the Creator. Furthermore, within the context of her nêhiyaw culture, where words are sacred and binding, such a vow would not have been taken lightly. From his birth, Ahenakew's dual path was set.

## Edward Ahenakew's Dual Path: Christianity and okihcitawiyihtamowin (Thinking through the Worthy Men's/Providers' Society)

As a young child, Ahenakew attended the reserve missionary school taught by his uncle Louis Ahenakew. Then, at the age of eleven, he left the reserve to attend the Emmanuel College Boarding School in Prince Albert.[22] After teaching at the John Smith missionary school, he attended Wycliffe College in Toronto.[23] He achieved great success with his studies, as the following excerpt from the history of the Saskatchewan Anglican Diocese articulates:

> With the establishment of Emmanuel College in Saskatoon, he transferred his theological studies there and graduated with the Degree of L.Th. and a B.A. from the University of Saskatchewan. He was appointed a missionary at Cedar Lake on a temporary basis, and after his ordination to the Priesthood in 1912 was appointed to assist Rev. J.R. Matheson at Onion Lake. When Mr. Matheson suffered a paralytic stroke and was unable to continue an active ministry, Edward Ahenakew became responsible for the seven or eight reserves of the Mission which he served well and conscientiously.[24]

One reason he "served" the reserves so well was that he could communicate with the members of his parish. In 1976, the late kêhtê-ayak Norman Burns stated: "Today, hardly anybody goes to church. When we do go, our minister, who is from Kinistino, speaks English. Before, when Edward Ahenakew was a minister, everybody went because he spoke in Cree and we were all able to understand him."[25] In 1918, the flu epidemic hit nêhiyaw territory and, as Maria Campbell describes in *Halfbreed,* "so many of our people died that mass burials were held."[26] During this time period, Canon Ahenakew "helped care for the sick who were unable to access transportation for outside medical care."[27] After bearing witness to the suffering and deaths of his people, and with the goal of providing future assistance to them, Ahenakew received a leave from the church to attend the University of Alberta's Faculty of Medicine to become a physician.[28]

Upon successfully completing three years of medical study, Ahenakew fell ill due to the extreme circumstances in which he was living. He recounted this experience to W. Bleasdell Cameron for an article in *The Western Producer* in 1950:

> "I had very little money," he said, "and was obliged to practice the most rigid economy. I had a small room in an apartment block over the river and I used to buy a good size piece of beef ready roasted; this I placed on the sill outside my window where it froze solid. I lived on this frozen meat and little else. When one piece was finished, I bought another. "Well, after a time I began to feel not too well and it wasn't a great while after until I was down and out. One of the doctors examined me. 'Young man,' he said, 'you're trying to kill yourself; what do you think you are, a polar bear trying to live on frozen meat!' He said my stomach was almost paralyzed so I left the University and did not go back. I was ill for a year though I never stopped working."[29]

This narrative speaks to the strength of Ahenakew's character and spirit. Not only did he live in abject poverty during medical school, but Ahenakew would have been one of the few Indigenous persons in the college – if not the only one. Because the school was in Alberta, he would not have had familial or community support. The demands of undertaking medical studies on one's own are difficult, let alone while facing the other obstacles Ahenakew describes. In the foreword to *Voices of the Plains Cree,* Cuthand adds to the frozen-meat narrative by citing a letter sent by Ahenakew in 1922: "I have been in hospital here (Lloydminster) since I came back from Edmonton (nervous breakdown) and am only getting on my feet again."[30] The University of Alberta's Faculty of Medicine was arguably Ahenakew's "Thickout Hills"; however, in a fashion similar to that of his kôhkom, Ahenakew was determined to help his people. This sense of responsibility to the people is in keeping with nêhiyaw culture. Like the nêhiyawak leaders before him, and of his era, Ahenakew had a profound sense of wâhkôtowin and his place within it.

Ahenakew was also grounded in a nêhiyaw sense of being in terms of his responsibilities and obligations as a nêhiyaw napêw. This grounding emerged from Ahenakew's close kinship ties to some of the most prominent nêhiyaw families of his era. Speaking to Ahenakew's experience in residential school, where two of his cousins make him feel at ease when he first arrives, Stan Cuthand states in the introduction to *Voices of the Plains Cree*: "As they would in later years, this web of family relations connected him with a larger community and eased his transitions from place to place."[31] Ahenakew was a member of nêhiyaw leader atâhk-akohp's family; he also had kinship ties to other leaders. He was, in the Western worldview, the "grandnephew of Chief Poundmaker" and "Star-Blanket"[32]; however, in nêhiyawiwin, pîhtokahânapiwiyin and atâhk-akohp would be his mosômak. His kinship was also extended to other leaders such as mistawâsis (Big Child), kâ-mihkosit pêwayis (Red Pheasant), and wataniy (Wuttunee).[33] As his description of the kisêyiniwak (Old Men) shows, these nêhiyaw leaders had a profound influence on Ahenakew:

> The role ... of Old Man, has been an institution of Indian Life through the centuries ... Old Men have had a responsible and important position to fill with the band. In a sense, they have supplied our moral code, taking the place both of historians and legal advisers. It was the Old Men who were the influence for good, who sought to right wrongs and to settle disputes; it was the Old Men who were qualified to speak, for they had passed through most of the experiences of life, and their own youthful fires were burned out ... An Old Man often had the gift of eloquence, enhanced by descriptive language and by superb mastery of gesture ... All these stories were hoarded in the minds of Old Men[;] they were kept intact, unchanging, entrusted through the years by one generation to the next. An Old Man dared not lie, for ridicule that was keen and general would have been his lot, and his standing as a teller of authentic events would have suffered. Of necessity then, his veracity had to be unimpeachable, and this, together with well-developed powers of observation, made him an authentic repository for the annals of his people, a worthy medium through whom the folklore of previous generations could be transmitted.[34]

The respect in Ahenakew's words shows that he did not sacrifice his sense of nêhiyaw being in taking on the role of canon for the Anglican Church. In comparing the kisêyiniwak to an "institution," Ahenakew emphasizes how, collectively, they represent Euro-Canadian organizations such as the churches and the universities. Ahenakew's respect for the kêhtê-ayak and his kinship ties ensured that Ahenakew learned from leaders such as kâ-pitikow, also known as piyêsiw-awâsis. When he went to kâ-pitikow's reserve to recuperate from the

*Figure 1* pîhtokahânapiwiyin (Poundmaker). Treaty 6
nêhiyaw leader and one of Ahenakew's mosômak.
*Saskatchewan Archives Board, R-B8775*

illness he suffered upon leaving medical school, Ahenakew spent his time collecting the man's oral narratives; this collaboration, *Voices of the Plains Cree,*
was edited by Ruth Buck.

Ahenakew also wrote and published an Anglican newsletter, the *Cree Monthly*
*Guide,* written in nêhiyaw syllabics, and helped to prepare a nêhiyaw-English
dictionary. Ahenakew had few contemporaries, but nêhiyaw Joseph Dion from
Long Lake and Mike Mountain Horse of the Kainai Nation were writing at the
same time that he was. As Cuthand states:

*Figure 2* Treaty 6 nêhiyaw leaders. Standing *(left to right)*: Louis O'Soup and NWMP interpreter and scout Peter Hourie. Seated *(right to left)*: Treaty 6 nêhiyaw leaders. atâhk-akohp (Starblanket), kâh-kwîwîstahâw (Flying in a Circle), and mistawâsis (Big Child). These leaders, along with pîhtokahânapiwiyin above, were some of the Old Men Ahenakew felt were so crucial to nêhiyaw society. Photo taken at the unveiling of the Brant Memorial in Ontario, 16 October 1886. *Library and Archives Canada, C-019258*

*Figure 3* kâ-pitikow/piyêsiw-awâsis (Thunderchild). Ahenakew wrote and published several of kâ-pitikow's oral narratives about nêhiyaw life. These narratives provide valuable insight into the nêhiyaw world before the reserve era. *University of Saskatchewan, University Archives and Special Collections, MSS C550/2/5.18a*

These writers knew enough of the cultural context of the old times to respect them, and although they were Christians they did not want the beliefs of their fathers to be forgotten or discounted ... they spoke their languages, had an instinctive feeling for their people, and had a profound respect for the values of their own communities. They saw themselves defending their communities against ugly stereotypes and condescension through their writing.[35]

All of these writers are examples of how Indigenous peoples synchronized the English language with their own respective cultures and, in doing so, maintained and preserved not only their cultures, but also their languages and worldviews. In addition to his writing, Ahenakew was also active in the League of Indians, a political organization initially formed in what had become Ontario by F.O. Loft, a Haudenosaunee (People of the Longhouse) veteran of the First World War. He sought to improve the lives of his people and other Indigenous nations. Loft travelled extensively "to unite Indians nationally through common concerns with the federal government Indian policies," and he "faced tremendous opposition from the federal government" during a time when Indigenous people were being "charged by police for 'violations' of the existing Pass laws."[36] One of the first meetings in western Canada was held in 1921 at Thunderchild. Rarihokwats states: "The platform was to create unity to battle against oppressive Indian Affairs policy, to promote religious freedom, and to regain the right to travel outside the reserve without passes, demanding that no further land surrenders be undertaken, that economic programs be instituted, and generally, that the spirit and terms of the treaties be honoured and respected."[37] Ahenakew was aware of the oppression his people faced and attempted to take action through his involvement in the League.

As *Voices of the Plains Cree* indicates, Ahenakew was very cognizant of politics and the needs of the people: "The principal aim of the League, I would say, is equality for the Indian as citizen – equality, that is, in the two-fold meaning of privilege and responsibility; and to achieve this objective, our first emphasis must be upon improved educational and health programs."[38] Because of his skills and, I would argue, his respect for the kiseyiniwak, Ahenakew was elected president of the League of Indians of western Canada. The nêhiyaw leaders that Ahenakew spoke so highly of, such as kâ-pitikow, and those of his generation supported Ahenakew in this key political role. These leaders needed someone who could converse in both nêhiyawêwin and English. Ahenakew was, as Cuthand articulates, "the voice of many people during his term."[39] The fact that he held such a prominent position speaks to his reputation among the people as a leader.

Ahenakew continued to be active in the League from 1919 until 1932, when, after a trip to Ottawa on behalf of the League, "the Indian Department urged the bishop to tell him to attend to his duties as a churchman and not to meddle with the affairs of the state."[40] Ahenakew's position as a minister did provide him with a certain amount of power, which he recognized; however, he was still held in check by the Church. Cuthand, recalling a narrative about Ahenakew told to him by his father, states: "They had many talks and he told my father that he believed that white people discriminated against Indians. He felt that the only job an Indian could have was to be a minister in the church because in the church there would be no discrimination."[41] He goes on further to articulate how Ahenakew was "loyal to the Anglican church to the end of his days," although "the church did little to reward his long service."[42] Some might argue that, as an Anglican missionary, Ahenakew was a symbol of assimilation working to convert his people – similar to the argument that English has only served to colonize Indigenous peoples. This critique is a simplistic dichotomy, however, placing Indigeneity in an "either/or" category alongside Christianity. As other essays in this volume emphasize, the categories of "Indigenous" and "Christian" were not mutually exclusive and often intersected in complex and contradictory ways.

Many scholars writing about Ahenakew emphasize this loyalty to the church and his commitment to nêhiyawak as a sign that he was conflicted in his dual roles. Deanna Reder writes: "On one hand he was a fierce critic of government policy and bitter at the prejudice he experienced within the church and in general society. On the other hand he was known by his community to be a devout Christian, loyal to the British Royal family and a devoted Anglican cleric."[43] Reder, citing Cuthand, goes on to articulate how Ahenakew was "caught between two worlds, and was often more loyal to the church."[44] These two characteristics are also reiterated in Goodwill and Sluman's narrative about nêhiyaw leader John Tootoosis. They also cite Cuthand in their interpretation of Ahenakew: "it can be seen from his writings that his heart and instincts were very much with the League. It must have been difficult for him, as it has been for so many Indians, to be thus pulled in two different directions at the same time, but John and others who knew him then felt that Edward's loyalty was first to the church."[45] Ahenakew may have experienced difficulties, but were his roles intrinsically conflicted?

Citing Brundige, Reder concludes that Ahenakew's roles were in opposition to one another and, subsequently, posed a problem that was "a personal one for Aboriginal people under colonization" since "how are we to make sense of our life if we are caught between two opposing narratives?"[46] Inherent in these conclusions regarding Ahenakew as a man whose "position was particularly conflicted as well as scrutinized" is the notion that Christianity and nêhiyawiwin are antagonistic to one another.[47] Although Ahenakew experienced hardship and conflict as a nêhiyaw napêw and as a Christian minister during his lifetime, as did many others of that generation, the two roles are not necessarily "opposing narratives" if one applies the Haudenosaunee theory of "complex understanding."

Onondaga scholar David Newhouse articulates the theory of complex understanding as being rooted in Haudenosaunee thought. This theory "doesn't work in an either-or fashion. A phenomenon is not one thing or another but all things at one time," creating "a constantly changing reality that is capable of transformation at any time."[48] In her article, Reder asks: "Given the generic expectations of autobiography produced in the 1920s, how would Ahenakew, bilingual and literate, an activist and a cleric, a Cree and a Christian, be able to express his opinions and experiences, especially when some of what he articulates is in opposition to himself?"[49] This question places Ahenakew's various roles as antagonistic to one another and makes the argument that, in order to adapt to dominant expectations and have the power of self-expression, he would have to be in opposition to himself. However, instead of viewing Ahenakew as being either a Christian minister or a nêhiyaw leader, the lens of complex understanding allows for fluidity between the two roles. Ahenakew was capable of "transforming" – not only himself but nêhiyaw culture, language, and worldviews – into English in order to make known "the view that the Indians have of certain matters affecting their lives" in order that "others may glimpse what we feel and experience."[50] Ahenakew's reality was a "constantly changing one," but he approached it with a great deal of intelligence and foresight.[51] His reality was also one that was deeply grounded in nêhiyaw-îsîhcikêwina (Cree rituals/culture/ways) and mâmitonêyihcikan.

From the time of his birth, Ahenakew was exposed to nêhiyaw-îsîhcikêwina and mâmitonêyihcikan. His mother's vow to give him to the ministry in exchange for his life is also rooted in nêhiyaw culture and one that would have been impressed upon him as a matter of honour and obligation.[52] By nêhiyaw laws of being, he was bound to the Creator to become a Christian minister. Ahenakew saw how there could be a crossing over between the two spiritualities. Miller, citing Paul Wallace's diary, describes the conversation between Ahenakew and Wallace when Ahenakew was initiated as an okimaw (leader/chief) by the kisêyiniwak:

> [It was] a most impressive ceremony, in the presence of between seven hundred and eight hundred Indians from Saskatchewan and Alberta. Two chiefs placed their hands on his shoulder, and outside, then two others placed their hands on the shoulders of two past chiefs. For half an hour the ceremony continued, and he walked backward and forward while the chiefs prayed over him. I asked if such prayer was at all like our Christian prayers. "Yes" he replied quickly, "like the prayers of the Old Testament."[53]

Wallace goes on to describe Ahenakew as being a "real chief" instead of a "departmental one," with the difference being that "the real chiefs are elected in accordance with the old traditions of the people. The Department Chiefs are chiefs only on the reserves."[54]

Ahenakew was, indeed, a leader of the people; in order to be recognized as such by nêhiyawak, he would have had to have the ability to "walk backward and forward" – to walk in the old traditions and the new ones. As a nêhiyaw napêw, an Anglican minister, a writer, a language speaker, and a leader of the people, Ahenakew was an okihcihtâw (a worthy young man/provider) of his era. He drew upon the traditions of the Old Ones within the nexus of Christianity, showing how nêhiyaw culture is a living, dynamic one.

## The Foundations: "Folklore" and the âtayôhkêwina

In 1929, *The Journal of American Folklore* published Ahenakew's "Cree Trickster Tales." Founded in 1888, the periodical arose out of the American Folklore Society, comprising "a collective of university-based humanities scholars, museum anthropologists, and private citizens – including author Mark Twain and US President Rutherford B. Hayes."[55] William Thoms first used the term "folklore" in Europe in 1846 for "subject matter [that] was 'more a Lore than a Literature' ... to refer to oral genres such as tales, songs, riddles, and proverbs, as well as customs and beliefs."[56] Even from this early definition, the privileging of the written is apparent, as is the idea that the oral is more fallible.

*Figure 4*  Edward Ahenakew, ca. 1910. *Saskatchewan Archives Board, R-B11359*

Thoms's definition of folklore and the discipline of anthropology were foundational to *The Journal*'s mandate. In the first issue, published in 1888, the editorial "On the Field and Work of a Journal of American Folklore" outlines the journal's principal research areas in terms of collection, one of which is the "Lore of the Indian Tribes of North America (myths, tales, etc.)."[57] The notion of the need to preserve the culture and history of the "vanishing Indian" in the face of "civilization" is at the forefront in terms of the materials *The Journal* wished to collect:

A great change is about to take place in the condition of the Indian tribes, and what is to be done must be done quickly. For the sake of the Indians themselves, it is necessary that they should be allowed opportunities for civilization; for our sake and for the future, it is desirable that a complete history should remain of what they have been, since their picturesque and wonderful life will soon be absorbed and lost in the uniformity of the modern world.[58]

The romanticization of Indigenous societies as "picturesque and wonderful" is present in this description as is the notion that, once "civilized," Indigenous peoples will no longer have histories or cultures. Thus, it is up to societies and journals such as that of the *Journal of American Folklore* to document and record Indigenous "lore" for the sake of preserving "what they have been."[59] In an article on the writings of Warren, Standing Bear, and Ahenakew, nêhiyaw historian and scholar Winona Wheeler notes how early Indigenous authors were well aware of the social and cultural positions of their peoples. She states: "No doubt they were influenced by the ethnographic rush into Indian country and by growing public interest in Indigenous lore during this period. However, each also had more resolute purposes."[60] As Wheeler further specifies, Ahenakew wrote to inform non-Indigenous readers and to critique "the demoralizing impact of colonial rule";[61] however, he also wrote for isiniywak (the people).

### Writing for isiniywak: The Intercultural Dialogue of Paul Wallace and Edward Ahenakew

Ahenakew's collection of the âtayôhkêwina was one of the first collections of nêhiyaw oral narratives to be recorded in English and, subsequently, published. Wheeler articulates how Ahenakew, along with other Indigenous writers like Warren and Standing Bear, "were pressed by an urgency to record the sacred teachings, histories, philosophies, and ways of life of their people before the destructive assimilating effects of 'civilization' wiped them from collective tribal memories."[62] During this era, Indigenous people were still being severely restricted. The pass system was in place, policies preventing thirst dances and other ceremonies were enforced while unofficial policies like starvation were encouraged, residential schools were rampant, and Indigenous peoples were not recognized as "citizens" despite the fact they had served in the First World War. The threat of losing these teachings was reflected in Ahenakew's lived experiences. As a man educated in two knowledge systems, and as an Anglican clergyman, Ahenakew had access to avenues his people would not have had otherwise, avenues such as that provided by Paul Wallace.

One of the reasons Ahenakew's "Cree Trickster Tales" was published was because he received assistance from historian, anthropologist, and folklorist Paul Wallace, whom he met when he attended the University of Alberta. As Miller states: "One of the most significant influences on Edward Ahenakew and his writings was his friendship with Paul Wallace, a graduate student at the University of Alberta and later professor of English at Lebanon Valley College, Annville[,] Pennsylvania, who specialized in editing and publishing collections of historical documents."[63] Miller notes that, although Wallace "believed Ahenakew could be a doorway between Cree knowledge and outsiders' appreciation of it," he also "compartmentalized his friendship with Ahenakew."[64] In other words, Wallace placed Ahenakew in various metaphorical boxes: Ahenakew was the "Indian" informant with a wealth of information that Wallace's profession could make use of, he was Wallace's peer at the University of Alberta,'he was a fellow writer and historian, and he was a friend.

Initially, Wallace appears to edit Ahenakew's work with his permission.[65] The editorial board of the *Journal* had also corresponded with Wallace, desiring that Ahenakew write "'additional notes to increase the scientific value of the narratives."[66] The final text was published with only a few explanatory notes and without credit or thanks to Wallace, so it is unclear whether Wallace in fact did edit the narratives. Either way, Ahenakew's friendship with Wallace continued, and he continued to send Wallace information about nêhiyaw life, culture, and traditions, as is evident in a letter dated 10 June 1948. In the letter, Ahenakew expresses his happiness about Wallace's son following in his father's footsteps: "I am so glad that he too is interested in a work that needs to be done now."[67] Almost twenty years after publishing "Cree Trickster Tales," Ahenakew was still pressed by the urgency to record nêhiyaw histories and cultural practices.

Although Miller writes that "what is indeterminable was whether Ahenakew cared about what was actually published when his purposes seem to have been thwarted by the editorial process and scholarly standards required,"[68] Ahenakew's initial purpose is clear both in his letter to Wallace and in his description of how he "worked to entertain partly and also to be as near to the actual form of the legends [as possible]."[69] One of the functions of the âtayôhkêwina is to "entertain," and the fact that Akenakew wanted to be "near to the actual form" of the narratives shows how he respected kâ-pitikow and the responsibilities of receiving and carrying these narratives. As the next generation from the Old Men whom he spoke so highly of and whom he likened to an institution wherein truth in telling stories is foundational, Ahenakew was aware that his own "veracity had to be unimpeachable."[70] Grounded in nêhiyawi-mâmitonêyihcikan, Ahenakew "demonstrated respect for [his] teachers, [he] humanized rather than objectified [his] scholarship."[71] He was a scholar ahead of his time. Ahenakew might have been frustrated in regards to the process of publishing, but he was dedicated to ensuring that the core of nêhiyawak, the âtayôhkêwina and kistêsinâw/wîsahkêcâhk, were preserved for future generations.

Although written in English and published in an anthropological journal, Edward Ahenakew's "Cree Trickster Tales" is a map of nêhiyaw-isîhcikêwina, nêhiyawi-mâmitonêyihcikan, and nêhiyawi-itâpisiniwin for those who are seeking to find their way. The importance of these sacred narratives and of kistêsinâw/wîsahkêcâhk to nêhiyawak culture and sense of being cannot be underestimated. For nêhiyawak, the âtayôhkêwina demonstrate our relationship to land, articulate a set of laws that govern people, and contain both our spiritual history and our philosophies. They mark wâhkôtowin and show us what happens when those relationships are out of balance. In addition, our understandings and interpretations weave around these narratives to animate the living present. By publishing a section of the âtayôhkêwina, Edward Ahenakew has given us the opportunity to kiskinômâsowin; we can guide ourselves into nêhiyaw mâmitonêyihcikan thought, theories, and paradigms. He created multiple dialogues between the nêhiyaw and the English world. By doing so, Ahenakew created new discursive possibilities, which we are still learning from, and he ensured that there was a path to help us find our way into the world of our ancestors.

kinanâskomitinâwâw for taking the time to read this chapter.

## Appendix: Cree Glossary of Terms

| | |
|---|---|
| atâhk-akohp | Star-Blanket/Sandy Lake First Nations |
| âtayôhkanak | Spirit Beings |
| âtayôhkêwina | Sacred Stories |
| ê-kî-mâyahkamikahk | 1885 – when/where it went wrong |
| isiniywak | the People |
| kâ-mihkosit pêwayis | Red Pheasant |
| kâ-pitikow | Thunderchild |
| kêhtê-ayak | Old Ones |
| kikâwinâw-askiy | Our Mother – Earth/Land |
| kinêpiko-maskotêw | Snake Plains/mistawâsis First Nations |
| kisêyiniw | Old Man |
| kisêyiniwak | Old Men |
| kîskanakwâs | Cut Sleeve, Edward Ahenakew's grandmother |
| kiskinômâsowin | education/guiding yourself |
| kistêsinâw/wîsahkêcâhk | Our Elder Brother/Spiritual Being |
| kôhkom | your grandmother |
| mêmêkwêsisak | Little People; Spirit Beings |
| mistawâsis | Big Child |
| mosômak | grandfathers |
| napêw | man |
| nêhiyaw | Cree |
| nêhiyawak | Cree people and Métis people |
| nêhiyaw-îsîhcikêwina | Cree rituals/culture/ways |
| nêhiyawi-itâpisiniwin | a Cree worldview or way of seeing |
| nêhiyawi-mâmitonêyihcikan | Cree consciousness/thinking |
| nêhiyawêwin | the Cree language |
| nêhiyawiwin | Creeness |
| nêwo-nâkiwin | the Fourth Stop – Mont Nebo |
| nimosôm | my grandfather |
| nôhkom | my grandmother |

| | |
|---|---|
| ohkoma | her/his grandmother |
| okihcihtâw | a worthy young man/provider |
| okimaw | leader/chief |
| pahkakos | A Skeletal Spirit/Being |
| pâstâhowin | transgression/when one does something wrong it comes back to him/her |
| pîhtokahânapiwiyin | Poundmaker |
| tâpwêwin | truth |
| wâhkôtowin | kinship/the way we relate to one another and the rest of Creation |
| wataniy | Wuttunee |
| wîtihkow | A being of cannibalistic darkness; greatly feared |

## Acknowledgments

I would like to acknowledge the Social Sciences and Humanities Research Council and the Gabriel Dumont Institute for supporting my research. I also acknowledge Maria Campbell, my Uncle Phillip Ledoux, Neal McLeod, the late Jerry McLeod, and the late Charlie Burns for their assistance in helping me to understand who Edward Ahenakew was and the era he lived through.

## Notes

1   In similar style to Leanne Simpson's *Dancing on Our Turtle's Back,* I translate terms only once in the text and then include all terms in a glossary at the end of the chapter. I, too, am not a fluent speaker of nêhiyawêwin – I am a language learner. However, my teacher and mentor Maria Campbell, along with many other language speakers, has told me it is essential to use my language, to think through it, and to include it whenever I can as it helps keep the language alive, encourages learning, and denotes cultural pride. Further- more, although most styles italicize "foreign" languages, it is my position that nêhiyawêwin must be placed beside English in an equal textual position. I am using English as a means of discourse; however, I am placing nêhiyaw language within this text as a theoretical and a living space – a space where words carry spiritual power and a space that I call home. nêhiyaw words are also not capitalized according to the convention of the orthography built by Leonard Bloomfield, Ida McLeod, Freda Ahenakew, and H.C. Wolfart. I take responsibility for any errors in this chapter. See Leanne Simpson, *Dancing on Our Turtle's Back: Stories of Nishnaabeg Re-Creation, Resurgence and a New Emergence* (Winnipeg: Arbeiter Ring, 2011), 26 and throughout.

2   Although many Indigenous scholars demarcate a line between "nêhiyaw" and "Métis," I include both together (in keeping with a teaching from Maria) in order to recognize the fluid kinship lines and to recognize their shared worldview in the context of the territories this essay is referring to. When I use the term "nêhiyawak," I am referring to those who see the world through nêhiyawi-itâpisiniwin (Cree way of seeing/worldview).

3   Gregory Scofield, *Thunder through My Veins* (Toronto: Harper Flamingo, 1999), xvi.

4   I've added the feminine pronoun for the ease of readers unfamiliar with Indigenous languages and thought – for instance, in Cree, there are no gendered pronouns, although there are distinctions made between genders within the language.

5   Scott Momaday, *The Man Made of Words: Essays, Stories, and Passages* (New York: St. Martin's Press, 1997), 16.

6   Maria uses this term to explain the power and sacred nature of words: each word carries with it a number of meanings and history; thus we must be very careful with what we say and how we say it.

7   kistêsinâw/wîsahkêcâhk is the Sacred Being who is at the centre of the âtayôhkêwina. Where I come from, nêhiyawak do not use his real name, wîsahkêcâhk, until snow is on the ground. When the ground is bare, we call him kistêsinâw, or Elder Brother. I use both terms here in keeping with this understanding.

8   W.F. Payton, *An Historical Sketch of the Diocese of Saskatchewan of the Anglican Church of Canada* (Prince Albert: The Anglican Diocese of Saskatchewan, 1974), chap. 21, n.p.

9   Ibid.

10  Ibid.

11  Ibid.

12  Ibid.

13  Ibid.

14  Dale Turner, *This Is Not a Peace Pipe: Towards a Critical Indigenous Philosophy* (Toronto: University of Toronto, 2006), 91.

15  Joe Couture, "Explorations in Native Knowing," in *The Cultural Maze,* ed. J. Friesen (Calgary, AB: Detselig Enterprises, 1991), 63.

16  Willie Ermine, "Aboriginal Epistomology," in *First Nations Education in Canada: The Circle Unfolds,* ed. Marie Battiste and Jean Barman (Vancouver: University of British Columbia, 1995), 104.

17  Noel Dyck, *What Is the Indian "Problem": Tutelage and Resistance in Canadian Indian Administration* (St. John's: Institute of Social and Economic Research, Memorial University of Newfoundland, 1991), 56.

18  Kurt Boyer, "1885 – Aftermath," *Our Legacy,* http://scaa.sk.ca/ourlegacy/exhibit_aftermath.

19  Emma LaRocque "challenges Western intellectual conventions with their hegemonic, canonical assumptions," noting that Indigenous voices and discourses must be read differently. She articulates how writing and researching within an Indigenous space sometimes requires the citation of generous portions from Indigenous narratives "without excessive intrusion." Citing Zimmerman's call for a "critical approach that allows for 'extensive quotations … to stand for themselves,'" LaRocque states she is "re-citing the documents because they have not been readily available to readers, nor have they received the hearing they deserve." I agree with both LaRocque and Zimmerman in critiquing the Western convention that frowns upon the use of long quotations; due to the nature and complexity of Indigenous narratives, Indigenous oral traditions, and Indigenous methodologies, there are times when a long quotation is needed in order to articulate the full meaning or intent of the words. In this manner, I, too, challenge the discursive "authority" of Western practices in order to clear more pathways to Indigenous ways of being. See Emma LaRocque, *When the Other Is Me* (Winnipeg: University of Manitoba Press, 2012), 12.

20  Ruth Buck, "The Story of the Ahenakews," *Saskatchewan History Magazine* 17, 1 (1964): 23.

21  Edward Ahenakew, *Voices of the Plains Cree,* ed. Ruth Buck (Regina: Canadian Plains Research Center, 1995), x.

22  Buck, "The Story of the Ahenakews," 12.

23  Payton, *An Historical Sketch,* chap. 21, n.p.

24  Ibid., chap. 21, n.p.

25  Saskatchewan Indian Cultural Centre, *kâtâayuk [kêhtê-ayak]: Saskatchewan Indian Elders* (Saskatoon, SK: SICC, 1976).

26  Maria Campbell, *Halfbreed* (Toronto: McClelland and Stewart, 1973), 20.

27  Charlene Crevier, "Edward Ahenakew," in *The Encyclopaedia of Saskatchewan,* ed. Blair Stonechild et al. (Regina: Canadian Plains Research Center, 2006), http://esask.uregina.ca/entry/ahenakew_edward_1885-1961.html.

28  Ibid.
29  Payton, *An Historical Sketch,* n.p.
30  Ahenakew, quoted in Stan Cuthand, foreword to *Voices of the Plains Cree,* by Edward Ahenakew, xiii.
31  Ibid., xi.
32  Crevier, "Edward Ahenakew."
33  Ibid.
34  Ahenakew, *Voices of the Plains Cree,* 10.
35  Ibid., xx.
36  Rarihokwats, "Historical Notes on the League of Indian Nations," *A Four Arrows Historical Sketch,* 19 October 2001, 10.
37  Ibid., 12.
38  Ahenakew, *Voices of the Plains Cree,* 85.
39  Cuthand, "Introduction," *Voices of the Plains Cree,* xx.
40  Ibid., xviii.
41  Ibid.
42  Ibid., xviii.
43  Deanna Reder, "Understanding Cree Protocol in the Shifting Passages of 'Old Keyam,'" *Studies in Canadian Literature* 31, 1 (2006): 60.
44  Ibid., 60.
45  Jean Goodwill and Norma Sluman, *John Tootoosis: Biography of a Cree Leader* (Ottawa: Golden Dog Press, 1982), 154.
46  Reder, "Understanding Cree Protocol," 60.
47  Ibid., 61.
48  David Newhouse, "Knowledge in a Multi-cultural World" (keynote address presented at the First Nations Technical Institute 14th Annual PLA Conference, 2003), 4.
49  Reder, "Understanding Cree Protocol," 61.
50  Ahenakew, *Voices of the Plains Cree,* 9.
51  Newhouse, "Knowledge in a Multi-cultural World," 4.
52  Ahenakew, *Voices of the Plains Cree,* x.
53  David Miller, "Edward Ahenakew's Tutelage by Paul Wallace: Reluctant Scholarship, Inadvertent Preservation," in *Gathering Places: Aboriginal and Fur Trade Histories,* ed. Caroline Podruchny and Laura Peers (Vancouver: UBC Press, 2010), 257.
54  Ibid., 257.
55  "About the American Folk Lore Society," *American Folklore Society,* http://www.afsnet.org/?page=AboutAFS.
56  Rosalyn Blyn-LaDrew, "Geoffrey Keating, William Thoms, Raymond Williams, and the Terminology of Folklore: 'Bêaloideas' as a 'Keyword,'" *Folklore Forum,* 27, 2 (1996): 5.
57  *Journal of American Folklore* 1, 1 (April–June 1888): 3–7.
58  Ibid., 3.
59  Ibid.
60  Winona Wheeler, "Guidance from Early Fourth World Indigenous Resistance Literature in the Americas: The Historical Writings of Warren, Standing Bear and Ahenakew," in *Understanding and Interrogating Fourth World Literatures,* ed. R.S. Patteti (New Delhi: Prestige International Publications, 2011), 8. At the time of writing, this article was still in press and permission was granted by the author to cite draft.
61  Ibid., 8.
62  Ibid.
63  Miller, "Edward Ahenakew's Tutelage," 251.

64 Ibid., 257.
65 Ibid., 259.
66 Ibid.
67 Edward Ahenakew to Paul Wallace, 10 June 1948, Boas Linguistics Collection of the American Philosophical Society, Collection 68 – Wallace Papers, Philadelphia North American Archives, Philadelphia.
68 Miller, "Edward Ahenakew's Tutelage," 258.
69 Ibid., 259.
70 Ahenakew, *Voices of the Plains Cree,* 10.
71 Wheeler, "Guidance from Early Fourth World Indigenous Resistance Literature in the Americas," 7.

# Part 3
# Contemporary Encounters

# 7

# Aporia, Atrocity, and Religion in the Truth and Reconciliation Commission of Canada

*Siphiwe Dube*

> *Even today, religious traditions perform the function of articulating an awareness of what is lacking or absent. They keep alive a sensitivity to failure and suffering. They rescue from oblivion the dimensions of our social and personal relations in which advances in cultural and social rationalization have caused utter devastation.*
>
> – HABERMAS, *BETWEEN NATURALISM AND RELIGION*

THIS CHAPTER BEGINS WITH the observation that recent public discussions about the Indian residential schools in Canada serve as a stark reminder of Christianity's problematic role in Canadian Indigenous history. In light of this troubled history, this chapter examines the possible roles for religion within the mandate of the Truth and Reconciliation Commission of Canada, also known as the Indian Residential Schools Truth and Reconciliation Commission (henceforth the TRCC, or the commission). Specifically, I address the complex ways in which Christian discourse – encompassing both the religious language and religious institutions of Christianity – informs the commission's aim of truth-finding and reconciliation.[1] Admittedly, the observations highlighted here are early observations, and ones that privilege my own politics of reading religion, specifically Christianity, in ambiguous terms.

This chapter argues that the presence of, and the role assumed by, Christian discourse in terms of both its direct involvement in the residential schools and in the TRCC's proceedings reveals ambiguity regarding Christianity's role in the process of responding to the residential schools experience. On the one hand, Christianity seems to provide a language that gives voice to encounters between Indigenous peoples and the morally horrifying residential schools experience. At the same time, it seems to provide a way to go beyond such horror by abrogating it in the hope of moving the Canadian nation forward towards reconciliation. Given the complex colonial relationship between Christianity and Indigenous communities in Canada, this ambiguous position of Christianity in the TRCC is both troubling and potentially fruitful. In many ways, this ambiguous double role of Christianity at the TRCC is nothing new. As is argued in earlier chapters in this collection by Elbourne, Fehr, and Beeds especially, throughout the nineteenth and twentieth centuries Christianity inhabited a complex position as both a weapon of colonialism and as a source of political and spiritual empowerment for Indigenous peoples. The purpose of this chapter is to explore this ambiguity in the twenty-first century by asking what role Christian institutions and discourse play in addressing issues of truth and reconciliation in the TRCC.

A series of questions shape my approach. Given the unambiguously invested and negative roles assumed by the Anglican, Presbyterian, Roman Catholic, and United churches in the atrocity of the residential schools, what role is permissible for the same religious institutions in the process of truth-finding and reconciliation on which "Canada" has now embarked?[2] What role does Christianity have in imagining a new space of encounter and exchange as that created by the TRCC as a public institution for truth-telling, witnessing, and reconciliation? Is it possible to regard the presence of Christian institutions at the CRTC as contributing to the decolonization process broadly conceived in this book? Moreover, if the TRCC is to be inclusive in its approach by providing "a holistic, culturally appropriate and safe setting for former students, their families and communities in which to share their experiences with the commission," how do the experiences of individual Indigenous Christian Canadians in particular figure into the negative discourse surrounding the role of the Christian churches in the residential schools?[3] Indeed, what of the Indigenous traditions such as knowledge mobilization circles that are now being evoked (as part of the reconciliation processes) in response to the assimilationist discourse of the residential schools? Is this evocation a reiteration of the colonial impulse, or is it something that stands outside the assimilationist logic of colonialism that informed the residential schools?

Other chapters in this volume speak to such tension by stressing that to acknowledge the significance of the history of Indigenous-Christian encounter is not necessarily to accept a single narrative of this history. Moreover, as the editors of this book note in the introductory chapter, it is problematic to reduce Indigenous-Christian encounters to simply assimilation or survival strategy. That it is to say, since residential schools were run under the auspices of Christian religious institutions, it is arguable that their participation is indispensable to the TRCC.[4] To dismiss the contributions of Christian institutions to the commission outright would limit Christianity to its being a wholesale instrument of colonialism. Hence, because of the way contemporary popular

Canadian history elides Christianity's investment in the Canadian nation-state and nationalism, the concern of this chapter is partly to challenge the elision of religion in contemporary Canadian history by pointing to Christianity's significance in the particular historical moment of the residential schools and how such a moment continues to haunt Canada's historical narrative. To that end, I believe that engaging the religious dimensions of the TRCC illustrates the kind of critical, dialectical, and interdisciplinary approach taken seriously by this volume in general with regards to Christian encounters and exchanges with Indigenous communities and their histories. In paying attention to both the past and present investment of Christianity in this particular colonial encounter, I hope to acknowledge both the TRCC's formative contribution to the whole of Canada's reconciliatory and nation-building project and recognize its limitations in achieving such a process of reconciliation due the strained relationship posed by Christianity as an inspiration for both the residential schools of the past and for the commission tasked with addressing the morally horrifying aspects of the residential schools.

This chapter analyzes the TRCC through a number of theoretical lenses while grounding this theoretical analysis through examination of second-hand accounts of the TRCC's first national event, drawn from both the commission's website and journalist Marites N. Sison's Special Report on the TRCC for the *Anglican Journal*. Theoretical analysis provides the opportunity to ask questions that might not otherwise be possible to ask within the strictures imposed by the language, processes, and spaces set up by the commission. Theory in this context provides us with the tools to think critically about the TRCC and what it has to offer those who participate in it. It also offers us the opportunity to examine the commission's limitations without completely losing hope in its possibilities. Given the historical emphasis of the other chapters in this volume, a theoretical analysis also offers distance from this history and the chance to imagine other possibilities not otherwise suggested by an examination of the historical record. By reflecting on the ideological underpinnings of the TRCC and what it hopes to achieve, the aim is that those who have a stake in the TRCC will be better able to engage the commission's capacity to consider truth-finding and reconciliation processes as part of the larger project of addressing the clefts in Canada's history. Of course, as critical race theorist bell hooks notes in her essay "Theory as Liberatory Practice," "Theory is not inherently healing, liberatory, or revolutionary. It fulfills this function only when we ask that it do so and direct our theorizing towards this end."[5] That is to say, unless all those vested with the power to engage in the process of transformation envisioned by the TRCC are intentionally self-reflexive about this process, the commission's mandates will remain only as potential.

## Some Background

The TRCC is part of the 2006 *Indian Residential Schools Settlement Agreement* (implemented in September 2007) between the survivors of the residential schools (or representatives thereof), the federal government, and the churches that administered the residential schools. The Commission aims to document and expose a hidden chapter in Canadian history that saw over 150,000 First Nations, Inuit, and Métis children taken from their families and forced into mostly church-run schools as part of the federal government's policy of assimilation from the late nineteenth century onwards.[6] The last residential school closed in 1996. During this decade, hundreds of former students, often called "survivors," sued the government of Canada and the churches that ran the residential schools for widespread physical, emotional, and sexual abuse suffered at these schools. The anger of the survivors caused an upsurge that forced an out-of-court settlement. This settlement included a revised agreement that mandated the TRCC, along with funds for commemoration and financial compensation for former students.

While the everyday operation of most schools was left up to the discretion of the individual churches themselves, the government of Canada officially sanctioned and financed the schools. In this sense, the government of Canada supported the missionary project of the churches because they fulfilled the aim of the government to assimilate Indigenous communities into the mainstream white Anglo-Canadian society.[7] Indeed, the relationship between the "Canadian State" and the "Christian churches" has been historically framed by an ambivalent codependence and a paternalistic stance towards the Indigenous communities of Canada by both sets of institutions, whereby the "civilizing missions" of the Christian churches and the Canadian nation-state aligned at critical points in relation to the Indigenous communities. The residential schools issue is one such major alignment. It should be no surprise, then, that the TRCC today has to struggle with this ambivalence as well in both its practice and constitution.[8] As a result, the role of the churches in the proceedings of the TRCC has been left open and ill defined. It is this ambiguity about the role of the churches in the TRCC that must be examined in order to further elucidate the ambivalence present in the spaces of encounters and exchanges dating from the colonial era to the present.

## Theoretical Locations

### Aporetic Religious Responses to Mass Atrocities

The ambiguous role of Christianity and Christian churches in response to mass atrocities is not a new problem per se, but the Canadian context offers new conditions under which to consider this ambiguity and how the TRCC might harness or engage it critically for its own purposes. A recent volume co-edited by Thomas Brudholm and Thomas Cushman addresses this issue more generally as a problem of religion and from diverse disciplinary perspectives. In particular, the essays by Peter Dews, Jennifer Geddes, and Arne Grøn speak specifically to my concern about the problems raised by the ambiguity of Christianity in the case of residential schools, even though they speak of "religion" in general and in the context of mass atrocities broadly. While these scholars are not dismissive of the positive role that religious discourse plays (or can play) in the context of responding to mass atrocities, they all highlight the two-pronged nature of this discourse and warn that care should be taken in appealing to religious discourse as a response to mass atrocities. They all perceive the role of religion as lying uncomfortably between necessity and impossibility. Geddes notes, for example, how religion functions in the context of the double bind posed by mass atrocities: it seems both necessary to speak about what happened and impossible to do so adequately.[9]

While speaking of religion in general as aporetic runs the risk of universalizing, and essentializing at the same time, disparate understandings of meaning-making beliefs, institutions, and practices (among many things), this chapter focuses on Christianity in order to contextualize the discussion of religion's role in mass atrocity for Canada and the atrocity of the residential schools. Following Grøn, who argues that a religious response to mass atrocity is *aporetic* in the sense that it can be described only in terms of ethics, on the one hand, and that it seems to find no direct ethical answer on the other.[10] That is, religion (Christianity in the context of the TRCC) can, in responding to atrocity, voice hope against despair (where the only seemingly possible response is to give up hope). On the other hand, echoing Jürgen Habermas, "religion can interpret evil by restoring a world in which humans can also morally re-situate themselves."[11] In this sense, the Christian religion in the context of the TRCC both reveals and tames the atrocity of the residential schools that it addresses. The significance of this ambivalence will be made clearer in the discussion of the official responses of the churches so far to the TRCC. For now, I want to draw attention to the way this chapter is informed by other scholars' discussions of religious ambivalence in the context of mass atrocities.

As I have noted elsewhere about the religious dimensions of the TRC in South Africa, the use of Christian discourse by that particular commission focused largely on its abstract and symbolic use of Christian rituals of prayer and confession, and Christian notions of forgiveness and reconciliation in the commission's attempts to restore a world marred by apartheid atrocities.[12] That is to say, the use of Christian discourse in the TRC of South Africa was touted by the commission itself as having less to do with the exposition of particular theological doctrines of Christianity per se (despite the leadership of this commission being shared by two Christian clergy) and more to do with harnessing the ambivalent nature of Christianity's ability to speak to both the atrocity of apartheid and the hope of post-apartheid South Africa, despite the fact that apartheid ideology also relied on certain Christian tenets. In this case, the dominance of Christian discourse was very clear and problematic for a country negotiating a new democracy.[13]

## Habermas, Religion, and the Public Sphere

While Dews, Geddes, and Grøn address the problem of religious ambiguity in the context of ethics, Jürgen Habermas provides another perspective from political philosophy. Of particular significance for this chapter is Habermas's recent reminder regarding the increasingly public role that religion has come to play in modern "Western" (some might even say postmodern) societies.[14] Habermas attaches a significant political function to religion and art, both of which serve to translate private experiences into public discourse.[15] In this sense, it can be argued that, despite the preponderance of secular language in the Canadian public sphere, Christian discourse in the context of the TRCC actually plays a significant mediation role of not only giving voice to very personal experiences of residential schools trauma in a public forum but also providing a language with which to share personal experiences in public in the political sense by challenging the normative historical record that would otherwise elide discussions of the problematic colonial political power dynamic that manifests very clearly in the residential schools. This form of public religion, in other words, has the explanatory power to help individuals and communities navigate the confluences of Christianity as idealized within its core message of acceptance and the particular instantiation of this religious tradition as a vehicle for atrocity.

In "Faith and Knowledge," for example, Habermas suggests that modern secular discourse might do well to pay attention to the power of religious language.[16] Moreover, in another essay, "Transcendence from Within, Transcendence in this World," Habermas argues that "since a philosophy which has become self-critical does not trust itself any longer to offer universal assertions about the concrete whole of exemplary forms of life, it must refer those affected to discourses in which they answer their substantial questions themselves."[17] That is to say, religion might be able to give meaning to life experiences that otherwise baffle other forms of knowing and apprehending the world, such as legal discourses or other value systems. In this sense, Christianity, as a public religion, offers an alternative to the unguarded pluralism of secularism.[18] In short, the public use of religious or Christian discourse can contribute meaningfully to making us conscious of the limitations of secular discourse and can remain indispensable as the bearer of a semantic content easily dismissed by non-religious discourses because of its explanatory power.[19] The importance of Christianity as an explanatory tool in public discourse about Indigenous issues is of consequence for the TRCC in particular because of the ways in which the personal experiences of certain Indigenous communities and individuals, unfortunately, have found voice in the Canadian public sphere only by being deemed as religious or spiritual rather than "political" – this in a context where the politics of Indigenous communities in Canada constantly come up against mixed responses from both white and non-white settler communities. The salience of the title of this volume, *Mixed Blessings,* serves as an apt iteration of this ambivalence.

However, even if one grants Habermas the benefit of the argument regarding the opening up of channels through taking public religion seriously, the fact remains that the use of religious ideas and discourse in response to mass atrocity is fraught with ambiguity, especially when the religious tradition in question is culpable.[20] Moreover, such ambiguity and ambivalence are problematic in determining adequate responses to the gravity of the residential schools experience outside the limited context of Christian discourse. That is, we must wonder at the possibility of reconciliation when Christianity is also implicated as a culprit, as in the case of the residential schools. Does Christian discourse retain a positive role, providing explanatory power and answering substantial questions as Habermas argues? Or is it possible that Christianity's ambiguity in the TRCC gives blanket clemency to the churches that were heavily involved in the traumatization of Indigenous communities across Canada?

## The TRCC: Between Christianity and the Residential Schools Trauma

Arguably, within the context of the TRCC, the significance of Christian discourse lies precisely in that space between conveying the shame of the residential schools experience, à la Habermas, and allowing for the containment of this shame. Given the emphasis on traditional Indigenous practices in some of the proceedings of the TRCC so far, as well as the high level of engagement by some of the churches, such as the Anglican Church and the United Church of Canada, with the commission, Christian discourse is clearly deemed integral. Consequently, Christianity can be said to provide a language out of the aporetic bind it creates for the Indigenous participants of the TRCC in that it works both apophatically and redemptively. That is to say, by pointing to the residential schools trauma as something beyond our human capacity to know or understand, while at the same time seeking to bring closure to the trauma, Christian discourse in the TRCC functions ambivalently. It would be easy to accept the active role of the churches in the commission were it simply a case of separating bad "religion" from good "religion" and assuming that good intentions count more than bad experiences. This is not the case, however, and the overwhelmingly engaged, although somewhat complex, role of Christianity in the colonization of Indigenous populations around the globe calls into question the value of separating the good message from the bad messenger. In addition, such ambivalence grants undeserved clemency to Christian religious institutions involved in the residential schools trauma to play both sides of the trauma with minimal guilt – arguments of hybridity and complex negotiations of religion and colonialism notwithstanding.

As examples from the first national event of the TRCC (held in Winnipeg, Manitoba, on 16–19 June 2010) demonstrate, there is palpable discomfort among Indigenous people concerning the presence of clergy and the use of Christian discourse in the TRCC's proceedings. For example, during the opening ceremony in Winnipeg, along with blessings and ritual drawn from varied Indigenous traditions, the crowd also heard the chair of the commission, Justice Murray Sinclair, recite the "Lord's Prayer." Archbishop Fred Hiltz, primate of the Anglican Church of Canada, remarked that he was "'surprised' that churches were given a prominent role in the opening ceremonies." In his evaluation, "The TRC 'gave us an opportunity that they didn't have to give us ... they were very generous in including us to the extent that they did.'"[21] Although Hiltz put it mildly, his discomfort arguably reflects a broader tension within the TRCC concerning the issue of how to acknowledge that Christian discourse was a big part of the residential schools trauma while also providing hope for those seeking to address the effects of this trauma.

In general, the TRCC's first national event received praise not only from Justice Sinclair but also from former Governor General Michaëlle Jean and high-ranking church clergy. Sinclair, for example, called the event a "special, excellent start."[22] The National Indigenous Anglican bishop, Mark MacDonald, called the event "a movement that can't be stopped. This is a ceremony that's just beginning ... It was not just truth-telling and hearings in the western sense, but ceremony in which the truth was told ... Survival was celebrated as well ... God came and was here listening to the hurts and the pain."[23] However, this positive praise, particularly in the statements of Sinclair and MacDonald, does not fully convey the complex reception that the TRCC's first national event received.

At face value, it would seem that the positive reception elides the complexity of the Christian churches' role in both the residential schools system and the TRCC. However, this would be an inaccurate representation of the complicated ways in which the commission has been received by both "survivors" and the churches involved in the residential schools saga. One of the key events high-lighting this complexity was a forum entitled "Native Traditional Spiritualities in Conversation with Christianity," which took place on the second day of the event. During the forum, MacDonald presented a complex picture of his role as an Indigenous Anglican priest and bishop. Other panellists, who also spoke of their complex relationship with Christianity, included Sister Eva Solomon, a Catholic nun of the Sisters of St. Joseph; Kona Cochrane, a lay Anglican from the diocese of Rupert's Land; and Reverend Margaret Mullin, an ordained Pres-byterian minister of Ojibwe and Irish/Scottish descent. The forum was sponsored by the Anglican, Presbyterian, Roman Catholic, and United churches, and featured clergy representatives who also ran an inter-faith tent where they of-fered reflections and interacted with event attendees.

As Marites Sison observes with regards to the forum, each of the panellists spoke of their struggles to balance the benefits of their Christian faith, the nega-tive legacy of Christianity in their lives, and the teachings of the elders of their communities. For example, Mullin is noted as saying, "We are the same people, living under the same sun, created by the same God."[24] Sr. Solomon echoed this point: "The 'sin' of the churches that operated the schools was to be a part of colonization, to think that what they offered us was superior to what God had already given us."[25] Both these observations clearly separate the teachings of Christianity as Mullin and Solomon understand them from the enterprise of colonialism with which the churches were connected. Sison further notes that Cochrane "spoke about 'the great benefit' of walking both native spiritual trad-itions and Christianity. 'I don't judge anyone,' she said, noting that when she went through a rough patch, both [traditions] have 'picked me up, dusted me up, and said, you're okay.'"[26] The comments of the panellists resonate with other chapters in this volume that emphasize the complex ways that Indigenous people have historically approached Christianity as something that can be usefully "managed" and integrated to offer them a degree of power, even as it embroils them in colonialism.

Articulations of the use of Native spirituality and Christianity by participants at the TRCC demonstrates how this pattern continues into the present, and how Christianity continues to play an ambiguous role, as it is tied simultan-eously to the negative personal experiences associated with residential schools and the positive discourse of healing that it provides in the context of the TRCC. By pointing to the ability of their Christian faith to meet their personal needs, while at the same time separating religion from the institutional failures of the churches involved in the residential schools system, the panellists preserve what they deem to be the ethical integrity of the Christian tradition. This integrity is distinct from the churches as religious institutions. William Asikinack, head of Indigenous Studies at the First Nations University of Canada and a student of the residential schools for five years, makes the same observation: "when you separate the philosophy of Christianity from the operation of the church, it's not that much different from traditional first nations beliefs."[27]

Consequently, by emphasizing the distinction between the form and content of Christian discourse, and noting similarities between Christianity and the beliefs and practices of Indigenous communities, Asikinack highlights further the ways in which the truth-content of Christianity, which is supposedly distinct from its institutional form, is able to carry itself in positive terms into the public space of the commission. The result is the further confirmation of not only the significant role of Christianity in responding to the atrocities of the residential schools at the TRCC but also the way in which ambiguity can be seen as working in favour of the churches at the expense of individual trauma. That is to say, while the delineation is useful, such a distinction (between personal Christianity and the institutional church) considers largely the individual utility of religious tradition in addressing traumatic experience. It is not as effective as a tool to address the broader community experience of the residential schools trauma. Such a symbolic interaction limits what can be brought to bear against institutions, especially the ways in which traumatic experiences have systemic and systematic ramifications for particular communities.

Peter Yellowquill, a former residential school student and a member of the Anishinaabe Nation from Long Plains in Manitoba, shares the opinions of William Asikinack. Summarizing a *Globe and Mail* interview with Yellowquill prior to the first national event, interviewer Patrick White notes that "for most former students, the religious presence will be an example of reconciliation in action – victims and perpetrators joining to share stories of abuse and hardship. But some like Mr. Yellowquill would rather dispense with the holy undertones, insisting that the sight of religious figures could stifle their disclosures."[28] Arguably Yellowquill's uneasiness about the presence of clergy points to the ways in which the commission's embrace of Christianity and the participation of Christian churches in the TRCC are problematic for former students who do not see the value of Christianity beyond its hurtful role in the residential schools. Others use similar arguments to oppose the commission on the grounds that the commission ignores the issue of justice and offers false reconciliation. One of the most prominent spokespeople for this group is former United Church minister Kevin Annett, who has rallied with protesters at some of the TRCC's national events, calling for the legal prosecution of the churches that ran the residential schools.[29] The dissent of Yellowquill and Annett illustrates the ambivalent nature of the commission's engagement of Christian discourse in its approach to addressing the atrocity of the residential schools: Christianity is both the source of the atrocity and the means to address it.

## Following in the Footsteps of the Official Apologies

While the proceedings of the TRCC themselves present the most striking illustration of the ambiguity of Christian discourse in addressing the issue of residential schools, earlier precedents point to the same ambiguity. These include the official apologies offered by various churches in the 1990s, as well as the state apology offered by Prime Minister Stephen Harper on 11 June 2008 on behalf of the Government of Canada. While the apologies by the churches and the state are of a different historical period than the TRCC, they highlight similar ambiguities with respect to the role of Christianity in the reconciliation process. They also make clear the direct link between the relative silence about residential schools in church discourse and the minimal presence of this history in discourses on Canadian nationalism.

While the Anglican, Presbyterian, and United churches have offered official apologies, the Roman Catholic Church has yet to offer an apology that clearly identifies its role in the residential schools system.[30] The closest that the Roman Catholic Church has come to an official apology is a statement expressing sorrow, offered in a private conversation between Pope Benedict XVI and a delegation from the Assembly of First Nations on 29 April 2009.[31] Interestingly, the lack of an official apology by the Catholic Church stands in contrast to the 1991 apology offered by the missionary Oblates of Mary Immaculate in Canada, one of the Church's missionary organizations that operated residential schools.[32] This contrast is not surprising, however, given the institutional claim that the "Catholic community in Canada has a decentralized structure," a statement used to absolve the official Church from making commitments that are institutionally binding when it is suitable to do so.[33] In this instance, the disjuncture between the private expressions of apology and the Church's reluctance to make a public institutional apology, while it perhaps suggests that problematic practices within the Church are abnormalities rather than institutional norms, is evidence that the Catholic Church in Canada has opted for a "privatization" of the apology process. The result is an ambiguous condemnation of the residential schools system that somewhat limits what can be deemed both legally and ethically binding for the Roman Catholic Church as an institution.

The apologies from the other three churches – Anglican (1993), Presbyterian (1994), and United (1986, 1998) – are arguably more articulate in their apportioning of blame. There is no attempt in the written apologies of these churches to completely disassociate the practices of individuals or the individual church dioceses that ran the residential schools from the church institution as a whole.

That said, all the apologies share one thing in common: there is no mention of justice, whether in the sense of due process or in the sense of a divine punishment (an arguably significant theme in Christian theology).[34] Instead, all the apologies use the language of reconciliation and the shared journey of healing and seeking forgiveness before God – even though what constitutes reconciliation is not clearly defined.[35]

In light of this lacuna between Christianity's general theological claim of the pursuit of justice and the absence of this theme in the apologies of the churches responsible for the residential schools, the focus of this chapter – the ambiguous role of Christian discourse – gains even greater purchase. Indeed, the original focus can be widened to ask: what role can Christian institutions play in the TRCC without imposing their understanding of truth and reconciliation on the commission? What kind of justice is possible under such circumstances? The lack of any defined discussion of justice in the apologies ultimately means that the current context of the TRCC is one that privileges forgiveness for the perpetrators of the residential schools atrocity rather than justice for the wronged "survivors." Thus, the extent to which reconciliation is achieved through the transformation of structures and institutions of self-actualization, such as religious, civic, civil, legal, and political institutions (the churches and the TRCC in this context) – what Cyril Adonis calls "true reconciliation" – remains largely "an Indian problem" in the Canadian context.[36] That is, "true reconciliation" is impossible when only one side bears both the burden of proof and self-actualization. To this end, the absence of testimonies from nuns, priests, and government officials from the TRCC's proceedings does not bode well for the type of transformative reconciliation envisioned by the TRCC itself.

While it is possible to read the placement of responsibility for self-actualization on the "wronged" community as a negative process, we should recall Habermas's observation regarding the possibility of religion allowing those affected by trauma to answer their substantial questions themselves. In other words, what the TRCC might be able to succeed in doing is shifting the national perspective away from the gaze of paternalism that has informed the relationship between the Canadian state and Indigenous communities, especially the longstanding and ambiguous "right of self-government" approach that has placed the burden on Indigenous communities to be solely responsible for dealing with the aftermath of the residential schools trauma. Arguably this shift would make possible a move towards truly autochthonous processes of self-determination, healing, and reconciliation for Indigenous communities in Canada, even while acknowledging that such a shift relies on the problematic ground of Christian discourse. In other words, the absence of justice in the church apologies can in fact provide the space for justice to be envisioned in various ways by the communities that have the highest stakes in the project of the TRCC: the First Nations, the Inuit, and the Métis of Canada.

## The Third Mirror of the TRCC: A Non-Conclusion

What should be clear from the analysis above is that from the perspective of the participants in the forum "Native Spiritualities in Conversation with Christianity," and arguably from the perspective of the commission itself, a distinction should be made between the message of Christian reconciliation as an ideal and the messengers, such as the churches as the institutions of Christianity. That Christian discourse has been allowed to have a prominent role in the commission's institutional habitus suggests that participants and commissioners have accepted this distinction, and why not? After all, as the comments by forum panellists demonstrate, the message of Christianity made it possible for them to make meaning of their traumatic experiences as victims of the residential schools system. In Habermasian terms, Christian discourse makes it possible for "survivors" of the residential schools to articulate their personal experiences in the public space offered by the commission. This implies that, were Christianity's presence completely jettisoned, the truth-finding and reconciliation processes of the commission would be even farther away from any viable concept of reconciliation because of the limitations imposed by other frames of reference for the TRCC, such as those from legal and political perspectives.

My critique of the use of Christianity in the TRCC notwithstanding, the well-publicized "success" of the South African TRC and some of the more publicized praise for the TRCC so far suggest that the use of Christian discourse is not as problematic as I make it to be. It could be argued, for instance, that the actual experience of sitting through an event that acknowledges one's suffering (such as the human rights violations hearings of the TRC of South Africa and at the national events of the TRCC so far) reveals that Christian discourse in fact provides "survivors" with a language with which to apprehend both the past and the future with a better sense of self. Given that many "survivors" reference Christianity and their conversion to Christianity as key to their healing journeys following their experience of residential schools trauma, it is clear that for these "survivors" Christianity remains central, both in their schooling as children and now in their healing as adults. For these "survivors," Christianity is not ambiguous, but a source of truth and healing. This is true to the extent that some "survivors" have even called for the acknowledgment of similarities between Indigenous religious traditions and Christianity when giving their witness testimonies, as noted in the discussion of the first national event above. In this context, it might seem that my critical perspective on Christianity's

ambiguous role in the TRCC is a red herring: shouldn't the aim of the commission – regardless of the discourse employed – be the achievement of
reconciliation and healing?

In fact, arguably, the ambiguity of Christian discourse is precisely what
also gives it legitimacy as a way to create what Arne Grøn refers to as "radical
narratives."[37] These radical narratives offer a way out of the bind for both
churches and individual adherents by separating the institutional practices from
the "pure" message of Christianity. In other words, although I have critiqued
this delineation above for its limitations, it seems possible to balance the
Habermasian call to elevate the positive role of religion in general (and Christianity specifically) in the public sphere (its ability to express private experiences in the language and context of the political) with the negative instance
reflected in its public use as a discourse of assimilation in the context of "post-
residential schools" Canada.

In this light, it may be that Christian discourse proves itself more worthy than
not in the capacity of the TRCC to achieve reconciliation. This might be the
case, especially, if we look more critically beyond the institutional Christian
churches and their conflicted power struggles and focus on individual narratives
of reconciliation. In this sense, the response to the aporia of religion might
prove less of a problem and more of an opportunity to move forward. Moreover,
paying attention to the positive side of the aporetic role of religion in the TRCC
might provide Canadian society with a language with which to respond to the
national trauma and rifts caused by the residential schools experience. That is,
the ambiguity of Christian discourse in the TRCC might be useful for chron-
icling evil and lamenting the cries of the victims of the residential schools – an
approach that also remains true to the experiences of the "survivors" as aporetic
as well. Consequently, and only maybe so, this use of Christian discourse might
constitute an ethically responsible way for the TRCC to address the role of
Christianity in responding to the trauma of residential schools in Canada.

However, this chapter argues that Christian religious discourse succeeds in
not being deemed a costly alternative by the state precisely because it is used
by the TRCC (and the South African TRC before it) in an ambiguous way. This
strategic use of religion potentially allows for healing, but it also downplays
Christianity's dominant role and responsibility in the residential schools trauma.
The prevalence of Christian notions of forgiveness, truth, and reconciliation
in the official language of both the TRCC and the South African TRC – which
many supporters have noted finds resonance in other religious traditions as
well – is precisely the cause for concern. One of the most disconcerting effects
of this ambivalent presence of Christianity in the TRCC is that those who choose
not to participate in the rituals identified as part of everyone's experience, albeit

in different forms, are excluded from full participation in the broader normative practices of truth-finding and reconciliation. The ambiguity, in other words, has the uncanny ability to silence narratives of dissent if they don't fit into the reconciliation model of Christian forgiveness on offer. Moreover, given that, during the negotiations of the settlement that established the TRCC, religious institutions took a very defensive legal approach to the historical problem of the residential schools, the overwhelming presence of Christian discourse in the subsequent proceedings of the TRCC is a further point of concern.[38]

The question of whether the TRCC's notion of reconciliation actually represents the restoration of prior good relations is especially significant if we take into account the fact that the religious practices of Indigenous individuals and communities in Canada now encompass a variety of traditions, some of which seem contradictory to Christianity in nature. Also, given the very colonial basis of the trauma of the residential schools experience as a civilizing project, an enterprise intimately tied to the missionary work of the Christian churches in Canada, the question of whether (including the extent to which) such trauma requires a language other than that of Christianity needs to be considered carefully.

To the extent that these issues reflect the problems of ambiguity identified earlier as informing the commission's discourse, it is important that there not be forged too easy an alliance between Christian religious discourse and the TRCC's aims of truth-finding and reconciliation. Such an alliance has the potential to undermine and subsume the individual traumas that constitute the collective and national trauma. Indeed, the foregone conclusion of such an alliance – namely, that this ambiguity is almost an impasse, one that will require self-directed healing from the Canadian Indigenous communities – is disconcerting. In this sense, the onus remains only on the wronged Indigenous communities to positively re-inscribe the religion in question (in this case Christianity) so that it still makes sense, despite the glaring anomalies. This is no great consolation and certainly not "true reconciliation."

## Notes

1  Following Michel Foucault, I rely on the definition of "discourse" as a system of thoughts and references that operate by the power of exclusion and interconnection. In this sense, religion, both as a broad system and in its particular instantiation in Christianity, operates on exclusionary notions of ideas of community, belief systems, liturgical practices, and so on, such that the languages and institutions of religion can be perceived to differ from non-religious languages and institutions, and imbue its users with specific power relations. While such difference does not capture the complexity of the relationship between religious and non-religious discourse, it does give frame to this chapter's discussion of religion as discourse. See, for example, Michel Foucault, *Archeology of Knowledge*, trans. A.M.

Sheridan Smith (New York: Pantheon Books, 1972); Michel Foucault, *The Birth of the Clinic: An Archeology of Medical Perception,* trans. A.M. Sheridan Smith (New York: Vintage Books, 1973); Michel Foucault, *Discipline and Punish: The Birth of the Prison,* trans. Alan Sheridan (New York: Vintage Books, 1977).

2  While atrocity and mass atrocities are such broad concepts so as to encompass phenomena quite disparate in nature, this chapter follows the lead of Thomas Brudholm and Thomas Cushman in their use of David Scheffer's definition of the terms. The chapter's subsequent categorization of the residential schools experience as an atrocity is along the same lines. Brudholm and Cushman argue that atrocity crimes are "high-impact crimes of severe gravity that are of an orchestrated character and that result in a significant number of victims and merit international response ... Like evil, or indeed 'radical' evil, talk about mass atrocities is saturated with terms expressive of a certain sense of moral horror or extraordinary transgression. The acts and events in question are decried as 'unimaginable,' as 'heinous,' 'abhorrent,' 'cruel,' and 'inhuman.'" Thomas Brudholm and Thomas Cushman, "Introduction," in *The Religious in Responses to Mass Atrocity: Interdisciplinary Perspectives,* ed. Thomas Brudholm and Thomas Cushman (New York: Cambridge University Press, 2009), 6.

3  "About Us," Truth and Reconciliation Commission of Canada, http://www.trc.caindex.php?p=26.

4  It should be noted that there were some residential schools (in the Arctic at least) that were operated entirely by the federal government; it is not the case that all residential schools were operated by churches. Moreover, although there is agreement of church and government policy on assimilation in the late nineteenth century, by the 1950s the assimilation policy was more nuanced. There was talk of educating and modernizing "Indians" while allowing them to retain their cultural identity. For an in-depth discussion, see John S. Milloy, "Integration for Closure: 1946 to 1986," in *A National Crime: The Canadian Government and the Residential School System, 1879-1986* (Winnipeg: University of Manitoba Press, 1999), 189-210.

5  bell hooks, *Teaching to Transgress: Education as the Practice of Freedom* (London and New York: Routledge, 1994), 61.

6  Marlene Brant Castellano, Linda Archibald, and Mike DeGagné, eds., *From Truth to Reconciliation: Transforming the Legacy of Residential Schools* (Ottawa: Aboriginal Healing Foundation, 2008), 3.

7  As affirmed by Duncan Scott Campbell, former head of the Department of Indian Affairs (1913-1932). See Robert Choquett, "The Education of Canada's Amerindians," in *Canada's Religions: An Historical Introduction* (Ottawa: University of Ottawa Press, 2004), 301-6.

8  In this sense, the TRCC follows in the tradition of similar truth commissions, such as the South African TRC, which had to address the tensions between the seemingly oppositional paths of historical amnesia and protracted prosecutions of those deemed to be violators. While in the case of South Africa the perpetrators were offered the choice of amnesty in lieu of trials as a way of addressing their problematic participation in the reconciliation processes of the TRC, this has not been the case in Canada with regards to the churches as perpetrators of the violence of residential schools.

9  Jennifer Geddes, "Religious Rhetoric in Response to Atrocity," in *The Religious in Response to Mass Atrocity: Interdisciplinary Perspectives,* ed. Thomas Brudholm and Thomas Cushman (Cambridge: Cambridge University Press, 2009), 22-27.

10  Arne Grøn, "The Limit of Ethics – The Ethics of the Limit," in *The Religious in Response to Mass Atrocity: Interdisciplinary Perspectives,* ed. Thomas Brudholm and Thomas Cushman (Cambridge: Cambridge University Press, 2009), 41.

11 Ibid., 53–54.
12 Siphiwe I. Dube, "The TRC, Democratic Ethos, and the New Culture of Critique in South Africa," in *Healing South African Wounds"/Les Carnets du Cerpa/c no 7*, ed. Gilles Teulie and Mélanie Joseph-Vilain (Montpellier: Presses Universitaires de la Méditerranée, 2009), 211–32; Siphiwe I. Dube, "The TRC of South Africa: A Dialectical Critique of its Core Concepts" (PhD diss., University of Toronto, 2008).
13 The use of Christian prayer to open the human rights violations hearings in the context of South Africa was a very clear adoption of a Christian practice and liturgical ritual – something I've noted with regards to the TRCC as well. Yet the TRC of South Africa appealed to the use of prayer during the human rights violations hearings on the basis of prayer as a religious ritual in general rather than a Christian one per se, such that Archbishop Desmond Tutu (the chairperson) could override a request by other commissioners to observe a moment of silence instead. Arguably, in its "awareness" of the value of the ambivalence of religious discourse, the TRC of South Africa constructed religiosity as a model of South African national identity and used the model to its advantage and, some would add, with success.
14 Jürgen Habermas, *Between Facts and Norms: Contributions to a Discourse Theory of Law and Democracy,* trans. W. Rehg (Cambridge, MA: MIT Press, 1996), 360.
15 M.D. Walhout, "Introduction: The Public Muse," in *Literature and the Renewal of the Public Sphere,* ed. Susan VanZanten Gallagher and M.D. Walhout (London: MacMillan Press, 2000), 185.
16 Jürgen Habermas, "Faith and Knowledge," in *The Frankfurt School on Religion: Key Writings by the Major Thinkers,* ed. E. Mendieta (New York: Routledge, 2005), 327–28.
17 Jürgen Habermas, "Transcendence from Within, Transcendence in this World," in *Habermas, Modernity, and Public Theology,* ed. Don S. Browning and Francis Schüssler Fiorenza (New York: Crossroad, 1992), 229.
18 It should be noted, nonetheless, that Christianity is still problematic in a multicultural and plural context such as Canada since it privileges the problematic essentialism of logocentrism by locating reason within the realm of an originary source of all knowledge such as God rather than acknowledging heterogeneity.
19 Jürgen Habermas, *Postmetaphysical Thinking: Philosophical Essays,* trans. William Mark Hohengarten (Cambridge, MA: MIT Press), 51.
20 Brudholm and Cushman, *The Religious in Responses to Mass Atrocity,* 4.
21 Marites Sison, "'We've only just begun' work of reconciliation, says Archbishop Fred Hiltz," Special Report: Truth and Reconciliation Commission (TRC), *Anglican Journal,* 20 June 2010, http://www.anglicanjournal.com/articles/special-report-truth-and-reconciliation-commission-trc-9243.
22 Ibid.
23 Ibid.
24 Marites Sison, "Walking a Fine Line," Special Report: Truth and Reconciliation Commission (TRC), *Anglican Journal,* 17 June 2010, http://www.anglicanjournal.com/articles/walking-a-fine-line-9238.
25 Ibid.
26 Ibid.
27 "Former Residential Schools Students Say Their Feelings about Christianity Are Complicated," Bible League of Canada, 16 June 2010, http://www.bibleleague.ca/news-detail-inter.php?id=173, accessed 20 June 2010.
28 Patrick White, "Some Former Residential School Students Struggle with Church Presence at Reconciliation Event," *Globe and Mail,* 14 June 2010, http://www.theglobeandmail.com/

news/national/some-former-residential-school-students-struggle-with-church-presence
-at-reconciliation-event/article1604219/.

29  See, for example, Kevin Annett, "Hidden from History: The Canadian Holocaust – The
Untold Story of the Genocide of Aboriginal Peoples," http://www.hiddenfromhistory.
org, accessed 24 June 2010; see also http://canadiangenocide.nativeweb.org/index.html.

30  Sixteen Catholic dioceses operated schools, according to the Canadian Conference of
Catholic Bishops. "Catholic Statement of Regret on the Former Residential Schools,"
*Canadian Conference of Catholic Bishops,* http://www.cbc.ca/news/world/pope-expresses
-sorrow-for-abuse-at-residential-schools-1.778019.

31  "Pope Expresses 'Sorrow' for Abuse at Residential Schools: AFN's Fontaine Says He Hopes
Statement Will 'Close the Book' on Apologies Issue," *CBC News,* 29 April 2009, http://
www.cbc.ca/news/world/story/2009/04/29/pope-first-nations042909.html.

32  "An Apology to the First Nations of Canada by the Oblate Conference of Canada, *Canadian Conference of Catholic Bishops,* http://www.cccb.ca/site/images/stories/pdf/oblate
_apology_english.pdf.

33  "Catholic Statement of Regret on the Former Residential Schools."

34  For example, "He executes justice for the fatherless and the widow, and loves the so-
journer, giving him food and clothing" (Deuteronomy 10:18); "I said in my heart, God
will judge the righteous and the wicked, for there is a time for every matter and for every
work" (Ecclesiastes 3:17); "For we know him who said, 'Vengeance is mine; I will repay.'
And again, 'The Lord will judge his people'" (Hebrews 10:30); "For I the Lord love justice;
I hate robbery and wrong; I will faithfully give them their recompense, and I will make
an everlasting covenant with them" (Isaiah 61:8); "Beloved, never avenge yourselves, but
leave it to the wrath of God, for it is written, 'Vengeance is mine, I will repay, says the
Lord'" (Romans 12:19).

35  See "Anglican Church of Canada Apology to Native People," Anglican Church of Canada, 6 August 1993, http://www.anglican.ca/relationships/apology/english; "Confessions
and Apologies," Presbyterian Church in Canada, January 1994, http://www.presbyterian.
ca/healing/; "Apology to Former Students of United Church Indian Residential Schools,
and to Their Families and Communities (1998)," United Church of Canada, October 1998,
http://www.united-church.ca/beliefs/policies/1998/a623.

36  Cyril Adonis, reviews of Megan Shore's *Religion and Conflict Resolution: Christianity and
South Africa's Truth and Reconciliation Commission*; Antjie Krog, Nosisi Mpolweni, and
Kopano Ratele's *There Was This Goat: Investigating the Truth and Reconciliation Commis-
sion Testimony of Notrose Nobomvu Konile*; François du Bois and Antje du Bois-Pedain,
eds., *Justice and Reconciliation in Post-Apartheid South Africa*; and Ole Bubenzer's *Post-
TRC Prosecutions in South Africa: Accountability for Political Crimes after the Truth and
Reconciliation Commission's Amnesty Process,* all in *International Journal of Transitional
Justice* 4, 3 (2010): 509–18.

37  Grøn, "The Limit of Ethics," 46.

38  Megan Shore and Scott Kline offer an additional, perhaps corollary (different?) opinion
regarding the TRC of South Africa, which challenges my skepticism further: essentially,
they argue that religion was inescapable in that context. They note that "Because the
churches had been such a potent force in civil society under apartheid, they were one of
the few institutions that had both the organizational capability and the infrastructure
to assist in establishing and conducting a truth commission." Megan Shore and Scott
Kline, "The Ambiguous Role of Religion in the South African Truth and Reconciliation
Commission," *Peace and Change* 31, 3 (2006): 323. Yet while it is arguable that the involvement of religious organizations was crucial to the work of the TRC in South Africa, the

same does not apply in Canada. In the Canadian context, churches, along with the government of Canada, were the other major culprit in the establishment and sustenance of the residential schools. This fact challenges the argument for their direct involvement in the TRCC, even if we accept that the participation of religious organizations is inescapable purely on civil grounds.

# 8

# Decolonizing Religious Encounter?
# Teaching "Indigenous Traditions, Women, and Colonialism"

*Denise Nadeau*

I COME TO THE TOPIC of religious encounter as someone of mixed heritage raised in Quebec. My French ancestors, on my father's side, arrived in Quebec in the mid-seventeenth century, intermarried with the Mi'gmaq, and later with the Scots, and colonized part of Gespe'gewa'gi, the territory of the Mi'gmaq in the Gaspé Peninsula. My mother, from Ontario, was of Irish and English ancestry; both her parents were second-generation immigrants. I grew up in Montreal in a Catholic Christian household. I currently live in the unceded territory of the K'omoks Nation on Vancouver Island. I approach my research and teaching from this location – as someone raised and very implicated by my family history in white settler colonialism and with a responsibility to and for that history, and as someone trained as a Christian theologian. I acknowledge and am grateful for the lessons I have learned from Indigenous Elders and teachers whom I have met as a visitor in Coast Salish and Mi'gmaq homelands.

I have been teaching a course on Indigenous traditions, women, and colonialism at Concordia University in Montreal since 2006. It is a "special topics" course in the Religion Department, taught every second year; in 2011 it was cross-listed with the university's new First People's Studies Program. The focus of the course is not on traditions per se but on Indigenous women's experience of the impact of colonialism on their traditions, and how Indigenous women have survived and are now transforming the colonial legacy through recovery of their traditions. The story told in this course is that of colonization and de-colonization through the eyes of Indigenous women as carriers and guardians of their traditions. One of the learning outcomes of the course is that all students reflect on decolonization from their own locations, be they from an Indigenous, white settler, or racialized minority background.

In 2011, I was very pleased to be invited to be part of the project "Religious Encounter and Exchange in Aboriginal Canada." I went to the seminar in Saskatoon with considerable curiosity but also some skepticism as to what I would learn about Christian-Indigenous encounter in Canada. I had become very critical of Christianity and its role in colonialism and went to the workshop with a sense of obligation to explore this reality further. After hearing the papers of the various contributors, I realized that the relationship of Indigenous peoples to Christianity was complex. In fact, any portrayal of Indigenous women and men as passive victims of evil missionaries reinforced the very binary I was trying to overcome in my teaching. After the workshop, I returned to my teaching with a more nuanced understanding of Indigenous Christianity; I incorporated into the course curriculum readings that reflected the complexity of the history of the encounter between Christianity and multiple Indigenous traditions in Canada.

## Teaching Religious Encounter

A Mohawk youth I once met at an activist event in Montreal told me he hadn't considered taking my course because it was in a religion department. He reminded me that his tradition was not a "religion" but a way of life. In a sense, I am raising the question of how one can decolonize religious studies; I consider how it is possible to teach about Indigenous traditions while maintaining their epistemic integrity under the umbrella of religious studies in a university context.

The first challenge to consider is that much of what are called "Indigenous traditions" can be learned only in community and through experience. A large portion of Indigenous knowledge is not to be shared publicly and is only transmitted orally by traditional knowledge holders. Significant components of various traditions can be accessed only through understanding and speaking the language of that tradition. In other words, there are boundaries that limit what can be taught in the academy.

The second challenge is linked to the question of who can teach in the area of Indigenous Studies and in what ways one's teaching is linked to one's positionality. This not only speaks to the insider-outsider debate, but to the question of what story gets told, in what ways, and by whom. I was not raised in an Indigenous tradition, have no in-depth knowledge of any one Indigenous tradition, and am not an Indigenous-language speaker. My field of study, my personal history, and my experience for the past thirty-five years have been in the contact zone between Christianity and Indigenous traditions.[1] In my younger years, I co-facilitated with Réné Fumoleau the Denendeh Seminar, which was an exposure program to educate non-Native Christians about Indigenous solidarity with the Dene. In the past two decades, I have worked on the ground in the area of healing of violence against Indigenous and racialized women, and in education about residential schools and truth and reconciliation, as well as doing cultural training and anti-racism education alongside Indigenous women colleagues. Accordingly, I teach from this interfaith location and, as a settler scholar, I share my own decolonization journey in the academic classroom.

I come to the topic of pedagogy as someone who was first trained as a popular educator and spent more than twenty years using the tools of popular education in my work.[2] I remember going into what was then Fort Providence (Zhahti Koe) in 1987 as part of my field placement work as a masters of divinity student. For a week I led a popular-education training session for a group of Dene women service providers, hoping to help them raise awareness in the community about spousal assault. While all enjoyed themselves doing theatre exercises and sharing their reality in drawing and sculptures, after I left the community, there was no follow-up. Besides my being the white fly-in "helper," I was unaware that, while there were some similarities between popular education and Indigenous ways of teaching and learning – for example, building community, learning from each other rather than from experts, and developing a collective analysis – Indigenous ways of knowing incorporate and transmit cultural values and a worldview that are significantly different from that of popular education.

In order to give students a sense of Indigenous traditions, I realized I would have to incorporate, as much as possible in a university classroom, Indigenous methodologies in my teaching.[3] This meant centring Indigenous knowledge and ways of teaching and learning in the classroom, incorporating a decolonizing process, and working with the different specificities of tribal knowledges. My intention was not only to disrupt students' stereotypical and colonial understandings of Indigenous peoples and their traditions but also to invite them to question their own autobiographies and histories in relation to colonialism and a Eurocentric worldview.

The first two times I taught the course I had an average of fifteen students. The third time, the course was cross-listed with First Peoples studies and women's studies, and there were forty-four registrants. This immediately raised a physical challenge, as I always teach in a circle. We (the students and I) arranged the classroom into two concentric circles of tables, which had to be moved into place before and after the class. At Concordia University, the students come from a wide range of backgrounds, ethnicities, nationalities, and religious traditions. Usually 10 to 15 percent are students with some Indigenous heritage. The range of background knowledge in the class is wide – the First Peoples studies students have a good sense of the history of colonialism; the rest often know very little.

With this range of students in a large cosmopolitan city, I have various intentions in mind as I design the course. For the Indigenous students, I hope to reinforce and deepen their experiences of their heritage and support them to feel affirmed in their identities, and to provide space for them to contribute their knowledge and experience. For students from a white settler background, I support them to become aware of the reality of white settler colonialism and their implication in it, without their resorting to the default of guilt, shame, anger, or defensiveness. In the case of racialized students, both those whose families have recently immigrated to Canada and have an experience of colonialism from their countries of origin and those with a multi-generational experience of racism in Canada, it is important that they learn to critically question the Canadian and Eurocentric framing of Indigenous peoples, women, and their histories. As well, they can reflect on their own complicity in the ongoing colonial dynamic of land-based power relationships in Canada.[4]

The question of how the gaze of the settler student can be turned on her/himself rather than emphasizing knowledge of the "Native Other" is as important as affirming the cultures and identities of the Indigenous students in the class. To do this it is critical to have all students reflect on the observed differences between an Indigenous worldview and a Eurocentric one, and to do so in a way that is personal and that engages the emotions, spirit, and body, not just the mind. Teaching about Indigenous traditions and colonialism in this country called Canada is teaching about the present reality of which we are all a part. As one student said, "this course was challenging because we were closer to the subject and had no distance."

Accordingly, we discuss traditions and religion in relation to the Canadian Truth and Reconciliation Commission on residential schools; the Idle No More movement; the ongoing issue of the murdered and missing Indigenous women; problems of poverty and the lack of housing and potable water in many communities; and the fight by global corporations and governments to push forward large resource developments on Indigenous lands. Not only is an analysis of historical, gendered colonialism necessary in this context, but a call for advocacy and a commitment to bettering the conditions of Indigenous peoples in the present is part of the teaching and learning. Jeff Corntassel (Cherokee) calls for "insurgent education," which "inspires activism and reclamation of Indigenous histories and Homelands."[5] As Andrea Smith, a critical scholar of Indigenous studies, has said, "it is not enough to understand and describe Indian 'religious' experience; it is necessary to advocate for the survival of practices and the end of colonialism."[6]

The first part of this chapter addresses some of the issues in teaching about Indigenous traditions in a religious studies classroom. The second section will discuss briefly the methodological and theoretical framework that best contributes to understanding Indigenous traditions and women. In the third section, I describe the classroom teaching strategies that I use to support an Indigenous knowledges framework. I conclude by discussing the challenges facing settler scholars who are teaching or engaging with Indigenous traditions, and I offer some final reflections on the possibilities of decolonization in the religious studies classroom.

## Issues in the Study and Teaching of Indigenous Religious Traditions

The framing of Indigenous traditions as religions has been a relatively recent phenomenon. The academic study of religion, which emerged in the mid-nineteenth century in Europe, imposed the Christian imperial gaze and its essentially Western framework onto non-Western wisdom traditions – so, for example, Hinduism and Buddhism became "religions."[7] When the Europeans and their Christian missionaries first arrived in the Americas, they interpreted Indigenous traditions as pagan tribal practices and "devil worship." Until the mid-twentieth century, religions were defined by the extent of their faithful adherence to doctrines, the importance of their sacred texts, and what were true and false beliefs, all categories derived from Christianity.[8] This perspective ignored the changing, complex, and daily practice of religions and traditions where cultures, politics, economics, and ritual intersect.

For decades the study of "other" religions served to reinforce the idea of the evolutionary superiority of Christianity. If Indigenous stories and practices were studied, usually by anthropologists, there was an underlying assumption that there was an evolutionary progression from "mythical thinking" to rational thought. Those cultures informed by the mythical were considered inferior; this argument was used as the justification for colonial occupation. Euro-Western scholars reified and represented these traditions, rather than having practitioners represent themselves.

The legacy of this colonial framework lives on in the debate about how religious traditions should be studied. The belief that Indigenous traditions are best understood through objective, scientific research by outsiders has now been challenged by Indigenous scholars. I introduce this discussion early in the course through readings by Mary Churchill (Cherokee) and Michelene Pesantubbee (Choctaw), who both critique how Indigenous religious traditions have been traditionally taught and studied in American universities.[9] Churchill and Pesantubbee target the Eurocentric tendency to homogenize religious experiences in creating universal theories about religion. They argue for the importance of deconstructing Western interpretations of religion and reconstructing Indigenous ones by bringing Indigenous epistemologies into the field. Churchill, who teaches women's studies and Indigenous literature, argues for the emic study of religion, an insider approach, and applies her own Cherokee-centred analysis to the work of poet Marilou Awaiakta.[10] Both she and Pesantubbee illustrate how believers and practitioners of traditions can contribute greatly to the study of Indigenous traditions and reject the problematic binary of insider/outsider, objective/subjective that has been set up by some Western scholars of religion.

In choosing the readings for the course, I was guided by the words of Mescalero Apache scholar Inez Talamantez, a mentor of many Indigenous religion scholars. Building on Vine Deloria Jr.'s (Standing Rock Sioux) advocacy of Indigenous-centred interpretations of traditions, Talamantez has encouraged her students to do fieldwork, learn the language of the tradition they are engaging with, and listen to people – especially the language speakers in a community – so as to construct theories based on the Indigenous knowledge that is part of the culture and that respond to questions that are relevant to those cultures and communities.[11] Hence I focus on women who are living their traditions, renewing and adapting traditional practices and applying principles in these areas: language revitalization; health and healing; children, youth, and family; protection of land and water; and sovereignty and citizenship. Alongside a course pack of articles, I use two texts: Leanne Simpson's *Dancing on Our Turtle's Back* and Kim Anderson's *Life Stages and Native Women: Memory, Teachings, and Story Medicine*.[12] Simpson applies an Anishinaabe worldview and teachings to her reality as a contemporary Indigenous mother, scholar, and activist; she does so by integrating her language within a resurgence and decolonization framework that is specifically Anishinaabe. Anderson has worked with Cree, Métis, and Anishinaabe knowledge keepers to recover traditional practices of Aboriginal women throughout the life stages. All the course readings, films, and speakers represent images of women who are today reconstructing their traditions and, in doing so, exposing how colonialism has been gendered and how the task of decolonization is gender-specific. As these women apply their values, teachings, and laws from their specific traditions to address contemporary issues, the students learn how these traditions are connected to land and place.

Throughout the course, I need to repeatedly address the most common stereotypes and misinformation about Indigenous traditions. The first is that there is "*the* Indian religion" – that is, that there is one homogeneous tradition.[13] This view only serves an ongoing colonial agenda that disconnects Indigenous traditions from diverse cultures and their land base. I stress the distinctions between traditions, their connections to specific territories, and I provide readings from women from five different traditions – Haudenosaunee, Mi'gmaq, Anishinaabe, Cree, and Okanagan. To complement the readings, I invite in at least four speakers from different traditions. Because at least one speaker every year has some Christian practice and because many Indigenous women often identify both as Christian and traditional, I address the complexities of how Indigenous women relate to Christianity through a reading by Laura Donaldson (Cherokee). Reminiscent of the approach taken by other authors in this volume, Donaldson addresses how Indigenous women appropriated Christianity and adapted it to fit with their worldview.[14] This opens up the discussion of how it is possible for Indigenous women to hold two traditions side by side or in combination without contradiction.

Another stereotype is the romantic and essentialist notion of Indigenous traditions rooted in the image of a frozen past. Indigenous traditions have evolved and adapted through contact with other cultures, especially Christian Europe. As well, unlike the image most non-Indigenous students have of the term "Aboriginal spirituality," which for them connotes sweat lodges and vision quests, ceremonial practices are but moments in complex worldviews where all beings and interactions are sacred.[15] To consider spirit and ceremony abstracted from the culture, values, protocols, and laws of a tradition, as well as from the social, political, and economic spheres of life, distorts a tradition.

The question of the authentic Indian – that is, who is a "real Indian"? – is another major issue addressed by the course. It is important not only because of the stereotypes of the "vanishing Indian" and the "spiritual warrior" but also because there are usually Indigenous students in the class who are struggling with this issue themselves. There are generations of women disenfranchised by the Indian Act and its imposed divisions of Indigenous peoples into Status, non-Status, First Nations, Métis, and Inuit. Because of colourism and internal divisions within communities based on these categories, and because of the residential schools and the fostering out of Indigenous children, Indigenous students often come to the class with ambiguous feelings about their identity. We address the impact of the Indian Act and the question of authenticity and identity through the readings, and the speakers share how they have come to terms with this challenge in their own lives.

Central to the study of Indigenous traditions is the question of epistemology. Indigenous religious traditions are place-based. Land – and specific land – serves as an ontological basis of Indigenous worldviews. This is a fundamental difference from Eurocentric understandings of religion, which speak of "world religions" and religious practices that are often viewed as disconnected from land and place. In order to decolonize how Indigenous traditions are taught in the classroom, both teaching strategies and content need to reinforce how a place-based relationship to land informs Indigenous ethics of reciprocity, responsibility, and mutual obligation. What is common to all Indigenous knowledge systems is the emphasis on the relationship of land to cultural practices and traditions. As Inez Talamantez has said, "a land-based pedagogy involves helping students to understand the connections between Native American worldviews and the different ways in which traditions grow out of relationship with the land."[16]

At the same time that I stress the specificity of tribal traditions and connection to land, I address the reality of traditional practices in contemporary urban Indigenous life. The majority of Indigenous women live in urban centres and often – because of loss of status, lack of housing in their home communities, being Métis or of mixed heritage, or simply choosing to live in the city – do not have the option of having a specific language and land connection. Many Indigenous people in urban and even some rural areas practice ceremonies that are intertribal in nature. These practices are often referred to as "pan-Indian," a term that implies one "true" religion and serves to deterritorialize cultural traditions in a way that benefits the ongoing colonial efforts to exploit Indigenous lands. In reality these practices are intertribal and reflect how Indigenous peoples have always borrowed, adapted, or gifted to the multiple religious influences in their history. As Michelene Pesantubbee has pointed out, when Indigenous people participate in a Lakota sweat or a Plains Sundance, they don't think they are "practicing pan-Indianism."[17]

## Decentring Colonialism

The first time I taught the course, I chose to emphasize the contact zone of religious encounter, using a postcolonial feminist framework. I included white women's participation in imperialism and their role in the attempted subjugation of Indigenous women, as well as the patriarchal dynamics to which white women were subject. I used readings from Indigenous women who described the intersections of race, gender, and colonialism in their experiences of their history and erosion of their traditions. I included a few readings by non-Indigenous women who were examining the role of white women in the colonial project and, in particular, women missionaries.

However, my concern about teaching from a feminist postcolonial perspective is that the content can still reinforce the dynamic of Indigenous as "Other," leaving the non-Indigenous student still able to comfortably distance him- or herself from the issues. This framework does disrupt the dominant narrative of Canadian history and challenges stereotypes and myths, and students may gain more information about the colonial process as it affects women, but there is not much that is positive that can connect Indigenous students to their traditions. Colonialism is still the centre of the course. We have not succeeded in decentring either Christianity or the West, and the oppositional framework reinforces a Euro-Western worldview, and can still be interpreted as presenting the Indigenous woman as victim, despite readings to the contrary. As well, the occlusion of the centrality of land in this framework means that the students do not have the opportunity to learn about the core of Indigenous traditions nor address their own relationship to land and place.

Lorna Williams (Lil'wat), Canada Research Chair in Indigenous Knowledge and Learning at the University of Victoria, and educator Michele Tanaka, writing on cross-cultural pedagogy in the classroom, maintain that there is little room for Indigenous worldviews *"as articulated by Native people"* when the emphasis in the academy is "on the relationship between the colonized and the colonizer, a relationship founded on conflict and adversarial approaches." They add that "the challenge for the academy, which is based on Western perspectives of teaching and learning, is to create spaces within these foreign and alienating environments that provide an opening to the Indigenous world."[18]

To provide this opening I incorporate, as much as possible, Indigenous methodologies into my teaching. Indigenous methodologies flow "from an Indigenous belief system that has at its core a relational understanding and accountability to the world."[19] If students could engage with and understand what a relational understanding was, then the negative impacts of colonial Christianity, in terms of how it served to undermine this worldview, could be grasped more easily. My shift to an Indigenous methodological framework has been influenced by my long-term work with my Anishinaabe/Cree colleague Alannah Young. Between 2009 and 2011, we worked with practising knowledge keepers from several Coastal Salish communities in workshops on the truth and reconciliation process, and in staff and faculty Aboriginal cultural training at the University of Victoria.[20] Most of the teachings focused on language and land. At a session at the University of Victoria on protecting Indigenous intellectual property rights, Elder Marie Cooper (Wsanec) challenged our language, and suggested that "respect," not "protect," was the appropriate word to use in talking about Indigenous intellectual property rights. This was a shift from the defensive to a proactive application of Indigenous principles and values. The knowledge keepers kept stressing that knowledge must come from a heart place, which was a place of action, not reaction, and it is this heart knowledge which is at the core of Indigenous traditions.[21]

I incorporate many aspects of Indigenous methodologies into the classroom: the particularities of tribal knowledges; the ethics and protocols of the nation in whose territory we are; the practice of locating ourselves in relation to land, place, and ancestry; and allowing "learning through spirit."[22] All activities reinforce relations and relationships as central to Indigenous worldviews, illustrate the relationship between Indigenous languages and place, and counter the Eurocentric split between humans and nature. We learn about the oral transmission of Indigenous knowledge in storytelling and the importance of protecting this way of passing on knowledge. Usually at least two of the class speakers are storytellers. A speaker who is a singer teaches about the role of song and song protocols, and engages the class in singing. The films and readings incorporate Indigenous methodologies, and I experiment with different teaching tools.

## Teaching Strategies

I incorporate Indigenous values from the first session of the class. I use the circle teachings taught to me by Bernadette Spence (Cree) to introduce the principle of relationship and the interdependence of all relations. As Celia Haig-Brown articulates so well, the circle "interrupts the assumptions of those other heuristics – the line and the box, dualities and binaries."[23] From Stó:lō scholar and educator Jo-ann Archibald (Q'um Q'um X'iem), I have learned that "knowledge must be shared in a manner that incorporates cultural respect, responsibility, reciprocity and reverence."[24] I speak to these four values in the context of circle teachings and the protocols of how one relates in a circle and I introduce them as guidelines for classroom behaviour.

I emphasize *respect* in how we talk to each other. In the circle everyone's voice is sought, welcomed, and respected, even minority views. I model this by encouraging, without judgment, the opinions of those who disagree with me or a reading. I keep going back to principles and set the tone, so that students begin to feel more courageous in saying what they really think rather than trying to guess what I want to hear. I teach *responsibility* as a value in that we take responsibility for what we say and don't say, how we acknowledge our own history and location in Canadian society and speak and act from it. I model speaking from my own location throughout the course, and in admitting when I don't know something, often saying why. I always acknowledge from whom and where I have learned what I teach. As with the practice of acknowledging who has transmitted a public song or shared a story, the practice of giving credit maintains relationships and affirms our interdependence and is what Celia Haig-Brown calls "the oral equivalent to citation."[25] I explain how teaching the course is one of the ways I exercise my responsibilities as a settler and my way of giving back for all I have received. This relates to the principle of *reciprocity,* which I affirm in gifting speakers and in having students present the gifts and speak for the class. I encourage students to look for where and how the principle of reciprocity is expressed in their readings. I reaffirm how reciprocity is central to a mutual, responsible, and ecological relationship with land. Lastly, I constantly emphasize the *reverence* for the entire natural and human world that Indigenous traditions teach us, and I encourage the students to see that value as integral to the respect, responsibility, and reciprocity they can practise with each other.

In terms of local protocols, I begin the class with acknowledging the traditional territory of the Mohawk peoples in whose territory Montreal is located. I briefly introduce myself, my ancestry, and the territory from which I come and in which I presently live as a visitor. The practice of acknowledging territory affirms how land, spirit, and culture are connected and underlines that the territory is a homeland that is occupied and, in many cases, unceded. In 2011, in recognition of the protocol to honour relationships with the peoples on whose land we are, I was fortunate to have Orenda Boucher-Curotte, a Mohawk scholar of Kateri Tekakwitha and at that time my teaching assistant, provide a Haudenosaunee perspective throughout the course, as well as teach a session on Kateri. In 2013, Chief Kahsennenhawe Sky-Deer, representative for youth on the Mohawk Council of Kahnawà:ke and a language speaker, agreed to both open and close the course with the Ohenton Karihwatehkwen, the address of the Haudenosaunee people, as well as speak to issues in her community.[26]

After the opening, I explain the intentions/objectives of the course (see Appendix) and acknowledge how there is and will be an ongoing tension between Indigenous ways of knowing and Western ways of teaching and learning. I stress the importance of "deep observation" and listening. Lorna Williams links these skills to self-generated and self-motivated learning in Indigenous ways of knowing.[27] I encourage students to figure out the answers themselves rather than constantly asking questions, and I speak to the value of silence in the classroom. My purpose is not only to encourage the white speakers in the class to hold back, but to challenge the ways in which we learn. I use silence often, especially around difficult subject matter. After showing the film *Finding Dawn,* about the murdered and missing women, we held silence for several minutes to allow everyone to process their feelings about the film, including those who were quietly weeping.[28] In the course evaluation, several cited the moments of silence as one of the things they liked best about the class.

Several times in the course, I use a pedagogical process that Alannah and I have adapted from Métis educator Marjorie Beaucage. Marjorie developed the "Indian Act Medicine Wheel," an activity for members of churches and labour unions that incorporates an Indigenous worldview into teaching about the Indian Act and colonialism. Because the medicine wheel is not part of traditions on the West Coast, where I live, or of the Haudenosaunee people in whose territory I am a guest, I refer to the process as circle teachings. The process involves moving around the four directions and allows students to share in small groups something of their life stories in relation to some aspect of Indigenous worldviews. I facilitate aspects of this process at four strategic moments in the course, each usually taking about thirty to forty minutes of a 135-minute class.

The first time I do this is in the introductory class. I ask students to identify the four directions. They then place themselves in a direction that corresponds to their season of birth (using Haudenosaunee correspondence of seasons and directions). They introduce themselves in their small groups and reflect on what they know about their season of birth and then report back as a group. For many, a collective reflection on seasons is new to them; it is enhanced when there are Indigenous students in their group who share how the rhythms of the seasons affect community life and ceremony. This activity introduces them to one way in which time functions in Indigenous communities and how the seasons regulate human and other species behaviour, and how the two are interrelated. As well, in reflecting on the directions, I introduce the importance of space in traditions – and how the ceremonial directions, including the sky and earth, place us within the cosmos.

In the second session I ask the students to group again by the directions and share "Where is your granny from?"[29] This activity draws on Indigenous traditions of introducing oneself by ancestry and territory. I ask students to name their cultural heritage through their grandmothers, as well as identify in whose Indigenous territory she and they themselves grew up. To help them, I provide maps of Indigenous territories today, as well as the map of the Americas before 1492. I encourage those not born in the Americas to reflect on and research Indigenous presence in their homelands.

With these activities, I encourage students to begin exploring their own relationship with space and land, and their own histories within the colonial past and present. Settler scholar David Greenwood has pointed out that the erasure of Indigenous presence on land and the history of land is an intentional part of the placelessness of Western schooling. It is in the interest of the "larger disembedding culture of global capitalism" to undermine all people's relationship to land and place, so that the "breaking down of ties to home communities" can further the exploitation and extraction of human and natural resources."[30] It also serves the interest of white supremacy, as Indigenous claims are presented as being those of "outsiders" to the white settler state. The "granny activity" reveals how occupation of Indigenous homelands is cleverly obscured by the dominant narrative of the land called "Canada." It locates specific nations within specific territories and allows me to use this moment to both challenge pan-Indian notions of Aboriginality and to address the politics of naming, that is, how Indigenous peoples have been called Indians, First Nations, Aboriginal peoples, and so on, to undermine and erase how each tradition is connected to a specific language, land, and place.

As most students who enter a religion class have little knowledge of the history of Indigenous peoples in the land called Canada, I use a third activity called "the Stone Messages." Within a circle of twenty-four stones, I place pieces of paper, each with a moment of Indigenous history – either of oppression or resistance – underneath each stone. I include moments that have specifically affected women, such as Bill C-31 and the 1876 Indian Act, as well as those that are part of the experience of the nations in the region. The messages are placed in a nonlinear fashion. At the centre of the circle is a basket of medicines, which are there to affirm the reverence and respect with which we need to uncover the very difficult moments in this history. Quoting the late Vine Deloria Jr. (Standing Rock Sioux), I introduce the principle that in the Indigenous moral universe, "there are no coincidences and nothing has incidental meaning."[31] If a student ends up in front of a stone under which there is a piece of paper that has written on it a historical moment about which he or she knows nothing, it is for a reason. Each student (or pair of students) is asked to take responsibility for that moment of history, sharing what he or she knows about it and/ or inviting others who may know more to add their thoughts.

This process takes the entire class time. I ask for a few minutes of silence at the end so there is time to absorb what we have heard. With responses ranging from anger and "why didn't we know about this?" to sorrow, shame, and guilt, this activity has high emotional impact. To deal with this I ask students to debrief in pairs and then to comment in the large group. In the evaluation, a few students expressed frustration with the amount of information and its non-linearity, while others found the process opened up a new way of constructing a collective narrative.

In one of the final classes, when we are looking at the role of ceremony in Indigenous traditions, I invite students to divide into four groups by stages in the life cycle – in the East from conception to birth and walking; in the South, childhood and youth; in the West, adulthood; and in the North, grandmothers and Elders.[32] They then share their understandings of this stage of life and what ceremonies or rituals are associated with that stage of life for women in their cultures. This process allows them to connect their own life stories with Indigenous life-stages traditions.

The course still contains the tensions of grading. Though I can create space for some collective ways of teaching and learning, I have to deal with assessment and assignments. I agree with the late Patricia Monture (Mohawk) that you can't take all the hierarchy out of the classroom and that "being a teacher is a responsibility rather than a power, and a responsibility to make sure learning is happening."[33] I struggle to create a range of assignments that recognizes the diversity of students' gifts and competencies. I have students write a weekly journal, in which I invite students to reflect on what is new, disturbing, or shocking to them in each class and the weekly readings, and to respond, incorporating poetry, drawings, or news clippings when able. I include group film reviews, a paper on any topic of choice, and a mid-term exam. I am well aware that I need to break out of my own Eurocentric focus on writing and to create assignment activities, possibly with video or audio, that engage the whole person – body, mind, spirit, and emotion.

In evaluating what I am doing in the classroom I acknowledge I am only incorporating small elements of Indigenous ways of knowing and land-based learning into the class. Lorna Williams and Michele Tanaka, in their article on cross-cultural pedagogy in the university, have identified the essential elements of Indigenous ways of educating: inclusivity, community building, peer learning, and recognition and celebration of individual uniqueness.[34] I can hope to create some space for these through the small-group circle-sharing activities, group assignments, and classroom discussions. When a student told me he had almost learned the most from his fellow students, I was pleased.

## For Settler Teachers

Settler scholars and teachers face unique challenges in integrating Indigenous ways of knowing into classroom teaching about religious encounter. Jean Pierre Restoule, Anishinaabe educator at the Ontario Institute for the Study of Education affirms and, in fact, encourages settler scholars to teach Indigenous ways of knowing. In advocating for non-Indigenous teachers to do this, he stipulates that, instead of asking "Do I have the right to teach this material?" the settler scholar "must approach this task 1) from the position of what is my responsibility? And 2) that the settler scholar /teacher's learning has to be developed through relationships, which is a life time process."[35]

If Restoule can give some assurances to self-doubting settler teachers, he is making it clear that it is hard work, with considerable soul-searching. Over the past thirty years, through the relationships I have made, I have learned to be vigilant about appropriation, to avoid speaking for Indigenous peoples, and to begin to understand my own responsibilities. If you want to learn about Indigenous knowledge systems, you can't do it by simply Googling it; the understanding has to be developed over time through relationships. That is the work and commitment. Haig-Brown reiterates the need for years of education, listening, observing, and building relationships in Indigenous contexts so that the non-Aboriginal teacher can begin to understand the relationship and difference between cultural appropriation and "deep learning."[36]

All teachers need to teach from their own location, both the points of their privilege and the points of oppression, and to problematize their stance. This will encourage students to look at themselves and question why they might take a stand or position, and help them to grasp that everyone comes from different circumstances not of their choosing. This can support building relationships in the classroom across races and difference. Whether Aboriginal or not, instructors need to do research on local protocols and, wherever possible, include some of these protocols in the classroom.[37]

## Conclusion: Decolonizing?

Let's get back to the critical question: is teaching a course out of an Indigenous Knowledge framework likely to have a decolonizing effect on students and teachers, and decolonize, to some extent, the teaching of religious studies in this area? When taught within a framework that privileges Indigenous knowledge, students discover that there are multiple worldviews and knowledge systems. Teaching from an Indigenous knowledge framework privileges Indigenous voices, foregrounds the relationship with land and place, and allows students to know not only what was lost but also what has been regained through contemporary Indigenization. Students as well discover an Indigenous perspective on gender balance and women's roles that differs significantly from that of white feminism. They learn how the values and cultural roles of Indigenous women were specifically targeted for erasure by the churches and government, and how Indigenous women are now applying these values and laws to renew everything from child welfare to recovering the sacredness of water. Students are able to grasp the roots of colonial and gendered violence and, as well, discover how the recovery of traditional values will play a critical role in ending oppression for all. At the same time they learn how some Indigenous women are critiquing Indigenous "traditionalism," where traditions frozen in the past are used today for the exclusion of women.[38]

In using an Indigenous knowledge framework, I am acting on my responsibility to the Indigenous students who attend the class. In the university, these students experience epistemic violence on a daily basis, and so I can provide aspects of a framework to which they can relate. This opens up liberatory possibilities for non-Indigenous students as well. The abstract and "neutral" knowledge that is privileged in universities is in direct conflict with Indigenous epistemologies grounded in local homelands. While it may take years for non-Indigenous people to really "get" heart knowledge, it is critical for all students to be open to the possibility of a differently constructed universe where all parts of their being can be engaged – where, as David Greenwood says, "we can remember we are embodied and emplaced people connected to other embodied and emplaced people."[39] My colleague Alannah Young Leon and I call this approach an "All our Relations" pedagogy, where the interconnection between all living beings is affirmed.[40] At the same time, as this fosters what Australian educators Nakata et al. call an "epistemic awakening," the focus on decolonization supports students to examine critically their own decolonization process as well as the role religion can play in it.[41]

It would be difficult to summarize the students' evaluations of this course. Besides asking them to make the last entry of their journal a commentary on what they had learned, I provided my own evaluation form, which is more useful than university quantitative forms. Comments ranged from "I learned the value of listening and silence," to "the importance of relationships," to "the course has been life changing for me." All of the Indigenous students said they had gained pride in their identity. There were also the usual comments, such as "Why didn't you lecture more instead of putting us in small groups?"

I have chosen not to define "decolonization" in both this chapter and the classroom. For me it is a process that both colonizer and colonized need to go through, and it is profoundly different for both. The full meaning of decolonization will be apparent only to generations after me. While the process of decolonization may be achieved imperfectly in the classroom, teaching about colonialism through the lens of Indigenous knowledge systems and a gender perspective exposes all students to a way of perceiving the world that will inspire them to think about who they are, where they have come from, and who they can be. No less significant, it can open them up to a process of learning that moves from the head to the heart. That is where decolonization begins.

## Appendix

**Course: Rel 368- FPST 398 A**

*Religion in Indigenous Traditions: Indigenous Traditions, Women and Colonialism*

This overview looks at some of the many diverse religious traditions of the First Nations populations in North America. The course examines sacred stories, ceremonial patterns, life cycle rituals, and how these inform the daily life of Indigenous women. Consideration is given to the historical interaction of Indigenous government with religious practices.

It will examine how women from various Indigenous traditions of Turtle Island have affirmed, adapted, or renegotiated their traditions in the context of colonization and missionization. Readings, films, and speakers will include women who are developing practices of resurgence and renewal within their respective Indigenous knowledge systems and, through storywork and ceremony, are applying Indigenous principles, values, and laws. The course will consider how Indigenous women's understandings of their traditions can inform the decolonization of settler, diasporic, and Indigenous populations.

Course Objectives:

(1) Identify some of the issues and ethical considerations in the study and representation of Indigenous traditions, women, and religion.

(2) Identify and have a basic understanding of the concepts and application of Indigenous knowledge systems and how these disrupt prevailing Euro-Western concepts of knowledge.

(3) Discuss how colonial Christianity, missionization, and the policy and practices of assimilation impacted and continue to impact Indigenous women's lives, roles, and traditional practices.

(4) Examine and critically discuss examples of how Indigenous women are renewing and restoring traditional practices and principles in the areas of language revitalization; health and healing; children, youth, family, and community; the protection of land and water; challenging violence against Indigenous women; governance, sovereignty, and citizenship.

(5) Explore some aspects of Indigenous ways of knowing and learning in the classroom.

(6) Reflect on how Indigenous women's understandings of decolonization can inform decolonization and alliances between settler, diasporic, and Indigenous peoples.

## Notes

1 Mary Louise Pratt defines the contact zone as "the space of colonial encounters where people geographically, historically separated, come into contact with each other and establish ongoing relations, usually involving conditions of coercion, radical inequality, and intractable conflict." Mary Louise Pratt, *Imperial Eyes: Travel Writing and Transculturation* (New York: Routledge, 1992), 7.

2 The term "popular education" refers to an education approach first developed by Brazilian Paulo Freire. See Denise Nadeau, *Counting Our Victories: Popular Education and Organizing* (New Westminster, BC: Repeal the Deal Productions, 1996), available at http://www.popednews.org/resources.html.

3 For an introduction to Indigenous methodologies, see also Margaret Kovach, *Indigenous Methodologies: Characteristics, Conversations, and Contexts* (Toronto: University of Toronto Press, 2009).

4 Beenash Jafri, "Privilege vs. Complicity: People of Colour and Settler Colonialism," *Equity Matters Blog,* 20 March 2012, http://www.ideas-idees.ca/blog/privilege-vs-complicity-people-colour-and-settler-colonialism.

5 Jeff Corntassel, "Indigenizing the Academy: Insurgent Education and the Roles of Indigenous Intellectuals," http://blog.fedcan.ca/2011/01/12/indigenizing-the-academy-insurgent-education-and-the-roles-of-indigenous-intellectuals/, accessed 8 June 2012.

6 Andrea Smith, "Roundtable Discussion: Native/First Nations Theology: 'Dismantling the Master's Tools with the Master's House': Native Feminist Liberation Theologies," *Journal of Feminist Studies in Religion* 22, 2 (2006), 89.

7 Kwok Pui-Lan, *Postcolonial Imagination and Feminist Theology* (Louisville: Westminster/John Knox Press, 2005), 187–88.

8 For a contemporary discussion dedicated to the debates and tensions around the term "religion," see *Journal of American Academy of Religion* 78, 4 (December 2010).

9 Mary C. Churchill, "Out of Bounds: Indigenous Knowing and the Study of Religion," in *Reading Native American Women: Critical/Creative Representations,* ed. Ines Hernandez-Avila (Lanham, MD: Altamira, 2005), 251–68; Michelene E. Pesantubbee, "Religious Studies on the Margins: Decolonizing Our Minds," in *Native Voices: American Indian Identity and Resistance,* ed. Richard Grounds, George E. Tinker, and David E. Wilkins (Lawrence: University of Kansas Press, 2003), 209–22.

10 Churchill, "Out of Bounds," 262–64.

11 See Ines Talamantez, "Transforming American Conceptions about Native America: Vine Deloria Jr., Critic and Coyote," in *Native Voices: American Indian Identity and Resistance,* 273–89; and Ines Talamantez, "Images of the Feminine in Apache Religious Traditions,"

in *After Patriarchy: Feminist Transformations of the World Religions,* ed. Paula M. Cooey, William R. Eakin, and Jay B. McDaniel (Maryknoll, NY: Orbis, 1991).

12  Kim Anderson, *Life Stages and Native Women: Memory, Teachings, and Story Medicine,* foreword by Maria Campbell (Winnipeg: University of Manitoba Press, 2011); Leanne Simpson, *Dancing on Our Turtle's Back: Stories of Nishnaabeg Re-Creation, Resurgence and a New Emergence* (Winnipeg: Arbeiter Ring, 2011).

13  Michelene Pesantubbee, "Teaching Native American Religions as a Matter of Fact," "Teaching About Native American Religious Traditions: Pedagogical Insights" Panel, American Academy of Religion Annual Meeting, San Francisco, 20 November 2011.

14  Laura Donaldson, "Native Women's Double Cross: Christology from the Contact Zone," *Feminist Theology* 29 (January 2000): 96–117.

15  For a discussion of how the process of stereotyping Native American religions informs scholarly notions of Indigenous traditions in the field of religious studies, see Michael J. Zorgy, "Lost in Conflation: Visual Culture and Constructions of the Category of Religion," *American Indian Quarterly* 35, 1 (Winter 2011): 1–27.

16  Ines Talamantez, "Teaching Native American Religious Traditions and Healing," in *Teaching Religion and Healing,* ed. Linda Barnes and Ines Talamantez (New York: Oxford, 2005), 119.

17  Pesantubbee, "Teaching Native American Religions as a Matter of Fact."

18  Lorna Williams and Michele Tanaka, "Schalay'nung Sxwey'ga: Emerging Cross-Cultural Pedagogy in the Academy: Educational Insights," *Educational Insights* 11, 3 (2007), 2–3, http://einsights.ogpr.educ.ubc.ca/v11n03/pdfs/williams.pdf.

19  Margaret Kovach, "Indigenous Methodologies and Modified Grounded Theory Method," http://www.thesummerinstitute.ca/wp-content/uploads/Indigenous-Methodologies.pdf. See also Kovach, *Indigenous Methodologies.*

20  Le,Nonet Staff and Faculty Aboriginal Cultural Training Manual, University of Victoria, Developed by Alannah Young and Denise Nadeau, http://www.uvic.ca/services/indigenous/programs/lenonet/.

21  I would like to acknowledge Deb George (Quw'-utsun'), Cultural Protocol Liaison for the University of Victoria, as well as Ron George and Wayne Charlie (Quw'-utsun') for being role models of this teaching.

22  Mary Jeanne (M.J.) Barrett, "Nourishing the Learning Spirit: Dialogue on Learning through *Spirit,* 23–26 May 2008, Wanuskewin Heritage Park," Report for the Canadian Council on Learning's Aboriginal Learning Knowledge Centre, http://www.nald.ca/library/research/ccl/nourishing_spirit/nourishing_spirit.pdf.

23  Celia Haig-Brown, "Indigenous Thought, Appropriation, and Non-Aboriginal People," *Canadian Journal of Education* 33, 4 (2010): 925–50, 940.

24  Jo-ann Archibald, *Indigenous Storywork: Educating the Heart, Mind, Body and Spirit* (Vancouver: UBC Press, 2008), 38.

25  Haig-Brown, "Indigenous Thought," 938.

26  The Ohenton Karihwatehkwen, which means "the words before all else," is said by the Haudenosaunee to open and close civil and religious meetings and is said as a daily sunrise greeting.

27  Lorna Williams, "Weaving Worlds: Enhancing the Learning of Aboriginal Students," http://www.ccl-cca.ca/pdfs/Minerva/CCLMinervaLornaWilliamsMarch2008.pdf.

28  *Finding Dawn,* directed by Christine Welsh (National Film Board, 2006), DVD.

29  Larry Grant, Musqueam Elder, offered this name for the activity.

30  David A. Greenwood, "Place, Survivance, and White Remembrance: A Decolonizing Challenge to Rural Education in Mobile Modernity," *Journal of Research in Rural Education* 24, 10 (2009), 4.

31   Vine Deloria Jr., "If You Think about It, You Will See That It Is True," in *Spirit and Reason, The Vine Deloria Jr. Reader,* ed. Barbara Deloria, Kristen Foehner, and Sam Scinta (Golden, CO: Fulcrum, 1999), 40–60.

32   For a detailed discussion of life stages of Indigenous women, see Anderson, *Life Stages and Native Women.*

33   Patricia Monture, "An Interview with Patricia Monture Speaking about Inclusion within the Academy," *University Affairs,* http://www.universityaffairs.ca/an-interview-with -patricia-monture.aspx, accessed 26 March 2012.

34   Williams and Tanaka, "Schalay'nung Sxwey'ga Emerging Cross-Cultural Pedagogy," 2.

35   Jean-Paul Restoule, "Everything Is Alive and Everyone Is Related: Indigenous Knowing and Inclusive Education," *Federation Equity Issues Portfolio's "Transforming the Academy: Aboriginal Education" Series,* http://www.ideas-idees.ca/blog/everything-alive-and -everyone-related-indigenous-knowing-and-inclusive-education.

36   Haig-Brown, "Indigenous Thought," 925–50.

37   For an example of protocols to respect in one university context, see the Coast Salish Protocols at the University of Victoria, http://www.uvic.ca/services/indigenous/index. php/cultural-protocol.

38   Dawn Martin Hill, "She No Speaks and Other Colonial Constructs of 'the Traditional Woman,'" in *Strong Women Stories: Native Vision and Community Survival,* ed. Kim Anderson and Bonita Lawrence (Toronto: Sumach Press, 2003), 106–20.

39   Greenwood, "Place, Survivance and White Remembrance," 2.

40   Alannah Young Leon and Denise Nadeau, "Embodying All Our Relations Pedagogy," in *Embodiment, Pedagogy and Decolonization: Critical and Materialist Considerations,* ed. Sheila Batacharya and Renita Wong (forthcoming from Athabasca University Press).

41   M. Nakata, V. Nakata, S. Keech, and R. Bolt, "Decolonial Goals and Pedagogies for Indigenous Studies," *Decolonization: Indigeneity, Education and Society* 1, 1 (2012): 120–40.

# 9

# Autoethnography That Breaks Your Heart:
# Or What Does an Interdisciplinarian Do When
# What She Was Hoping for Simply Isn't There?

*Carmen Lansdowne*

I AM A MEMBER OF THE Heiltsuk First Nation from the Heiltsuk house of Wuyalitxv, hereditary chief Harvey Humchitt. I am also adopted into the Gwa'yasdams house of hereditary chief Rick Johnson.[1] My Heiltsuk name is Ga'gwaigilouk (which means "dearest one" or "sweetheart"), and my Kwakwala name is Kwisa'lakw (which means "woman who travels to many places far away"). It is customary for my people, much like the current trend of declaring one's "social location"[2] as a scholar, to declare our lineage before we speak. I am also an ordained minister in the United Church of Canada, and an indigenous theologian. When I declare who I am and where I am from, it is the beginning of both the deconstructive and the constructive tasks for me as a Heiltsuk (christian) theologian and interdisciplinary scholar.

Throughout this work, I side with George "Tink" Tinker in his intentional use of the lower case for adjectives such as "christian" in order to "avoid unnecessary normativizing or universalizing of the principal institutional religious quotient of the euro-west." This includes not capitalizing the "north" in "North America" in recognition that the geopolitical boundaries in America are artificially constructed.[3] The lack of capitalization also challenges disparities and divisions based on sociocultural and economic power that are signalled by "North," "Central," and "South" America. Also like Tinker, I capitalize "White" to signify the hegemony of White privilege that exists in my context.[4] "Whiteness" is not usually capitalized, so its capitalization serves as a visible rememberer of how much power is vested in the word "white" and in the racial construction of Whiteness. This power is often left unexamined, so the capitalization of "White" and "Whiteness" serves as a caricature of the hegemonic force. Lastly, words like "Heiltsuk," "First Nations," "Native American," and "American Indian" are capitalized because they are preferred terms of reference; "indigenous," in contrast, refers to indigeneity in general, and therefore remains lower case.

As this collection makes clear, the academy is no stranger to the troubled histories between indigenous peoples and churches; churches acted as both active and passive perpetrators of geographic, economic, social, and religious colonization in the name of christianity. Existing scholarship has traditionally focused on the relationship between indigenous peoples and their colonizers as an essentialized relationship of "conquered peoples" versus "imperial powers."[5] Despite this history of these multiple colonizations there exists a faithful, sometimes even growing, population of indigenous peoples who identify themselves as christian (Roman Catholic, Protestant, and Orthodox). Yet these christian indigenous identities exist on the underside of society, usually unseen and unheard by the denominations or churches to which they remain loyal. This invisibility is partly demographic – due to the large decimation of indigenous peoples, indigenous communities are often small – but it is also part of what scholar Laura Donaldson calls the "sanctioned ignorance"[6] of discourse in the academy. As black-studies professor George Lipsitz identifies, there exists a possessive investment in "Whiteness,"[7] a long-held blue-chip stock of churches in colonized lands. Against this investment, indigenous scholars in the disciplines of English, education, and theology (among others), in order to "reorder" the academy,[8] are beginning to articulate explicit characteristics of indigenous epistemologies that are common to different communities and distinct peoples.

The project I originally intended to undertake when I started working on this chapter was to engage the extant archival and other primary sources left by literate First Nations christians to explore their theological beliefs. I have always longed for a more engaged, more authentic-feeling history of First Nations christianity, one that broke through traditional historiographic disciplinary boundaries and sang a different song that would more accurately reflect my own understanding of the history of my people and the beautiful (as well as the oft-described ugly) reasons we converted. While I would argue there are some legitimate critiques of the work of those historians who are attempting to retell the history of Native christianit(ies), I was inspired to do this project because of the profound departure from the canon of missionary historiography from the Pacific Northwest Coast of Canada that is represented by Susan Neylan's *The Heavens Are Changing: Nineteenth-Century Protestant Missions and Tsimshian Christianity* (2003). I was inspired by her work and hoped that an exploration of extant writings of First Nations christians would guide me towards my own research projects. In particular, I felt that Neylan's model would be appropriate to the way in which I study both indigenous epistemologies and christian theologies of mission in that it brings together historical, theological, epistemological, and methodological approaches to a particular case study. By examining the primary and secondary sources related to the Crosby marine mission on the Pacific Northwest of British Columbia, I hoped to explicitly engage the academic practice of interdisciplinarity in a way that would create a new narrative about the interaction between First Nations in British Columbia and the Methodist missionaries who lived among them.

Susan Neylan's project approached the work from a historical perspective: she researched the history of interactions between the Crosbys and First Nations from primary sources left by First Nations writers.[9] I was interested in this particular mission because Thomas Crosby was a late-nineteenth-century Methodist missionary in the traditional territories of the Heiltsuk and Tsimshian peoples from whom I am descended. I am also an ordained minister in the United Church of Canada – that very liberal progeny of the Methodist Church in Canada. My ties to Crosby and the many legacies of his mission are therefore both geographic and theological. I hoped to conduct a study similar to Neylan's fascinating work, but with my primary focus on theology and missiology rather than history. In addition, I was also intentional in exploring autoethnographic writing that incorporates both scholarship on indigenous epistemology and story writing as a method of indigenous scholarship. Autoethnography is distinct from traditional qualitative ethnographic models of scholarship in that it focuses on the subjective experience of the researcher rather than the objective observation of the beliefs and practices of others. It is used increasingly (both explicitly and implicitly) by indigenous scholars as a methodology that is more epistemologically appropriate to our worldviews.[10]

Ethnographer Ruth Behar wrote an autoethnographic collection of essays on her fieldwork, titled *The Vulnerable Observer: Anthropology That Breaks Your Heart*.[11] After engaging in the research process for this project, I understand more clearly what she means by "the vulnerable observer," although I'm sure I mean something different from her anthropology "that breaks your heart." The vulnerability with which I now identify more fully is the willingness to write the personal into the academic, despite disciplinarian power politics that resist such a move. What better place, then, to venture into the world of subjective qualitative research than an interdisciplinary research project? It is not that autobiography is completely excluded in the academy. As Behar points out, "No one objects to autobiography, as such, as a genre in its own right. What bothers critics is the insertion of personal stories into what we have been taught to think of as the analysis of impersonal social facts."[12] I understand Behar's experience of "anthropology that breaks your heart" to mean the articulation of the deep, personal investment that anthropologists have in their work. It breaks your heart because you expose your own investment – your own sense of compassion. I did something similar in this project, but rather than expose my subjectivity in relation to a topic, I made myself the subject being acted on by the topic: my heart is broken over and over again by the failure of the church, of the academy, and of society in general to represent the vast heterogeneity of indigenous experiences of colonization – both good and bad. It seems as though the still-dominant Amer-european colonialist thinking that rationalized residential schools and forced sterilization of Native women still reigns supreme, although in much more politically correct and convenient ways. In my experience, whether the stories told are success stories or tragedies, they are almost always still told in service of the colonialist drive to keep indigenous peoples oppressed and disappearing from national narratives (despite even the most self-aware, best intentions of the author) – and that is heartbreaking.

The autoethnographic writer is, by nature of her project, quite possibly putting herself in the path of direct confrontation or dismissal of her work. But the stakes are even higher than the potential resistance to her methodology. Vulnerability also requires *good* writing, not just vulnerable writing. If a scholar writes in a traditional empiricist framework of study, the worst that can happen with good scholarship is that it might be boring. For a vulnerable scholar explicitly incorporating the personal into the scholarly, *boring* has additional ramifications: "a boring self-revelation, one that fails to move the reader, is more than embarrassing; it is humiliating."[13] I now understand in a more embodied way exactly how I am being vulnerable. The experience of engaging autoethnography in this project has left visceral and emotional imprints that continue to shape my research and writing. While my research may be interesting to me, I worry it still may be boring and/or academically subversive. And so in naming that fear (and in naming the hope that my vulnerability will *not,* in fact, be boring), I will continue.

## What Breaks My Heart

My proposal for this project was ambitious. I had not looked at the primary written historical sources, nor had I really paid attention to how widely spread across Canadian (and British!) archival depositories the primary sources were. I thought it would be possible for me to replicate the type of work that Susan Neylan did in *The Heavens Are Changing.* If I had really considered where Neylan's sources were, I might have realized how large an undertaking I was proposing.

Vulnerability 1: I underestimated the impact that the geographical separation of various archival collections would have on my work. I also grossly overestimated the number and comprehensiveness of extant written records (in English) left by First Nations christians.

It was ambitious not only in the way I meant to "decode" the missiology/theology of First Nations christians in the Pacific Northwest but also in how I assumed that there would be something different – some kind of signifier that would set apart the epistemologies of different coastal peoples in nineteenth and early twentieth centuries in British Columbia. I realize in retrospect that this is a universal limitation faced by all scholars who rely on archives, and in a way it has left me with a new compassion for settler scholars, including those contributing to this volume, who are trying their best to recreate histories from the same incomplete records. Though I did my undergraduate studies in history, I am not a historian; I am a theologian. I made assumptions based on my practice of writing academic theology that grossly underestimated the time, resources, and determination required to do successful archival research. While I maintain my (sometimes vociferous) critiques of the discipline of history, after doing this work and engaging with historians in the workshop leading to the publication of this volume, I have a new appreciation for the dedication of historians.

Vulnerability 2: I underestimated the impact that early missionizing (during the colonial and early Canadian periods) had on First Nations expressions of culture and faith. I will discuss this vulnerability more completely later in this chapter when discussing Native missionaries such as James Starr and W.H. Pierce.

As I read in preparation for this chapter, I oscillated back and forth – primary historical documents found in the archives and other records, then theory, then secondary sources, then theory, then back to primary sources. There was no "systematic" undertaking of the sources I gathered; my intention was rather to try to approach the work in a way that the past and present would stay connected.

My research experience at the archives of the British Columbia Conference of the United Church of Canada marks the beginning of my heartbreak (as I realized Vulnerabilities 1 and 2 were connected). I was disappointed that I did not find what I was looking for. I was hoping I would find something that had been overlooked or ignored; instead I had to acknowledge I was hoping for something that doesn't exist. And yet it does: I am haunted by the quotes from liberation theologian Marcella Althaus-Reid and First Nations novelist Lee Maracle that I've used in other works, about the "grand narratives"[14] of indigenous peoples that have been systematically erased and yet at the same time persist in language we can no longer articulate. Marcella Althaus-Reid writes, "the destruction of the Grand Narratives of the Americas did not come as the result of a hermeneutics of suspicion, or the realization of the trace in the text, that element which is a movement leading us towards what the text tries to occult, hide and negate. No, economic exploitation was the deconstructive clause, the doubting interrogation of naturalized, assumed authoritative narratives."[15] In her fiction writing, Lee Maracle suggests that the grand narratives, although assaulted, are still carried in the bodies, although they can no longer be spoken:

> Grace has left their bodies. They are rendered stiff and tense by the knot of shame that sits stuck in their throats. It needs to be expressed, pushed up and out so they may sing again, but five centuries of "Hush, don't cry" holds the expression of their shame still. Under it lies a dangerous grief. They now tread heavily upon the back of their mother. Lunging from place to place, they plant seeds but don't bother to watch them grow. They water nothingness as though this water will somehow recreate life without their participation. Many have acquired the jerky movements, the bad skin and the hard, strident song-less voices of the newcomers. Their world has lost its future. Cut off from considering their past, they list in the momentary context of the present. Consideration requires a spiritual sensibility, one that sees life from all its jewel-like angles. [They] don't see life; they barely feel their existence. They avert each other's gaze. The reflection of grief and shame in the eyes of others mirrored back at them is too terrifying to contemplate. They mark time. Time is the enemy of the dispirited. [They] wander aimlessly, killing time in small pieces.[16]

We wear the grand narratives in the scars on our psyches. And in our survival. And in our faith.

I became aware of both resenting and appreciating the work of Susan Neylan in her chapter on Arthur Wellington Clah.[17] I resented her for telling a story that is not hers, and was grateful to her for doing so; I resented the ways in which it so conforms to the dominant disciplinarity of history, but at the same time her work is to be celebrated because she values and honours both his story and his faith. I don't want to resent her or any of the historians whose work I read. But at what point do we *change* the status quo? I hear informal talk at conferences about historical methodologies perpetuating cultural hegemonies: "Well, yes ... It's unfair but it's the way it is." Or worse (spoken *to me*): "Your methodology makes me uncomfortable!" Well, I should hope so, sir ... I should hope so. Because what I do is not easy. I straddle two worlds with great hope – hope for transformation. Hope that my readers will take my people seriously, that they will take our history seriously ... that they will take our present seriously. Hope that they will *learn* (when will they really learn?) that our history is the reason for our present situation.

That our history is the raison d'être of our present situation is exactly why I feel compelled to write in a new way; it is why I employ this risky autoethnography. In my mind, to do otherwise is to allow my subaltern voice to be assimilated into the hegemony of existing disciplinarity.[18] And I know I do this risking that this particular work (or subsequent work) will be considered "too personal."

Behar still echoes in my head:

> But if you're an African-American legal scholar writing about the history of contract law, and you discover, as Patricia Williams recounts in *The Alchemy of Race and Rights,* the deed of sale of your own great-great-grandmother to a white lawyer, that bitter knowledge certainly gives "the facts" another twist of urgency and poignancy. It undercuts the notion of a contract as an abstract, impersonal legal document, challenging us to think about the universality of the law and the pursuit of justice for all.[19]

This history is personal. The conversion of Heiltsuk and other First Nations on the coast of what is now British Columbia is personal. Missiology, because I am a christian, is personal. It is *all* personal. It is personal to the point that when I read scholarly theology, history, critical theory, I sometimes recoil against (what seems to me) the harsh impersonality of it. I feel like a woman standing behind thick, soundproof, bulletproof glass, screaming at the horror of Native realities in 2012, yet no one in the academy can hear me. And it breaks my heart.

But there is strength in numbers, and I am not alone. I have not been alone since I decided to write this piece this way; I did not come up with this idea on my own. In fact, I was inspired by my younger brother, who employed auto-ethnography as the primary methodology for his master's thesis. He was (in my opinion) incredibly vulnerable, and ethically responsible. His intention was to get rid of what he called "carried shame" so that he would be able to work through his own issues and be a more stable and self-aware therapist for his clients, his family, himself.[20] In the methodology section of his thesis, he engaged in a written conversation with quotations from the work of Carolyn Ellis and Art Bochner, the leading proponents of autoethnography. He did this in order to outline how he intended to use (and why he was attracted to) this form of writing:

> ART: "Our enthusiasm for autoethnography was instigated by a desire to move ethnography away from the gaze of the distanced and detached observer and toward the embrace of intimate involvement, engagement, and embodied participation." (Bochner & Ellis, 2006, p. 433-435)
> CAROLYN: "I want to demonstrate my passion for autoethnography through a story or a conversation that shows multiple voices and positions. I want people to feel the story in their guts, not just know the "facts" in their heads." (Bochner & Ellis, 2006, p. 435)

ROBB: This is why autoethnography appeals to me. I feel the journey I have taken in this thesis is a story about what is deep in my guts. I want the reader to feel that. I don't want to control what the reader feels but I want them to have a sense of the tensions I am grappling with. I was caught off guard by the first autoethnographies that I read (Ronai, 1995; Keats, 2000). I found myself absorbed in their stories. I was brought to tears on several occasions. I had not experienced depth like that in any academic writing. I was not absorbed in a voyeuristic way. I was personally invested. My understanding of the subjects these authors wrote on was impacted from my different locations – as a father, as a counsellor, as a man. I knew at this point that this was the methodology that I needed to use on my own journey. I can't see how a detached observation could ever penetrate what I have tried to express in my thesis. There is so much I didn't even know about myself that has been uncovered through the writing process.

ROBB: What is the relation between evocation and autoethnography?

ART: "Evocation is a goal, not a type of autoethnography. I wouldn't think of applying the term "autoethnography" to texts that are not evocative." (Bochner & Ellis, 2006, p. 435)[21]

My brother is not the only First Nations scholar I know who chose to write in an autobiographical and evocative way. Although less explicit in her use of autoethnography as a method, Patricia June Vickers uses poetry, photography, and evocative personal writing in her doctoral dissertation, "Ayaawx (Ts'msyen ancestral law): The Power of Transformation." Vickers also writes of how to process the visceral reaction of integrating the academic with the real – that is to say, the academic study with life as a Native person in Canada (or the United States, or anywhere for that matter). She writes, "When I first attempted to write this dissertation, there was a gnawing sensation that seemed to be in my gut. As I consciously sat with 'it' (resistance, repulsion, anger, fear, cynicism), there was no particular place of abiding. The 'it' was under my skin, in my head, a feeling in my bones, and most of all, a darkness in the depths of my soul."[22] While I am not sure that I experienced necessarily the intensity of emotion that my brother and Patricia Vickers experienced, it is good to know that there is a common "something" that needs deconstruction, something – some truth – that needs to be named by First Nations scholars writing in the academy.

There is a kind of liminal space in interdisciplinarity that has the ability to express a longing to confront the status quo through writing. This is especially true for indigenous writers. There is anger at colonization. There is reclamation of culture and identity. There is frustration that to reclaim culture and identity then puts us in a position to be questioned on the authenticity of our

"Indian-ness" and/or to be questioned about the degree to which we've assimilated (a question posed often most vociferously by Native colleagues). Over the
course of my graduate studies, I find that fiction and poetry most often express
the connection between history and reality. These genres are not as bound by
scientific method as the rest of the academy. They can express in more adequate
ways how my heart is broken:

> *Hanging from the cross*
> *Hanging from the cross*
>   *They keep asking us*
>   *What's wrong with us*
>   *We keep saying back*
>   *What's wrong with you*
>   *What's wrong with you*
>   *Is what's wrong with us*
> *Hanging from the cross*
> *Hanging from the cross*
>   *Indians are Jesus*
> *Hanging from the cross*
> *Hanging from the cross*
>   *In the name of the mother*
>   *The child*
>   *And the human spirit*
>   *Indians are Jesus*
> *Hanging from the cross*
> *Hanging from the cross*
>   *We weren't lost*
>   *And we didn't need any book*[23]

It seems that this is "how it is": "We weren't lost / And we didn't need any
book." And most Indians have feelings ranging from nihilism to rage about that.
And yet some of us chose, still choose, and will continue to choose, to convert
to christianity. This includes the original meetings between First Nations in
north America as well as the contemporary choice for Indians to convert (or to
remain christian). It even extends to those "oh-so-unpopular" Indians who did
*not* have a negative experience in the boarding schools of the US or the residential schools of Canada.[24]

The late nineteenth century and the early twentieth century, when the Crosby
missions began, were a context of the overt partnership of missionizing and
civilizing intentions in colonial contexts. "That Christian Missions, as a

civilising agency, have done priceless service to the Child-Races of the Empire is unquestionable," said J.N. Ogilvie in his 1923 Duff Lecture at the University of Edinburgh.[25] A minister in the Church of Scotland and a member of the Royal Society, Edinburgh, Ogilvie outlines well the ways in which christian missionaries sought to "elevate" the racialized others to whom they ministered:

> To give these races a written language and the beginnings of a literature; to school them, so that the rudiments of education are theirs; to train them in the many industries that contribute to a people's progress; to bring to their women a new position, a new hope, and new life; to transform their lives by the gracious ministry of healing; to elevate the home and the family; to commend and enforce a new and higher morality for the individual and for society; and to be largely instrumental in ending those baneful practices that have degraded and disfigured the life of the Child-Races for long centuries – these are services whose value can hardly be over-estimated.[26]

While it appears that Ogilvie's point is focused on the "secular" and "civilizing" work of christian missions, he reminds his readers later that "however striking and useful the civilising work may be which they accomplish among the Child-Races of the world, their master-purpose remains spiritual."[27] What is the specific theology of mission that undergirds the missions of that time and context, if it is not simply the confluence of salvation and civilization?

From what I understand in the history of the conversion of the Heiltsuk, it was the theological concepts of hope and forgiveness that were new to our people and which made the gospel message of christianity attractive in a rapidly changing context of active settling of Native land by euro-Canadians and new immigrants from Europe (including my paternal great-grandfather, who was from England). A family anecdote has my (maternal Heiltsuk) great-grandfather questioning the church about why White people were so crazy as to go and fight in the First World War. He said that we had converted to christianity (after careful study of the bible) in part because the concepts of hope and forgiveness were new to our people and gave us an escape from the patterns of traditional warfare. If Whites were good christians, my great-grandfather asked, how come they were going to war? As I will outline later, theological understandings of God and of creation within coastal First Nations traditions and christianity were actually quite compatible. As Alan Morley notes in his biography of the Rev. Dr. Peter Kelly (the second First Nations man ordained by the British Columbia Conference of the Methodist church), "the factors in their decision [to convert], after the lapse of a century, cannot exactly be determined; however, by the testimony of the Indians themselves, their previous religious beliefs in many ways paralleled the illustrative legends and parables of the Bible, but, as they said, 'offered no hope.'"28

While this specific work is an interdisciplinary examination of mission history and indigenous epistemologies, as I explained earlier, the problem/subject of the work is me. That is the evocation of autoethnography: that my writing about myself will call to something in you as we respond together to the "subject" about which I am writing. Therefore, the problem/subject of this work is also the legacy of Methodist missionary Thomas Crosby and his missionary endeavours on the Pacific Northwest Coast. I have not chosen to engage in a chronological progression of the Crosby mission. This is partly because the resources I would have liked to use do not exist. This is also in part because I define the "Crosby mission" to mean not only the presence of Thomas and Emma Crosby as missionaries on the coast but also the legacy of that mission and the ways it has manifested over the past one hundred and twenty years. I am part of that legacy. My village is part of that legacy. My denomination is still part of it.

## On Interdisciplinarity and History

Like all First Nations history, the telling of missionary history is not simply a telling of the past. It is political. It matters. It matters to my people because it is so completely connected to our present. To make a moral pronouncement (since I'm being vulnerable and personal), it *should* matter to all people. The primary "problem" for me is finding extant "records" of First Nations theology. But that problem is just one piece of a larger context in which I am thoroughly an "insider." As an ordained Heiltsuk woman, I cannot be anything but an insider in this study. What appeals to me about the problem-based model is that my subjectivity is expected, not frowned upon (as it would necessarily be by more "disciplinarian" historians). In his book *Silencing the Past: Power and the Production of History*, Haitian interdisciplinary anthropologist Michel-Rolph Trouillot writes about the ways in which disciplinary positivism has earned itself some scorn in this respect. He writes, "Indeed the professionalization of the discipline is partly premised on that distinction [between historical process and historical knowledge]: the more distant the sociohistorical process is from its knowledge, the easier the claim to a 'scientific' professionalism."29

This is not in itself a bad thing. The problem lies in relation to power and what I believe is the general failure of the discipline of history to see power as problematic. While certain theorists (Foucault, to name the obvious) have influenced the work of individual historians, it seems to me that this has not had a substantive effect on the discipline as a whole. This has serious implications for history as told (or not told) from the perspective of the margins – in this case, from the perspective of First Nations. For example, when I was in my early twenties, *BC Business* magazine published an op-ed piece in which the author said that oral history was whatever the latest spokesperson to take the stand wanted to say.[30] I was compelled to write a very lengthy, scathing critique of this perspective (which was published in a very shortened, edited form), explaining that traditional oral history was rich with protocol and, when this was followed, I found its practice to be a much more reliable form of "historical truth" than that of White scholars who "interpreted" the past of First Nations, with no connection to the people or their historical or contemporary struggles.[31] From the positivist perspective (whether it is acknowledged or not), "history is a story about power, a story about those who won."[32] The other end of the disciplinary spectrum in history is the constructivist position: that histories as told from different perspectives are just different fictions in a range of fictitious presentations of history.[33] Regardless of which end or at which point along the spectrum one finds oneself as a historian, the issue of power continues to be set aside and only rarely addressed by historians, and even then often inadequately. In fact, Trouillot argues that "the more important an issue for specific segments of civil society, the more subdued the interpretations of the facts offered by most professional historians."[34]

It is precisely this apolitical turn in history – or rather the turn *away* from the political – that is difficult for people on the margins (who also produce their own histories outside of the academy). The fact that history is produced outside of disciplinary boundaries has been largely ignored, according to Trouillot.[35] More importantly, "even the best treatments of academic history proceed as if what happened in the other sites [sites other than the ones investigated in a particular history] was largely inconsequential. Yet is it really inconsequential that the history of America is being written in the same world where few little boys want to be Indians?"[36] The fact that Trouillot values power in the production of history (something I value in the construction of missiology), as well as ambiguity (which is necessary in an autoethnographic account of a problem), helps me to negotiate a methodological and factual obstacle in the work I have undertaken.

## I Did Not Find What I Wanted but Found What I Needed

When I first surveyed Susan Neylan's *The Heavens Are Changing*, I assumed that the written records left in archival deposits would be mainly from First Nations clergy. I did not realize how few of us there were. I also did not realize until I read further into Neylan's book the importance that lay preachers and "catechists" played in maintaining the missions in our traditional territory. I did not realize we had even had people who played such roles until I was home (in Bella Bella) for Christmas in December 2010. I was asked to preside at a service at Darby Memorial United Church in my hometown (it was packed – nine people showed up!). When I was in the small, cold, disorganized church office changing out of my alb back into my winter coat, I saw a drawing – a portrait – I had never noticed before. It was coloured pencil on black paper. I cannot remember the exact title under the portrait, but the man in the picture was Mr. James Starr – a travelling missionary lay preacher. And he was First Nations!

I spent the next week at home dreaming of the records I would find of James Starr and men (and women?) like him when I arrived at the United Church Archives in Vancouver the following week. What I was hoping to find were sermons. Where else would one hope to find insight into the theology of First Nations christian leaders over the past 130 years? It has become clear to me after reading the accounts of Thomas Crosby and W.H. Pierce, however, that no such thing exists. In Crosby's *Up and Down the North Pacific Coast by Canoe and Mission Ship,* he speaks of how the people would memorize scripture and as much of the sermons (preached by White men) as they could, and then they would repeat them as lay preachers or during Bible study or to themselves as personal comfort during times of distress.[37] Even though I live in an age where I write my sermons in full text (and then save them as PDFs on my computer), these faithful preachers did not have written copies of their sermons. There are memories, however, like those outlined in the biography of Peter Kelly, of the thoughtfulness and thoroughness of First Nations deliberations on conversion: "It was characteristic of the coast Indians' integrity that they debated the new religion with honesty, respect, solemnity and in detail. The early converts adopted it only when convinced in soul and mind and then dedicated themselves to it completely. That was, in their circumstances, an almost superhuman task, but they carried it out."[38]

Trouillot's work is also helpful for me in the "factual void" that exists in Pacific Northwest Coast Native theology. He writes, "Silences enter the process of historical production at four crucial moments: the moment of fact creation (the making of *sources*); the moment of fact assembly (the making of *archives*); the moment of fact retrieval (the making of *narratives*); and the moment of retrospective significance (the making of *history* in the final instance)."[39] The remainder of his work in *Silencing the Past* is dedicated to uncovering different strategies for deconstructing silences in history. In Chapter 2, Trouillot uses extant sources to tell the story of a forgotten figure in the Haitian revolution. He writes, "The evidence required to tell his story was available in the corpus I studied, in spite of the poverty of the sources. I only reposition that evidence to generate a new narrative. My alternative narrative, as it develops, reveals the silences that buried, until now, the story of the colonel."[40] This is precisely the method that Neylan undertook in *The Heavens Are Changing*. My "problem" remains that I cannot resolve it by this methodology. I have history that is created in retrieval and retrospective, but I have no material sources to use in the creation of facts or archives. How, then, do I *prove* the narrative of my people's faith from a historical perspective without the weight of materiality behind it?

If, as Trouillot suggests, "the play of power in the production of alternative narratives begins with the joint creation of facts and sources,"[41] then this points to why the subaltern *cannot* speak in terms of retelling missionary history to uncover the theological perspectives of First Nations converts (specifically those who undertook leadership positions in missionizing the Pacific Northwest Coast).[42] There are no facts or sources. But I believe that, because it is possible to uncover the silences in the acts of retrieval and retrospective (two processes in the creation of history that are compatible with oral traditions), we must simply look out of the past and into the present in order to understand again the past.

There is a tension between the "saving souls" motivation of the missionaries and the "hope for the future" felt by the First Nations. Neylan writes, "'Indians' were warlike, superstitious, cruel, inhumane, devilish, drunken, debased and heathen,"[43] according to missionary perspectives of the time. She goes on to write, "Yet, if First Nations were so irredeemable, the project of missionization would have been pointless,"[44] explaining that, despite common perceptions of Indians as "heathen/pagan" or even "barbarian," missionaries would have to believe in the humanity of the heathen in order to think they could be saved at all. She concludes that "the missionaries' accounts of the Northwest Coast temper negative descriptions of indigenous cultures with admiring portrayals of work habits, cleanliness, respect of elders, and other characteristics[,] which frequently allowed them to decry the decline of such values in their own societies."[45]

I struggle with this. I'm not sure I believe it. I have no proof to the contrary, but there is too much documentation that points in a slightly different direction. From reading the accounts of the region's two most well-known missionaries of the time, Thomas Crosby (Methodist) and William Duncan (Anglican), there is no indication that the "virtues" they valued in Native communities were inherent. I read into their accounts that they believe they taught these "christian" values to the communities. Further, that the "success" of teaching these values to the "wretched Indian" was put forward as an example of what Neylan notes as the propaganda and publications necessary for the financial support of missions.[46] Given the difficulty of separating what was deemed "positive" in Indian culture and what was not, I find it helpful to read outside of the direct accounts.

The cross-cultural confusion strikes me as funny: Sherman Alexie funny.[47] Indian Agent (of the federal government of Canada) William Halliday writes that "all who have worked amongst the Indians, either as missionaries, as medical officers, or as workers in either fields, have been extremely struck by what might be called, for want of a better definition, their lack of moral sensibility. They seem to utterly lack the fine feeling which we commonly call sentiment, and their ideas are very gross."[48] While he might have termed their ideas "gross," I think that without really *listening* and learning (something which, in his position, I don't think would have been possible), Halliday couldn't possibly understand the strength of Indian morality, different as it was from his own. More importantly, though, I think Halliday (and others) didn't understand our humour.

There is an example in the same chapter – one of the examples Halliday uses to illustrate our "gross ideas" and lack of sentiment – where I think he simply didn't get it. After a long conversation in mixed Kwakwala, Chinook, and English, Halliday and an Indian named "Joe" had an exchange that made me laugh out loud. Joe's wife had died three days before their conversation (presumably of TB – "He [sic] die because he have no more wind."[49]). After passing on his condolences, Halliday writes:

Our conversation then turned to some difficulty he had been having over a trap line, which I promised to get adjusted satisfactorily for him, and as I turned away, he said to me: "Mr. Halliday, what do you think if I marry Queen?" I looked at him in amazement, and said: "Why do you ask me that question? Queen has a husband already." A smile broke over his face, and he said: "But that is no matter, he like me better."[50]

I repeat: Sherman Alexie funny. But not everyone "gets" Sherman Alexie.

## Are There Any Primary Sources?
W.H. Pierce was the first ordained Methodist minister of First Nations heritage on the coast of British Columbia. The fact that he was mixed Scottish and Tsimshian was not lost on his missionary colleagues (or on historians writing about Pierce and other missionaries on the coast). Although the construction of race (or, rather, the taxonomy of race) is a western concept, Pierce was considered (and would still be considered by some scholars) to be not "fully" Indian. In histories as well as archival sources, it is interesting to note that Pierce's race is generally not mentioned, unless it serves the purpose of emphasizing the good work of the missions so as to command financial support from the wider church. In such instances, he is often referred to as "our Indian brother" or "the Indian missionary."

While I lament the absence of overtly theological primary sources, my purpose is not entirely lost, for I have the autobiography of W.H. Pierce. It is not until the second half of his autobiography that it is even evident that Pierce had any training in traditional ways of life at all (other than his stating so). Like Crosby and Halliday's accounts of their work from a White perspective, Pierce is aware of the changing landscape of Native life on the coast and devotes a good portion of the book to ethnographies that explain the "old ways" of life. It is here that we encounter some recollection of traditional North Coast cultures mixed with the "mimicry" of a hybrid identity in a context of active colonization.

Most notably, the first lines of the second part of his autobiography, *From Potlatch to Pulpit*, begin with "Before the Gospel was preached by the Missionary the natives were ignorant, superstitious, degraded, wild and cruel."[51] This is not unfamiliar in the historiography of north American colonization of First Nations. What is interesting is the indication that Pierce has some apprecia-tion for the traditional ways he was taught by his maternal grandfather before his conversion and calling as a missionary. Under the heading "Superstitious or Old Heathen Beliefs," Pierce acknowledges an important ambivalence as a "mimic" of western christian culture:

> Without exception, the Indians all believed in One as the Creator of all things, and this One lived far away somewhere in the sky ... They believe that if a man lived a good life and did kind deeds, that he would live in happiness somewhere and be rewarded. While if a man lived a bad life and cared only to be selfish, mean and cruel, he would be rewarded accordingly and have no happiness evermore.[52]

Pierce becomes an ambivalent figure of mimicry here. By "mimicry" I mean the term used in postcolonial studies to identify the ways in which the colonized are forced to "mimic" the colonizers.[53] However, the copy is never exact; the edges are blurry and so (in Pierce's case) he never becomes fully White, despite the fact that his writing is aimed at a White audience that expects him to live up to a White ethic of civilization. On the one hand he separates himself from "the Natives" by signifying Indians and Natives with the definite article "the." In addition, he parrots the hegemonic racist discourse of his day that was the preface to the ethnographic section of his autobiography.

Where I find Pierce's writings *most* important, however, is in his description of the potlatch. I have long intuitively felt that the potlatch is one of the places of theological crossroads that allowed christianity to make sense to First Nations on the coast. If the theology Pierce outlines in the "superstitions and old beliefs" is an accurate portrayal, then it is especially interesting to note the distinction that he makes between traditional potlatching and post-contact "feasting." After describing the mechanisms whereby families/crests contributed (materially) to the potlatch and the systems of resulting obligation that were established, Pierce is very clear:

> The real potlatch, conducted in the early days, before the whites came, was very different from the modern feast. There were rules and regulations to govern every move and these were strictly adhered to ... There were rules to guide the dances, the whole of the feast, and the young people.
>
> During the potlatch the wisest and best speakers were chosen to give lectures for the benefit of those who had come together to enjoy themselves. These lectures taught them how to respect themselves and to honor those who were in authority as their chiefs. The young people were instructed to lead pure lives and shun all forms of evil ...
>
> But alas! How different is the Potlatch of today. Amongst the natives it is the root of all evil and the big mountain of sin against which the missionaries have to fight.[54]

He goes on to highlight how the destruction of traditional society *before* conversion to christianity was the chief problem with respect to the potlatch. The decimation of populations due to disease – especially influenza, tuberculosis, and smallpox – left the traditional hierarchies in question and allowed for "commoners" to throw potlatches that did not conform to the strict rules and regulations of the potlatch. Nor, conceivably, did they uphold the traditional forms of banking and increasing power, wealth, and prestige through political alliances and intermarriage as had been done for centuries before. Pierce also indicates that "mixed with the potlatch of today is the white man's dance, which to the native is a great attraction." That, in conjunction with the presence of alcohol, was "the source of much evil."[55]

It is not, then, the potlatch in its traditional form to which Pierce objects; contrary to popular stereotypes that potlatching cultures were "animist" and devil worshippers, Pierce highlights that the potlatch tradition was already upset by the time he was doing missionary work in the late nineteenth century. Unlike White observers, Pierce does not reject the traditional culture because he understands it. What he rejects is the nihilistic behaviours that came from the introduction of disease and alcohol, which he understands as having destroyed the original goodness of the old system. It is important to mention one final characteristic of White-Native relations at the time of Pierce's writing, in which he argues against patronization of the potlatch.[56] He says, "there are many intellectual whites who uphold the potlatch, and consider that the natives have a right to enjoy themselves in this way. It is quite evident that they see only the surface and have no conception of the undercurrent."[57]

Each section of the ethnographic part of Pierce's autobiography has hybrid ambivalences that cast doubt on the sincerity of his opening statement. For example, despite the tendency of Halliday to portray the Kwakwaka'wakw as taking marriage lightly (which he did in his misinterpretation of Joe's words about marriage and in subsequent examples), Pierce notes that marriage was undertaken seriously and for life – especially in the high-ranking families. Further, even though Pierce has mimicked the dominant settler perspective that Indians were lazy and so forth, in the section titled "Training of Children" Pierce highlights how "laziness, they were told[,] would bring ... poverty and disgrace amongst their people and cause them to be a laughing stock to everyone. On the other hand, to be industrious ... meant that they would command self respect and honor, and always have plenty and thus be ready to alleviate any distress amongst the unfortunate."[58] This statement is in almost direct contrast to that of Halliday, who writes, "There is one very material difference between the Japanese and the Indians, and this is in the fact that the Indians have absolutely no parental control over their children."[59]

## Coming Full Circle

I am not entirely sure that this project achieves what I had hoped it would achieve when I originally conceived it. That is not a comfortable fact for me to admit, but in my commitment to be vulnerable and engage in autoethnography, I must admit it if I am to have integrity in telling you the story of this study. I read much more than I integrated into my writing. But at the same time, I feel that I have progressed farther than I would have if I had simply summarized all of the documents that I read in the archives. What was important about the other archival records I read was this: they were mainly from national First Nations theological consultations in the United Church of Canada from the 1970s onward. Thus my choice to not integrate them into my writing at this time. It was a difficult decision because it was in those documents, reports, meeting minutes, and newsletters that I started to see more explicit theological reflection by First Nations in British Columbia. The existence of those later records confirms for me that I am on the right track in my intuitive sense about late-nineteenth and early-twentieth-century First Nations christianity, despite the absence of facts or archival records to prove my intuitions. A long line of spiritual leaders have followed in the theological footsteps of those whom I have discussed here.

It was suggested to me at the forum "Religious Encounter and Exchange in Aboriginal Canada," where the contributors to this volume first came together, that there might be more extant sources of interest to me, especially in London, England. I find this hopeful, and perhaps useful for future research projects. For the time being, my own primary research interest lies in constructive theology and missiology; the good thing is that the archives will be there waiting for me when I am ready to fall back down that particular rabbit hole. And for the first time in a long time, rather than feeling alienated by the discipline of history, the forum has given me the opportunity to build relationships with historians that (hopefully) will continue into the future, informing both their work in history and my work in theology. I am greatly indebted to those present for their careful, considerate, and enthusiastic feedback, critique, questions, and encouragement.

In reflecting on my experience at the forum, I don't think I can articulate how guarded I felt going into the meetings. I knew to some extent that I was an outsider, being primarily a theologian (although I had completed an undergraduate degree in history). For some reason, I had assumed there would be more First Nations scholars there, but despite the fact we were few, I must acknowledge what a superb job our convenors and the other contributors did at creating a safe and respectful place of dialogue and trust. Our conversations on the issues I raise in this chapter have given me hope: I felt as if the contemporary political concerns I raise as a result of my work were not only heard but to some extent integrated into the discourse. I know that the workshop has shaped me in new ways, both in terms of the history of religious encounter and exchange in Aboriginal Canada, but also in terms of my own research and pedagogy as a scholar.

I hope that when it is read in conjunction with the other contributions to this volume that my work will encourage readers to consider a more critical engagement with the political concerns of First Nations in Canada (and elsewhere), while they engage with more traditional historical discourse provided by my very accomplished colleagues. In my view, critical thinking is one of the most important skills gained in higher education, and even if my readers disagree with some or all of what I've written, perhaps shedding some light on how a Heiltsuk interdisciplinarian reads First Nations history will at least allow for reading with a different lens, even if only temporarily.

## Notes

1 The Heiltsuk First Nation is located in the central coast of what is now called British Columbia. Our traditional territory encompassed 5,000 km² of this coastal area. Now, 25 percent of our population lives on a small reservation, Waglisla (or Bella Bella), on Campbell Island. The remaining 75 percent live in Canadian urban centres. The Gwa'yasdams First Nation is part of the larger Kwakwaka'wakw peoples from the northern half of Vancouver Island and surrounding islands and inlets. The Gwa'yasdams traditional territory is found on and around Gilford Island, British Columbia.

2 As outlined in the *Dictionary of Feminist Theologies*, feminist theology requires an explication of personal experience and social analysis, and that "there is a communal aspect to

experiences, that they are socially located and connected to power and 'value-defined and interest-laden." See Ada María Isasi-Diaz, "Experiences," in *Dictionary of Feminist Theologies*, ed. Letty M. Russel and J. Shannon Clarkson (Louisville, KY: Westminster John Knox Press, 1996), 96.

3 Mignolo's *The Invention of Latin America* (Malden, MA: Blackwell Publishing, 2005).

4 George E. "Tink" Tinker, *American Indian Liberation: A Theology of Sovereignty* (Maryknoll, NY: Orbis Books, 2008), 1–2.

5 This idea was articulated by Michael Harkin in *The Heiltsuks: Dialogues of Culture and History on the Northwest Coast* (Lincoln: University of Nebraska Press, 2000) but is corroborated in the way other scholars articulate Christian mission history in North America. See especially Jan Hare and Jean Barman, *Good Intentions Gone Awry: Emma Crosby and the Methodist Mission on the Northwest Coast* (Vancouver: UBC Press, 2006); Susan Neylan, *The Heavens Are Changing: Nineteenth-Century Protestant Missions and Tsimshian Christianity* (Montreal/Kingston: McGill Queens University Press, 2003).

6 See Laura E. Donaldson, *Decolonizing Feminisms: Race, Gender and Empire-Building* (Chapel Hill: University of North Carolina Press, 1992).

7 See George Lipsitz, *The Possessive Investment in Whiteness: How White People Profit from Identity Politics,* revised and expanded (Philadelphia: Temple University Press, 2006).

8 See Rauna Kuokkanen, *Reshaping the University: Responsibility, Indigenous Epistemes, and the Logic of the Gift* (Vancouver: UBC Press, 2007); Devon Abbott Mihesuah and Angela Cavender Wilson, eds., *Indigenizing the Academy: Transforming Scholarship and Empowering Communities* (Lincoln: University of Nebraska Press, 2004); Gregory Cajete, *Look to the Mountain: An Ecology of Indigenous Education* (Skyland, NC: Kivaki Press, 1994); Curry Stephenson Malott, Lisa Waukau, and Lauren Waukau-Villagomez, eds., *Teaching Native America across the Curriculum: A Critical Inquiry* (New York: Peter Lang, 2009).

9 See Susan Neylan, *The Heavens Are Changing*.

10 The two leading scholars in autoethnography are Carolyn Ellis and Arthur Bochner at the University of South Florida. Indigenous graduate students who have used various forms of autoethnography as method include Sylvia Rae Cottell (University of Victoria), Robert B. Lansdowne (University of British Columbia), and Patricia June Vickers (University of Victoria).

11 Ruth Behar, *The Vulnerable Observer: Anthropology That Breaks Your Heart* (Boston: Beacon Press, 1996).

12 Ibid., 12.

13 Behar, *The Vulnerable Observer,* 13.

14 By "grand narratives" I refer to the postmodern concept of metanarratives as put forth by Lyotard and other postmodern philosophers. Rather than referring to a particular metanarrative, I am simply acknowledging that indigenous metanarratives existed prior to european contact.

15 Marcella Althaus-Reid, *Indecent Theology: Theological Perversions in Sex, Gender and Politics* (New York: Routledge, 2000), 16.

16 Lee Maracle, *Daughters Are Forever* (Vancouver: Raincoast Books, 2002), 25.

17 "Clah" was a Tsimshian catechist in the Methodist mission who left nearly fifty years' worth of daily written reflections on his faith. See chap. 6 in Neylan, *The Heavens Are Changing,* 161–75.

18 "Subaltern" is a term adopted by Antonio Gramsci to refer to groups who are subject to the dominant class in a society. Since I am First Nations, I consider myself to be a subaltern voice in north America.

19  Behar, *The Vulnerable Observer,* 13.
20  See Robert B. Lansdowne, "Buried Underneath: Uncovering My First Nations Identity" (master's thesis: University of British Columbia, 2009).
21  Lansdowne, "Buried Underneath," 27.
22  Patricia June Vickers, "Ayaawx (Ts'msyen ancestral law): The Power of Transformation," (PhD diss., University of Victoria, 2008).
23  John Trudell, "Epithet," quoted in James Treat, ed., *Writing the Cross Culture: Native Fiction on the White Man's Religion* (Golden, CO: Fulcrum Publishing, 2006).
24  See Scott Richard Lyon, *X-Marks: Native Signatures of Assent* (Minneapolis: University of Minnesota Press, 2010), 22–23, where he talks about the children in his community always choosing to interview his grandfather "Aub" about his negative experience in boarding school; no one ever wanted to interview his wife, Leona, who had a positive experience.
25  J.N. Ogilvie, *Our Empire's Debt to Missions: The Duff Missionary Lecture, 1923* (London: Hodder and Stoughton, 1924), 87.
26  Ibid., 87.
27  Ibid., 140.
28  Alan Morley, *Roar of the Breakers: A Biography of Peter Kelly* (Toronto: Ryerson Press, 1967), 14.
29  Michel-Rolph Trouillot, *Silencing the Past: Power and the Production of History* (Boston, MA: Beacon Press, 1995), 5.
30  Mel Smith, "Unholy Mess," *BC Business,* August 1998, 55–56.
31  Carmen Lansdowne, letter to the editor, *BC Business,* October 1998, 14–16.
32  Trouillot, *Silencing the Past,* 5.
33  Ibid., 5–6.
34  Ibid., 21.
35  Ibid.
36  Ibid., 22.
37  See especially chap. 6, "Municipal and Industrial Organization," and chap. 7, "Education and Social Work." Thomas Crosby, *Up and Down the North Pacific Coast by Canoe and Mission Ship* (Toronto: Frederick Clarke Stephenson, 1914).
38  Morley, *Roar of the Breakers,* 41.
39  Trouillot, *Silencing the Past,* 26.
40  Ibid., 27.
41  Ibid., 29.
42  Proposed as an answer to critical theorist Gayatri Spivak's now famous question, "Can the subaltern speak?" See Gayatri Chakravorty Spivak, "Can the Subaltern Speak?" in *Marxism and the Interpretation of Culture,* ed. Cary Nelson and Lawrence Grossberg (London: Macmillan, 1988), 271–313.
43  Neylan, *The Heavens Are Changing,* 79.
44  Ibid.
45  Ibid., 80.
46  Ibid., 81.
47  Sherman Alexie is an American poet, writer, and filmmaker of indigenous descent from multiple tribes. His work is intended to evoke sadness relating to Native realities in contemporary life, but he evokes this sadness through humour (quite often what is referred to as "Rez humour").
48  W.M. Halliday, "Morality," in *Potlatch and Totem and the Recollections of an Indian Agent* (Toronto: J.M. Dent and Sons, 1935), 141.
49  Ibid., 142.

50   Ibid.

51   William Henry Pierce, *From Potlatch to Pulpit: Being the Autobiography of the Rev. William Henry Pierce, Native Missionary to the Indian Tribes of the Northwest Coast of British Columbia* (Vancouver: Vancouver Bindery, 1933), 108.

52   Ibid., 118.

53   "Mimicry" is defined by Ashcroft, Griffiths, and Tiffin as "An increasingly important term in post-colonial theory, because it has come to describe the ambivalent relationship between colonizer and colonized. When colonial discourse encourages the colonized subject to "mimic" the colonizer, by adopting the colonizer's cultural habits, assumptions, institutions and values, the result is never a simple reproduction of those traits. Rather, the result is a "blurred copy" of the colonizer that can be quite threatening." See Bill Ashcroft, Gareth Griffiths, and Helen Tiffin, "Mimicry," in *Post-Colonial Studies: The Key Concepts*, ed. Bill Ashcroft, Gareth Griffiths, and Helen Tiffin (New York: Routledge, 2000), 139–42. See also postcolonial theorist Homi Bhabha's chapter "Of Mimicry and Man: The Ambivalence of Postcolonial Discourse" in Bhabha, *The Location of Culture* (New York: Routledge, 1994), 121–31. In particular, Bhabha notes that "colonial mimicry is the desire for a reformed, recognizable Other, *as a subject of a difference that is almost the same, but not quite*. Which is to say, that the discourse of mimicry is constructed around *an ambivalence*" (122) [emphasis in original].

54   Pierce, *From Potlatch to Pulpit*, 126.

55   Ibid.

56   This could warrant a much longer discussion on a particular possessive investment in "Whiteness" that upholds multiculturalism as a tenet of liberal society, without the requirement that cultures fully understand each other. There are still many from settler backgrounds who act as political or social "patrons" of Native culture, oftentimes to the disservice of the indigenous community as the practice can stifle internal indigenous dialogue, specifically when disagreements arise about history and cultural protocols. But that is the topic of a whole other chapter.

57   Pierce, *From Potlatch to Pulpit*, 127.

58   Ibid., 133.

59   Halliday, *Potlatch and Totem*, 219.

# Conclusion:
# Reflections on Encounter

*Tolly Bradford and Chelsea Horton*

THIS COLLECTION WAS NOT initially conceived as such. Our primary goal in organizing a gathering on "Religious Encounter and Exchange in Aboriginal Canada," as the workshop that inspired this book was titled, was to seek out and bring into conversation scholars who were exploring this topic from various vantage points. We aimed to curate a collection of essays that considered how Indigenous peoples in what became Canada have interacted with other religions, and Christianity specifically, over the past several hundred years. We hoped that these case studies might form a special edition of a journal, but we had few expectations for publication beyond that. We did not know what, if any, theoretical coherence and methodological common ground would connect workshop participants.

As the workshop took shape, however, it became clear there was an active and diverse group of scholars working on the topic. Discussions were rich and, despite moments of tension and disagreement, it was obvious that we all shared a goal of pursuing scholarship that promotes a closer understanding of the complex relationship between Christianity and colonialism in Indigenous Canada. Indeed, as the workshop unfolded and the essays that compose this collection were revised, it became apparent that there was a substantial rethinking about Indigenous-Christian interaction underway across various disciplines in Canada. This collection, while by no means comprehensive, endeavours to sketch out the major themes of this emerging scholarship and share the energy emanating from this interdisciplinary exchange.

Along the path from workshop to publication, we came to recognize, for one, that contributors productively focus their analysis on several separate (albeit also overlapping) sites of encounter: community, individual, and contemporary. Further, they collectively underline the importance of situating Indigenous interactions with Christianity in specific colonial contexts and contests for spiritual and political power alike. These contexts, this collection reveals, are at once transnational and, at least in the post-Confederation period, specific to

Canada. Contributors explore these shared themes from a range of methodological perspectives and (whether declared or not) social locations.

This collection is itself a site of encounter. Historians of settler heritage pre-
dominated numerically at the original workshop, as they do here.[1] Many of
these participants came away from the gathering more attuned to the politics
of their work, the need to expand their source base, and the need to render their
methodological processes more open and transparent. Similarly, scholars working in other disciplines came to recognize the practical limitations placed on
historians by the availability of documentary sources, and the commitment
that a number of these historians expressed to read and reflect this admittedly
skewed written archive as accurately as possible.

Where participants perhaps differed most dramatically was in their sense of
responsibility: why and for whom they research and write. Many of the historians, trained to sift carefully through the (mostly written) archival record, felt
responsible to that archival record. While these historians recognized the limitations of the sources they rely on, they were committed to reconstructing, as
much as possible, the contexts they learn about through the colonial and missionary documents, and sometimes oral narratives, that they interpret. Other
participants, conversely, expressed a more overt responsibility to challenge the
racism and colonialism that persist in present-day Canada. They further sought
to decolonize by cultivating and applying Indigenous methodologies, theory,
and knowledge. These scholars were responsible not only to a reflection of the
archive but to living Indigenous people and communities and to providing
meaning, hope, and understanding for past, present, and future generations.
These different responsibilities are intimately tied to the methodological differences apparent in this volume. In the end, there is no clear consensus or thesis
in this book about how to research this subject in a good way, nor how to reconcile the nuance of past events with the complex current legacies of Christianity and colonialism in Indigenous Canada. Instead, we are left with a deeply
textured scholarship about Indigenous-Christian encounter in this country.

These are timely issues in light of current events in Canada, where dialogue
about Indigenous-Christian encounter extends well beyond the academy. In
2014, Joseph Boyden's novel *The Orenda*, which tells a compelling, romantic, and
teleological tale of early interactions between Wendat, Haudenosaunee, and
Jesuit communities, was crowned CBC's "Canada Reads" champion.[2] The Truth
and Reconciliation Commission of Canada has brought the violent history of
the residential school system to much more public prominence and has called
for a process of reconciliation "based on a commitment to mutual respect."[3]
"Reconciliation," the TRCC notes in a summary of its final report, "is not an
Aboriginal problem; it is a Canadian one. Virtually all aspects of Canadian

society may need to be reconsidered."[4] As the TRCC concludes its mandate, and as further research into the schools begins, we are hopeful that scholars will cultivate comprehensive interpretations of Indigenous-Christian interactions, residential schools, and their legacies. These interpretations should balance the harsh realities of colonialism with the possibility that Christianity had, and continues to hold, deep spiritual and political meaning for some Indigenous people. Scholars must, simultaneously, grapple with the question of how their work engages with the process of reconciliation envisioned and articulated by the TRCC.

Reaching back to where we started, the canonization of Kateri Tekakwitha once again throws all of this into sharp relief. Among the many Indigenous people present in Rome for the 2012 ceremony was Chief Wilton Littlechild, himself a former residential school student and a TRCC Commissioner. Speaking to Anishinaabe writer Wab Kinew after the ceremony, Chief Littlechild shared, "I've forgiven, even more now, I think. For myself, the experiences that I've had, but also for my family." Kinew, in his own reflections, spoke of what he described as "a miracle of at least equal significance" to Jake Finkbonner's healing from flesh-eating disease: "that people treated so poorly by the church as children grew up to not only forgive but embrace it." Kinew also reflected on Pope Benedict's call for a "renewal of faith in the first nations," writing: "The truth about reconciliation is this: it is not a second chance at assimilation. It should not be a kinder, gentler evangelism, free from the horrors of the residential school era. Rather, true reconciliation is a second chance at building a mutually respectful relationship."[5] This is one interpretation of reconciliation, one that is open to Christianity, even as it distances itself from residential school history. The definition of "reconciliation," like those of "decolonization" and "encounter," is open and contested, and is likely to continue to shift as the findings of the TRCC are disseminated and, perhaps, promote meaningful change in Canada and Canadian institutions. The time is ripe for rethinking and dialogue around these processes, in the past and present, in the academy and outside. For as the stories of Kateri Tekakwitha and those who connect with her so vividly illuminate, the mixed blessings of Indigenous encounters with Christianity in Canada live on.

### Notes

1 This is less a balanced demographic reflection of the scholars exploring this subject than a product of the editors' professional networks.

2 For Wab Kinew's opening spoken-word defence of the book, see http://wabkinew.ca/the -orenda-spoken-word/. For thoughtful reviews of the book, see Hayden King, "Critical Review of Joseph Boyden's *The Orenda*: A Timeless, Classic Colonial Alibi," *Muskrat*

*Magazine,* 24 September 2013, http://muskratmagazine.com/critical-review-of-joseph -boydens-the-orenda-a-timeless-classic-colonial-alibi/; Allan Greer, "Hurons and Jesuits Revisited: Joseph Boyden's *The Orenda*," H-France, http://h-france.net/fffh/the-buzz/ boyden-the-orenda/.

3  Truth and Reconciliation Commission of Canada, *Honouring the Truth, Reconciling the Future: Summary of the Final Report of the Truth and Reconciliation Commission of Canada,* 2015, vi, http://www.trc.ca/websites/trcinstitution/File/2015/Honouring_the_ Truth_Reconciling_for_the_Future_July_23_2015.pdf.

4  Ibid.

5  Wab Kinew, "'It's the Same Great Spirit': Canonization of Kateri Is a Big Step toward True Reconciliation, but the Embrace Could Go Further," *Winnipeg Free Press,* 22 October 2012, http://www.winnipegfreepress.com/local/its-the-same-great-spirit-175193351.html. Kinew expands on these themes, and his father's personal relationship with Kateri and the Catholic Church, in *The Reason You Walk* (Toronto: Viking, 2015). See especially chap. 18, 201–16.

# Contributors

**Tasha Beeds** resides in the Anishinaabe Territory of the Mississauga Nation, where she is a professor and a PhD candidate in Indigenous studies under the direction of Maria Campbell, John Borrows, and Paula Sherman. She grew up with her mother's nêhiyaw and Métis family in the territories of Treaty 6. In addition to a number of print and online publications, Tasha has published articles in *Me Funny*; *Indigenous Poetics*; *Mixed-Race Women Speak Out*; and the *Canadian Journal of Poetry*. As a woman of nêhiyaw ancestry, a first-degree member of the Midewiwin society, and a Water Walker, she is dedicated to moving in Ceremony for the continual resurgence and revitalization of Indigenous thought, knowledges, and sovereignty in all forms.

**Jean-François Bélisle** is a historian who specializes in Latin American studies. His main research interest is oriented to the comparative analysis of the Andean and the Mesoamerican contexts. His chapter in this collection (co-authored with Nicole St-Onge) is one of the first analyses of Louis Riel's political and religious thought from a hemispheric perspective.

**Tolly Bradford** is an assistant professor of history at Concordia University of Edmonton, where he teaches Canadian and world history. His research examines the ways Christianity and other forms of cultural colonialism have shaped Indigeneity and colonial politics in settler societies, especially western Canada. He is the author of *Prophetic Identities: Indigenous Missionaries on British Colonial Frontiers, 1850–75* (UBC Press, 2012).

**Siphiwe Dube** is a postdoctoral fellow in the Department of Practical Theology at the University of Pretoria, RSA. His research focuses on the intersection of religion with critical masculinity studies, transitional justice, postcolonial feminist theory, and hip hop, exploring how the heterogeneous concept of the ambivalence of religion can be used in productive ways for both the academic study of religions and praxis application in social development projects. His work has appeared in the *International Journal of Transitional Justice, Religious Studies and Theology* and a number of edited book collections.

**Elizabeth Elbourne** is an associate professor and chair in the Department of History and Classical Studies, McGill University. Her research interests include religion, gender, and colonialism, particularly interactions between settlers and Indigenous peoples in the contested borderlands of the British Empire. She is also interested in biography. She is currently working on a book on imperial households and the histories of three interlinked family networks. Her past publications include *Blood Ground: Colonialism, Missions and the Contest for Christianity in Britain and the Eastern Cape, 1799–1852* (2003) and *Sex, Power and Slavery* (2014), co-edited with Gwyn Campbell. She was until recently co-editor with Brian Cowan of the *Journal of British Studies*.

**Amanda Fehr** is a PhD candidate in the Department of History at the University of Saskatchewan. She studies boundary maintenance, historical consciousness, memory, representation, and the relationship between political identities and personal experiences. Her doctoral research explores the intersections of religious and political expression during the twentieth century in Île-à-la-Crosse and English River. She has published articles on place making among the Stó:lō in British Columbia, and the role of the Virgin Mary in northwestern Saskatchewan.

**Chelsea Horton** is a research consultant working with Indigenous communities in Canada. She holds a PhD in history from the University of British Columbia, where she has taught on the subjects of Indigenous history, religious encounter, and women in Canada. Her research interests include oral history, identity, religion, and colonialism, and she has published and presented on the histories of Indigenous members of the Baha'i faith in North America. She lives on Vancouver Island, in the traditional territory of the Snaw-naw-as people.

**The Rev. Carmen Lansdowne** is a member of the Heiltsuk First Nation, an ordained minister in the United Church of Canada, and holds a PhD from the Graduate Theological Union in Berkeley, California. She currently serves as director of operations at Ecojustice, Canada's leading environmental non-profit, while maintaining independent scholar status by publishing and presenting her work in North America and internationally. Her research interests include Indigenous methods, comparative and decolonizing epistemologies, constructive theology, and Christian mission. Her previous academic publications include a chapter in *Theology and the Crisis of Engagement: Essays on the Relationship of Theology and the Social Sciences* (2013). She has also written for non-academic audiences through the United Church of Canada and the World Council of Churches.

**Cecilia Morgan** is a professor in the Department of Curriculum, Teaching, and Learning at the University of Toronto. She is currently writing a book on the travels of Indigenous people from British North America to Britain, Europe, and beyond, 1780–1914. She has also published journal articles and book chapters on the history of gender, culture, and colonial relations in nineteenth-century Ontario, as well as *"A Happy Holiday": English-Canadians and Transatlantic Tourism, 1870–1930* (2008). Her latest book is *Creating Colonial Pasts: History, Memory, and Commemoration in Southern Ontario, 1860–1980* (2015). Morgan's forthcoming books are *Commemorating Canada: History, Heritage, and Memory, 1850s–1990s* and *Better Britains? Settler Societies within the British Empire, 1783–1920* (both University of Toronto Press). Her new research project explores the lives of English Canadian actresses with transnational careers, 1860s–1940s.

**Denise Nadeau** is of mixed heritage (French, Irish, Scottish, and English) from Quebec. She is an affiliate assistant professor with the Department of Religion at Concordia University in Montreal. Her research focuses on settler-Indigenous relations, in particular on decolonization of the body and on settler erasure of Mi'gmaq memory on the land of Gespe'gewa'gi. She also works as a dance movement therapist, combining expressive art therapies and spiritual practices in the healing of racist and colonial violence. She currently lives in the traditional homelands of the K'omoks Nation.

**Timothy Pearson** is an independent researcher, editor, and writer. He holds a PhD from McGill University and has taught the history of early colonial encounters in North America at the University of Western Ontario and McMaster University. He is the author of *Becoming Holy in Early Canada* (2014) and lives in London, Ontario.

**Nicole St-Onge** is a professor of history and the director of the Institute of Canadian and Aboriginal Studies at the University of Ottawa. Her current research interests include nineteenth-century bison-hunting Plains Métis brigades, French Canadian employees of the American Fur Company between 1817 and

1850, and nineteenth-century mixed-descent families in the Upper Mississippi and Missouri river basins. Most recently, in collaboration with Brenda Macdougall and Carolyn Podruchny, she contributed to and edited *Contours of a People: Metis Family, Mobility, and History* (2012).

# Index

and the miraculous, 105, 108, 112–13. *See also* conversions; ritual

Bélisle, Jean-François, 9, 10, 85, 209

Benedict XVI, Pope, 1, 155

Betts, Gregory, 102–4

Beyer, Peter, 105

Big Child. See mistawâsis (Big Child)

boarding schools, 191, 203*n*24. *See also* residential schools

Bochner, Arthur, 189–90

Bouchard-Taylor Commission, 33

Boucher-Curotte, Orenda, 174

Bourget, Ignace, Montreal, 105–6, 115*n*30

Boyden, Joseph, 206

Bradford, Tolly, 209

Brant, Chief John, 10, 49, 56–57, 88

Brant, Chief Joseph, 10, 42, 45, 46, 53–55, 88

Brant, Christiana, 88

Brant, Isaac, 55–56

Brant, Lucy, 89

Brant, Molly, 42, 52–53

Brantford, Upper Canada, 84, 87, 95

Britain (18th c.): Anglicans and church-state authority, 41; discrimination against Catholics, 41–42; Mohawk alliances with military, 38, 42; Protestant dissenters, 40–41, 44; Queen Anne's gift of silver to Mohawks, 42, 50–52, 59*n*49; Royal Proclamation of 1763, 40, 45; SPG missionaries to Haudenosaunee, 41, 42, 43, 44, 45, 48, 49. *See also* Anglican Church, Northeast (18th c.); Mohawk/Kanien'kehá:ka (18th c.)

Britain (19th c.): Christian moral authority, 84–85; evangelicalism, 9, 85–86, 89–90; middle-class culture, 85–86

British Columbia. *See* Pacific Northwest; potlatch; Stó:lō Coast Salish; Tsimshian

Brudholm, Thomas, 149, 160*n*2

Buc, Philippe, 24

Buck, Ruth, 121, 128

burial sites, Stó:lō. *See* Stó:lō Coast Salish, I:yem memorial

Burns, Norman, 125–26

Cameron, W. Bleasdell, 126

Campbell, Maria, 120, 124, 126, 138*n*6, 138*nn*1–2

Canajoharie, 38, 43, 45, 48–49, 51

*Captive Histories* (Alfred), 51

Carey, John and Eliza Field Jones, 84. *See also* Jones, Eliza Field

Caribbean: missionary wives, 96–97, 100*n*71; scholars with Caribbean ancestry, 11

Carlson, Keith Thor, 63, 66, 75*n*1, 75*n*8, 76*n*17

Casanova, José, 104

Catholic Church. *See* Roman Catholic Church

cemeteries, Stó:lō. *See* Stó:lō Coast Salish, I:yem memorial

ceremony, as term, 23–24, 35*n*15. *See also* potlatch; ritual

Charlie, Captain, 68, 78*nn*43–44

Charlie, Cecilia and Suzanne, 76*n*10

Charlie, Patrick, 67, 77*n*36, 78*n*44

Chauchetière, Claude, 4

Christianity: aporetic response to mass atrocities, 148–49; as a public religion, 150–51, 153–54, 157–58. *See also* religion; ritual and Christianity

Christianity and Indigenous peoples: about, 2, 6, 183–84, 191; academic courses on Indigenous traditions, 169–70; autobiographies of Indigenous ministers, 197–200; belief in a divine god, 35*n*14; canonization of Kateri Tekakwitha, 1–2, 4, 14*n*10, 207; Christian belief in demonology, 36*n*36; Christian influences as more than colonialism, 76*n*18; complexity of encounter, 165, 169–70; Cree syncretism, 125, 133; Haudenosaunee theory of complex understanding, 132–33; historical exclusion of relationship, 71–72; intersection of traditional spirituality and, 131–33, 153–54, 157–58; mimicry, 198; and political and spiritual power, 6–8; scholarship on, 3–4, 183–85; TRCC forum on, 153, 157. *See also* contact zone; conversions; missionaries; Truth and Reconciliation Commission of Canada (TRCC)

Christianity and Indigenous peoples, workshop. *See* "Religious Encounter and Exchange in Aboriginal Canada" (workshop)